Global Visions
Beyond the New World Order

Global Visions
Beyond the New World Order

edited by Jeremy Brecher,
John Brown Childs, and Jill Cutler

South End Press
Boston

Cover design by John Moss
Text design and production by the South End Press collective
Printed in the U.S.A. on acid-free, recycled paper.
First edition, first printing

Library of Congress Cataloging-in-Publication Data
Global Visions: beyond the new world order/ edited by Jeremy
Brecher, John Brown Childs, and Jill Cutler.
p. cm.
Includes bibliographical references and index.
ISBN 0-89608—461-2 (cloth): $40.00 —ISBN 0-89608-460-4 (pbk.)
$16.00
1. International economic relations. 2. International cooperation.
3. Social movements. I. Brecher, Jeremy.
II. Childs, John Brown. III. Cutler, Jill.
HF1359.G58 1993
337—dc20   93-9615
                                                              CIP

South End Press, 116 Saint Botolph Street, Boston, MA 02115
99 98 97 96 95 94 93 1 2 3 4 5 6 7

Table of Contents

Part III
Globalization-from-Below:
Alternatives

Acknowledgements

The editors would like to thank the following:

For help identifying and tracking down potential contributors: John Cavanagh, John Feffer, Eleonora Castano Ferreira, Stan Gacek, Joanne Landy, Peter Rachleff, Primitivo Rodriguez, and Andrzej Tymowski;

For reading drafts of the Introduction and other material: Martin Bresnick, Tim Costello, John Feffer, Loie Hayes, Allen Hunter, Michael Pertschuk, Bruce Shapiro, and Peter Waterman;

For permitting reprinting of previously published material: *Z Magazine;* Longman Group U.K. Ltd., for permission to reprint Fang Lizhi's "Patriotism and Global Citizenship," translated by James H. Williams, from *The Broken Mirror: China After Tiananmen,* 1990; *Third World Resurgence* for pieces by Vandana Shiva and Martin Khor; and *Envio,* a publication of Universidad Centroamericana, and Central American Historical Institute, Georgetown University, for permission to reprint Xabier Gorostiaga's "Latin America in the New World Order";

And for translations: Josie Mendez-Negrete, David G. Sweet, and Joe Weiss.

We also want to thank the Race and Ethnicity Research Council at the University of California, Santa Cruz for their invaluable support in the development of this project.

Introduction

Globalization-from-Below

We live in an era of globalization. In the 1990s, says Xabier Gorostiaga, Rector of the Central American University, "Humanity itself is being discovered as one world, an inseparable unity, a communal home linked to a common destiny. That destiny is the product of a technological revolution, a revolution in information, social communication and transportation and also of a growing consciousness of the threat of collective suicide for having overstepped the bounds of the planet."

We have little experience of how to live as one world. In this book, people from diverse geographical and social origins grapple with how to turn our globalizing world into a common home.

Richard Falk, professor of international law at Princeton University, notes that two very different sorts of globalization are occurring. One he calls "globalization-from-above"—also known as the "New World Order"—based on the leading states and transnational business and political elites.

But Falk identifies another, less widely recognized type of globalization—"globalization-from-below." It consists of "an array of transnational social forces animated by environmental concerns, human rights, hostility to patriarchy, and a vision of human community based on the unity of diverse cultures seeking an end to poverty, oppression, humiliation, and collective violence."

Globalization-from-below inclines not toward a New World Order but toward a "one-world community." It is "an expression of the spirit of 'democracy without frontiers', mounting a challenge to "the homogenizing tendencies of globalization-from-above." It is based in a "global civil society" which seeks "to extend ideas of moral, legal, and environmental accountability to those now acting on behalf of state, market, and media."

Multifesto

This book might be called a manifesto for globalization-from-below, were not the very concept of a single position or perspective subsuming all others antithetical to its spirit of diversity. Perhaps it should be described as a "multifesto." Like the *Federalist Papers,* whose ideas helped shape the United States Constitution two centuries ago, it contains contributions by different authors coming from different starting points but presenting complementary perspectives tending in the same direction.

This book is designed to help initiate a dialogue which will establish globalization-from-below as a new paradigm for understanding and reshaping the world order. Its authors were selected, not because they would agree about everything (they don't), but because of the contribution they could make to developing that dialogue. Most of them are both scholars experienced in research and writing and activists with close ties to social movements.

Who should participate in discussing the future world order? Unfortunately, much of the debate in academic and policy circles seems to assume that the world's centers of wealth and power constitute a privileged "core" position from which to view the globe, and that only this small part of the world need be included in the dialogue about the world's future. This book presents a wide range of voices, many of them rarely heard in that debate, speaking not only of their local contexts, but of the global situation. They do so in a range of styles, from the academic to the vernacular and from the visionary to the concrete.

This book grows out of a symposium published in *Z Magazine* in which authors were asked to respond to an essay by Jeremy Brecher. For this book, scholars and activists from all over the world were invited either to respond to the original symposium or to contribute an article relevant to the theme "New World Order vs. One-World Community." The result is a book with 32 contributors from more than 20 countries on five continents and a few islands.

This book is divided into three parts: "Part I: New World Order vs. One-World Community: The Forum" debates the proposals for a global alternative presented in the lead essay, "The Hierarchs' 'New World Order'—And Ours" by Jeremy Brecher. "Part II: Globalization-from-Above: Critiques" examines the effort to perpetuate domination by internationalizing it. "Part III: Globalization-from-Below: Alternatives" addresses the problems and possibilities of a one-world community.

Globalization-from-Above

Globalization-from-above extracts resources from the natural world and from local communities in order to increase the wealth and power of the wealthy and powerful. It concentrates that wealth and power in organizations which use their control of people and resources to expand their domination and to fight each other. It transfers power and resources from the natural world to human domination, from communities to elites, and from local societies to national and transnational power centers.

Western media and politicians have purveyed a fairy-tale version of this process. The forces of capitalism and democracy defeated the "evil empire" of communism and oppression. Now the victors are supporting a worldwide outbreak of democracy and economic freedom, with the United States and other world powers preserving world order through the UN, while the free market brings peace and prosperity to all the world's people. The reality, according to Falk, is "the world as an homogenizing supermarket for those with the purchasing power" while those without it are "excluded and, to the extent required, suppressed by police, paramilitary, and military means."

Globalization-from-above is destroying communities and environments. Over the past two decades, as Indian author and journalist Vandana Shiva writes, there has emerged a recognition that our major environmental threats are caused "by globally powerful institutions like multinational corporations and multilateral development banks like the World Bank, which reach every city, village, field, and forest through their worldwide operations."

Haunani-Kay Trask, Director of Hawaiian Studies at the University of Hawaii at Manoa and a member of the Nuclear-Free and Independent Pacific Movement, describes the natural and human devastation caused by globalization-from-above in Hawaii and the Pacific: "Extreme U.S. militarization of our islands and increasing nuclearization of the Pacific Basin; exploitation of ocean resources (including toxic dumping) by Japan, Taiwan, Korea, the United States and others; commodification of island cultures by mass-based corporate tourism; economic penetration and land takeovers by Japanese and other Asian money; and forced emigration of indigenous islanders from their nuclearized homelands." The late Petra Kelly, founder of the German Greens, notes that even in Siberia, the "last untouched region of the world," there are "Japanese, German, U.S., and Korean companies" which are "exploiting every bit of it, burning down the last Siberian forest." The people there have no say-so; "all they know is that the companies destroy everything, and they have nothing from it—just poverty."

Globalization-from-above proceeds under the banner of a free-market economic liberalism which promises economic prosperity but which has delivered worldwide impoverishment and a growing polarization between rich and poor. As Cuauhtémoc Cárdenas, head of the Party of the Democratic Revolution (PRD), Mexico's largest opposition party, writes, it has become evident that "if one relies only on the effects of market forces, social contrasts become deeper and the gaps in the development of the economies become wider."

The failure of the free-market panacea is not limited to the Third World. Francis M. Deng, Senior Fellow at the Brookings Institution, former Sudanese Minister of State for Foreign Affairs and the UN Secretary-General's representative on the problem of displaced persons, observes that in what was the socialist Second World "economic liberalization and the introduction of market economies," initially hailed as reflecting "the victory of capitalism over communism or socialism, seems, at least in the initial phases, not to bring the instant prosperity which the peoples of these nations clearly aspired to and expected." Quite the contrary, "Both productivity and equitable distribution, even of essential commodities, have been severely curtailed, resulting in humanitarian disasters." And even the "First World," notes Saskia Sassen, author and professor of urban planning at Columbia University, is seeing "the decline in earnings among the lower third or even bottom half of the earnings distribution in most major developed economies," including Japan, and "the expulsion of growing numbers from the 'mainstream economy'"—i.e. the rise of "permanent unemployment."

Globalization-from-above is leading to equally radical polarization between different regions—what Gorostiaga calls "an avalanche of North against South." In the new international division of labor, as Cárdenas notes, Third World countries are assigned the role of "providers of labor and raw materials, captive markets to complement those of the industrialized countries, suppliers of agricultural products that require mild climates and of new zones for the expansion of First World tourism. They are also replacing the North as the site for production that threatens the environment and for disposing of toxic wastes." Never before in history, according to Gorostiaga, not even in colonial times, has such an extreme bipolarization of the world existed.

One result, according to Primitivo Rodriguez, Director of the Mexico-U.S. Border Program of the American Friends Service Committee, is massive migration from poor to rich countries. "Millions of displaced people and coerced immigrants have become a cheap and flexible labor reserve both within industrialized nations and in the 'borderlands' that divide the North and the South."

Globalization-from-above has marched under the banner of democratization, but hardly of a democratization that empowers people to control the real conditions of their lives. Hassan A. Sunmonu, Secretary-General of the Organization of African Trade Union Unity, notes that "Currently the world is talking about democracy," but "nobody is talking about its component of social and economic justice" because "the democracy the rightwing is trying to fashion" is "government of the rich, by the rich, on behalf of the people."

The actual result of such a fraudulent democratization is often repression. Cárdenas notes that impoverishment breeds social discontent, but often "there is no political will to really solve the problems" that generate the discontent. So instead there follows "the hardening of political regimes and the systematic cancellation, through the use of force and repression, of citizen and human rights."

The repression and impoverishment spawned by globalization-from-above have provoked religious and nationalist fundamentalisms, what Peter Waterman of the Institute of Social Studies in the Hague calls "an authoritarian populist communal response" to "both capitalist and communist modernization projects." The result is fertile soil for what author John Feffer describes as a worldview which "defines citizenship by blood, soil, language, religion, or some combination of these elements."

Globalization-from-above is eroding the power of national governments to control their own societies. According to Gay W. Seidman, professor of sociology at the University of Wisconsin, Madison and the University of Witwatersrand, Johannesburg and international editor of the *South African Labour Bulletin,* "Increased mobility of capital and new patterns of international investment have eroded nation-states' control over economic growth....Even in historically industrialized areas, social services and corporate taxes have been cut in the effort to retain investments....Even historically powerful nations find themselves competing with other nations, hoping to attract investments and jobs by offering companies a more attractive deal."

The increasing global concentration of wealth is matched by a parallel concentration of power. As Vandana Shiva notes, the Group of Seven (the "G-7" or "Rich Men's Club" of the world's richest countries) "dictate global affairs, but they remain narrow, local, and parochial" in the interests that guide them. The World Bank, for example, is not really a bank that serves the interest of all the world's communities: "It is a bank where decisions are based on voting weighted by the economic and political power of donors."

Proposals for a New World Order are often actually efforts to institutionalize and legitimate globalization-from-above through the United Nations. Guinean political scientist Siba Grovogui notes that "many Western policymakers have called for a reactivation of the UN in a manner that increases the policing role of the Security Council." They use images of "international cooperation, peace, and stability," but in practice, the New World Order they describe is one "dominated by the West, in which the Security Council, and the UN in general, lends legitimacy to Western interests and hegemony." Meanwhile, war and turmoil continue throughout much of what Francis Deng has dubbed "The New World Dis-Order."

The global concentration of wealth and power has not led to domination by a single country. Indeed, an important feature of the present conjuncture, according to Juan Palacios of the Center for Pacific Studies at the University of Guadalajara, is "the evident decline of U.S. hegemony, and thus the absence of a single, undisputed hegemon." Indeed, Palacios argues that today "it seems virtually impossible for any nation to become such a hegemon."

The consequence is what Gorostiaga calls "a new divvying up of world 'spheres of influence.'" Its origin, according to Palacios, is the deepening trend toward global stagnation that began in the early 1970s, which is giving rise to "an exacerbated economic competition among both nations and multinational corporations as investment opportunities have narrowed" and profit rates have concomitantly slumped. World commercial exchange in this era has increasingly turned into "adverserial trade," carried out not between nations but between regions, "as the nation-state is being undermined by the power of the multistate conglomerates that characterize this new economic order."

Palacios notes an emerging contradiction between "the formation of regional blocs" and "the transnationalization of productive operations across national, regional, or even continental borders." What seems to be emerging is a world of "regional multistate clusters" cut across by "an increasingly globalized network of shared production among nations" that will correspond to "a highly hierarchical international division of labor."

Globalization-from-Below

Globalization-from-below, in contrast to globalization-from-above, aims to restore to communities the power to nurture their environments; to enhance the access of ordinary people to the resources they need; to democratize local, national, and transnational political institutions; and to impose pacification on conflicting power centers.

During the 1980s, according to Falk, transnational activism by the environmental, human rights, and women's movements became "prominent for the first time in history." Amnesty International and Greenpeace were "emblematic of this transnational militancy." This "grassroots surge" featured "a shared conviction that upholding human rights and building political democracy" provide the common underpinning for desirable transnational change.

Gorostiaga similarly observes that "International social subjects are sending out calls in different forms, in all parts of the world, through political, religious, union, and NGO [nongovernmental organization] forums and, for the first time, they have begun to link up internationally." He lists such examples as the Japan-Asian People's Plan 21, which brings together hundreds of Pacific organizations; the Third World Network; and the Forum for People's Economics.

Of course there have been internationalisms in the past, but Peter Waterman points out that the former type was largely a "nationalist internationalism," in the sense of "attempting to win nation-states for peoples without them, and rights within them for workers without such." "The old proletarian and socialist internationalism, demanding or seeking a simplified unity," has been largely surpassed and replaced by "the pluralistic internationalisms of the new social subjects and movements"—movements that "recognize a democratic diversity as a source of strength." These movements have shifted attention from "national" problems to "global" ones "for which there are clearly no adequate national (or even *international)* answers." Waterman suggests that these "new internationalisms" be referred to in terms of "an uneven, diverse, and rich movement for global solidarity."

This new transnational linking is supported by a new communications technology, according to Nancy Stefanik, an electronic advocacy specialist who led the design of GLOBALink and other computer networks serving the international tobacco control movement. She points out that "a large number of initiatives involving a variety of technologies...are under way" and that "the technologies that support the globalizing of the economy are also facilitating political and social action that transcends national borders." The result is the "development of networks that empower citizen activists around the world and facilitate the formation of virtual communities that transcend traditional barriers to understanding."

Denis MacShane of the International Metalworkers Federation notes that, for the labor movement, "Global production requires global worker solidarity at the workplace level." Consequently, transnational electronic networking is becoming common in the labor movement. "E-Mail, fax, cheap travel" open up "immense liberating possibilities" because "it is now possible for the power game to be transferred from the hotel rooms where ideologues of the world met to workplace-based linkages confronting international capital."

Grassroots organizing has become pervasive throughout the world. Muto Ichiyo of the Pacific-Asian Resource Center in Tokyo observes that in the Asian-Pacific region, "Everywhere we see the patient, dedicated efforts to promote empowerment—of community people, ethnic groups, women, labor groups, urban slum dwellers, people organizing themselves against 'development' imposed from above, or asserting their independence and autonomy." The major popular political explosions seen in China, Korea, Malaysia, and many other countries in recent years "are in most cases prepared in these small-scale accumulated efforts of empowerment and 'conscientization.'"

Muto acknowledges that "The people are divided into a multitude of groups with their respective identities: gender, ethnic, religious, geographical, cultural, class, nation-state." But today, "these groups are being forced to live together under conditions imposed upon them" by a "state-supported global capitalism" which is organizing them into "a system of international and hierarchical division of labor." Popular struggle "begins on this terrain, in this divisive structure." It is "rooted in each group's identity," and "asserts the group's dignity as well as its immediate interests." But experience shows that interaction with other movements transforms a movement, helping it overcome "narrowness and oppressive practices inside it." In the process of transborder political action, people's groups and organizations gradually form themselves into transborder coalitions which produce an autonomy-based collaboration "cutting across the state barriers" and perhaps ultimately "replacing the interstate system."

Such transborder collaboration is occurring even among groups often presumed to be profound enemies. For example, Palestinian scholar Nahla Abdo, currently of Carleton University in Ottawa, describes the role the women of the *intifada* have played in "politicizing the Israeli women's movement" and "generating not only sympathy but also solidarity and support among various feminist groups internationally"— demonstrated by the formation of a number of Jewish organizations such as "Women in Black" and "Women Against Occupation" in Israel, Europe, and various North American cities.

Democratization

A central goal of globalization-from-below is democratization at every level from the local to the global. Evelina Dagnino, professor of political science at the University of Campinas in Brazil, notes that "the reestablishment of democratic regimes has been a widespread phenomenon in the past few years, sweeping the so-called 'Second' and 'Third' Worlds." But she adds that social movements are creating an alternative definition of democracy based on "the necessary enlargement of...democracy to include social and cultural practices" rather than just the state.

The result is a new conception of citizenship. "The struggles of the urban poor for housing, health, or education; of rural workers for land; of ecological groups for environmental protection; of women, homosexuals, and blacks for equal rights points in a single direction: the elimination of inequality in all its different forms and the building of a truly democratic society." It also implies "the right to be different and the idea that difference shall not constitute a basis for inequality." This notion of citizenship constitutes "an elastic system of reference able to encompass different expressions and dimensions of inequality: economic, social, political, and cultural."

Economic rights are central to this expanded concept of democracy. Gay Seidman describes how the powerful new industrial unions that have emerged in newly industrialized countries like Brazil, Korea, and South Africa have expressed a vision of democratization that included not only the right to vote but also "some kind of redistribution of resources and wealth." In countries that had "experienced authoritarian rule, popular movements tend to include not only political rights and civil liberties, but also socio-economic rights, as goals of the transition to democracy. For them, 'democratization' implies more than simply giving people the right to vote every few years; it includes an understanding that citizens are entitled to demand a living wage, a reasonable standard of living, and basic social services like education, health, and housing."

But this drive for democratization comes up against a maldistribution of power which is not only local and national but also transnational. For as Muto points out, "Most of the major decisions which affect the lives of millions of people are made outside their countries, without their knowledge, much less their consent." They are made "in the core countries, by their governments, by transnational corporations, or by collective agencies such as the International Monetary Fund (IMF), the World Bank, big power summits, or international business bodies."

Vandana Shiva draws the logical conclusion: "Democratizing of international interests is essential if genuine democracy is to exist at local and national levels." She sees an "Earth democracy," however, not as a further strengthing of existing international bureaucracies, but rather as "a lateral expansion of decisionmaking, based on the protection of local community rights where they exist and the institution of rights where they have been eroded." Local environmental rights, for example, would include "the right to information and the right to prior consent: any activity with potential impact on the local environment should require the consent of the local people."

Muto describes such an approach as "a new concept of political right and political action," which he calls "transborder participatory democracy." It asserts a universal "right of the people to intervene in, to modify, to regulate, and ultimately to control any decisions that affect them," no matter where those decisions are made. Transborder participatory democracy offers an answer to "the particular formation that oppressive power has taken in our time: the state-supported globalization of capital."

Transborder participatory democracy according to Muto describes "a world order clearly distinct from the conventional idea of world government or world federation, which presupposes states as the constituent units." It is based on "a new principle, by which not the state, but the people themselves can emerge as the chief actors in determining the course of world politics and economics."

New Constitutive Orders

In place of the current concentration of power in dominant states and transnational corporations, globalization-from-below implies a redistribution of power both upward and downward to a global but decentralized multilevel system. Political scientist Stephen R. Shalom argues that "democratic structures are needed at every level." At the same time, "People ought to participate in decisions in proportion to how much the decisions affect them." Decentralization—making decisions on lower levels—"tends to promote more participation, more individual initiative, more experimentation, and more diversity."

Globalization-from-below's simultaneous emphasis on local empowerment and on transnationalization may seem contradictory, even paradoxical. But in fact the two directions are interdependent. As Richard Falk puts it, the essence of global civil society is diversity, which "provides the ethos of the forms of global citizenship." John Brown Childs, professor of sociology and chair of the Race and Ethnicity Research Council at the University of California, Santa Cruz, notes that "the most positive possibilities for Planetary Community" are coming from "highly distinctive cultural/occupational/local groups who are increasingly working cooperatively with one another." These groups are grounded in "issues that operate at both local and global levels" and have "intersecting concerns" about environment, poverty, militarism, and elite control. Childs argues that "locally rooted, culturally grounded diversity," far from being an intrinsic barrier to planetary community, can be "fundamental to the growth of egalitarian cooperation."

According to Francis Deng, "A political, economic, social, and cultural system that autonomously utilizes local resources and resourcefulness within the framework of regional and global interaction and interdependency" can be designed to reconcile "the lofty ideals of unity" with "the imperatives of segmentation and fragmentation." As units of participation and social orientation, the family, the clan, and the tribe can be "complementary rather than antagonistic to the nation and the global order."

Diversity and local empowerment can be goals for global institutions, rather than barriers to their development. Petra Kelly, for example, proposed an "International Environmental Court," modeled on the World Court, to hear cases like the Chernobyl, Bhopal, and Rhine river disasters and an "Alternative Earth Council" composed of jurists, elders, and other experts from all parts of the world to review governmental policies on the environment; a prime function of such institutions would be to defend the power of local communities to protect their own environments. Conversely, decentralization does not abolish wider responsibilities; as John Feffer points out, "an expanded sense of citizenship" must "accede to principles agreed upon internationally" like the UN Declaration of Human Rights. Indeed, such a multilevel system would provide a more legitimate basis for intervention by the world community when governments fail to meet basic responsibilities to protect human rights, preserve the environment, and resolve disputes without violence.

While such a multilevel conception is surely different from the system of territorial states asserting total sovereignty and independence—the so-called "Westphalian Model" which has dominated international relations since the "Peace of Westphalia" in 1648—it does not necessarily imply the elimination of national identities. As Ben E. Aigbokhan, Senior Lecturer in Economics at Edo State University, Nigeria, and member of the African Peace Research Movement, writes, "Retaining national identities may not pose a serious barrier to a new world order conducive to peaceful coexistence with sustainable growth and development, so long as there are inter-boundary interests strong enough to make parties see themselves as having common interests to protect and promote."

A radical democratization may, however, require the empowerment of a far wider range of groups than those now recognized as nations. Sociologist Elise Boulding, secretary general of the International Peace Research Association and former international chairperson of the Women's International League for Peace and Freedom, sees a crucial role being played by what she calls "identity groups"—"all groups that have some sense of common history and common fate, recognizing that the common history may be at least in part mythical." She notes that "supposedly extinct ethnicities are reappearing at a rapid rate, and new ones are created as migrant streams from the Third World settle in First World societies and create new hybrid cultural identities." Such identity groups are storehouses of social and environmental "problem-solving skills." The resurgence of such identity groups may, in fact, be a response to "the failure of the modern nation-state to meet the needs of its diverse populations."

"A viable political future for the 21st century," according to Boulding, "may depend on a new constitutive order substantially modifying the present nation-state system, one that permits much wider participation of identity groups in shaping the polities of which they are a part." This means "shifting the locus of authority downward to regional and local units."

Elaine Bernard, a Canadian union activist who currently heads the Harvard University Trade Union Program, describes one country where the creation of such a "new constitutive order" may be on the agenda. The current constitutional crisis in Canada, she argues, "holds out the opportunity to restructure the Canadian state, not according to the dictates of business, but rather to meet the democratic and national aspirations of the population as a whole. With Quebecois demanding their right to self-determination, and a majority of Canadians now supporting indigenous peoples' right to self-government, Canadians have an opportunity to construct a new federal structure that assures self-government for national groupings."

Many cultural groups are divided among several nation-states. Jack Forbes, director of the Native American Studies Program of the University of California at Davis, proposes the development of "trans-state entities" which can function across national boundaries. The Inuit (Eskimo) people, for example, share a common heritage and common problems, but are divided among the United States, Russia, Canada, and Greenland. Forbes suggests that certain functions of government—such as education; Inuit-language radio and television; environmental protection; and authority over marriage, the structure of the family, the inheritance of personal property, and other matters often left to provincial authority— be turned over completely to an "Inuit governmental authority of multi-state character." Forbes suggests similar "cross-boundary sub-states" for such conflict-ridden areas of identity-group overlap as the Kurdish communities in Turkey, Iraq, and Iran and the Catholic and Protestant communities in Northern Ireland. He argues that "by abandoning ideas of exclusivistic and centralized states we may be able to find ways to solve ethnic clashes without recourse to violence."

Grassroots Sustainable Development

Globalization-from-above has extracted wealth and productive capacity from local environments and the people who live in them; globalization-from-below aims instead to enable people at the grassroots to develop natural and human capacities which they can control and nurture. As Martin Khor, director of the Third World Network in Penang, Malaysia, and managing editor of *Third World Resurgence,* points out, when economic institutions must compete for profit in order to survive, economic growth becomes a necessity. "Much of the world's output and incomes is channelled to a small elite (mostly in the North but also in the South), while a large part of humanity (mostly in the South, but also a growing minority in the North) has insufficient means to satisfy its needs."

The same dynamic has led to "the rapid depletion and contamination of resources, pollution, proliferation of toxics, and climate change threats." Social movements have striven to counter this dynamic by helping people to "regain their right to land and other resources" and to promote "their right to good health and adequate nutrition, to safety, housing, and a sustainable environment."

From the experience and needs of such movements, according to Gay Seidman, an alternative approach to political economy is beginning to emerge, stressing "bottom-up mobilization rather than top-down investment incentives." By developing organizations in "civil society, independent of the state, popular-movement activists hope to create a source of pressure...to insist that states respond to the needs of poor and middle-class citizens." Such efforts could be supplemented by economic development strategies which use government services in such areas as housing and electrification to "provide jobs and increase domestic market size. Rather than promoting investments in new export-oriented agriculture or manufacture, governments responsive to popular movements might promote private investment in social services which would first employ workers, and then increase consumption and markets."

Such alternatives require a reconsideration of current economic dogmas. Muto Ichiyo suggests that we "begin with basics—what we need for a decent living and how those things should be produced, distributed, and consumed. Value added (GNP) should cease to be the measure for economic activities. Instead, satisfaction of human needs in a human way should be our yardstick."

Muto maintains that this is neither "an image of a subsistence economy" nor "a call to go back to pre-modern society." It envisions "a new affluence" made possible by "accumulation at the grassroots level, by people themselves." In such a system, "people-to-people relations regulate the economy, and not vice versa."

But constructive efforts to encourage grassroots economic development are greatly limited by the power of global economic institutions. Therefore, according to Martin Khor, "the fight for democracy also has to be extended to the international arena where the lack of democracy is so obvious." Such institutions as the transnational corporations, the international banks, the World Bank, the International Monetary Fund, and the General Agreement on Tariffs and Trade should be made much more accountable to the public. "The public has the right because the public suffers the consequences if something goes wrong, whether it be the Bhopal residents dying from chemical poisoning, or the more than

100,000 farmers dying from pesticide poisoning annually, or the hundreds of millions of people suffering the social and economic effects of structural adjustment policies imposed by the World Bank and the IMF....Not only Southern governments but also local communities in our countries must have the opportunity to participate in the design of programs and the monitoring of effects."

Luiz Inacio Lula da Silva, "Lula," former metalworker and union activist, President of the Brazilian Workers Party, and runner-up in Brazil's 1989 presidential election, argues that the global concentration of power requires a transnational response because "there is no individual way out of the crisis." Every time a Latin American country tries alone to renegotiate better commercial, economic, or even cultural deals with Europe or the United States, "It's like placing a lightweight up against Mike Tyson—no matter how good he is, the odds are stacked against him and he ends up getting knocked out."

Gay Seidman indicates what some of the elements of a transnational response might be. At the governmental level, international trade agreements may prove "the only way for dependent economies to avoid constantly deteriorating prices for primary product exports, either by setting new terms of trade or by creating regional economic blocs to create semi-protected markets for fledgling industries." Social movements have already increased bargaining power vis-à-vis multinational corporations by "unions sending aid to workers on strike elsewhere"; going on strike themselves "to pressure their multinational corporate employers to recognize unions in their Third World subsidiaries"; and boycotting goods from regimes which repress labor, for example when "stevedores in several U.S. ports refused to unload South African goods during the 1980s." Organizations like Greenpeace have brought together people with common concerns from around the world in well-coordinated campaigns; the international consumer boycott of Nestlé prompted advertising restrictions on baby-food formulas; "an international grassroots anti-apartheid movement in the 1980s forced governments in the United States and Europe to impose economic sanctions on South Africa, undoubtedly speeding up the transition to democracy there. If popular mobilization were coordinated internationally, democratic states might find they gained more negotiating room: multinational corporations would find their options limited if they faced similar demands everywhere."

Elaine Bernard points out the growing cooperation among people's organizations in Canada, Mexico, and the United States in response to proposals for a North American Free Trade Agreement. In all three countries, "workers are struggling with governments which have adopted neo-conservative business strategies of low wage competition. In order to reject the business program of competitiveness though, labor and the popular movements need to develop in its place an alternative continental agreement on fair trade and development....This will require considerable rethinking of the role of government and sovereignty. Social charters can play an important role. Charters as statements of agreement among movements and people, not negotiated by governments, can help promote working people's rights—and not only their political and civil rights, but also their social and economic rights."

Conflicts and Contradictions

Notwithstanding their evident convergence, there are undoubtedly conflicts and contradictions among the various versions of globalization-from-below.

Some concern the proper categories for analysis. Gorostiaga, for example, writes that "the increasing division of the world, between a North of few people and many resources and a South with many people and few resources, is the axis of the current crisis." While acknowledging that "the terms 'North' and 'South' simplify the world's problems," he argues that "they also allow us to underline the dominant contradiction." Peter Waterman argues, in contrast, that we are seeing an "interpenetration of the local, the national, and the international" which lets us increasingly "see the world as one complex and contradictory capitalist whole" rather than as "divided into a homogeneous West opposed to a homogeneous East, or Three Worlds, or North and South, similarly homogeneous and opposed."

There are empirical disagreements, too. How much, and in what ways, for example, has the nation-state system been altered by recent changes? Primitivo Rodriguez suggests that the rise of "borderlands" like the Mexico-U.S. frontier "signals the end of 'national' identities and announces the birth of a new 'country' whose rules and mores are still undefined, but whose workers are bound together by the reality of being citizens of the global economy," a "'nation' without borders." Denis MacShane, in contrast, maintains that "it is the formation of the nation-state that is the single biggest global political surge that can be seen under way in the post-communist, post uni-polar world."

MacShane also points out that, within the project of globalization-from-below, different goals may compete. "The four 'E's'—economy, ethnicity, equality (of gender), and ecology—are often rivals in claiming priority as much as they are allies in forging complementary coalitions." He adds that emphasis on global versus national or local contexts may conflict. "The embrace of internationalism" may at times be "a mechanism for avoiding the difficult work of securing advances" within the domestic or nation-state context.

There are also conflicts between different orientations toward organization and institutionalization. Nancy Stefanik notes the rise of networks that "empower citizen activists around the world and facilitate the formation of virtual communities that transcend traditional barriers to understanding." She suggests that this constitutes a "revolution of consciousness," revealing "universal values of simplicity and cooperation, respect for Mother Earth, and concern for generations to come." But MacShane warns that "a constant appeal to a networking, friction-free, millenaristic post-political global community" carries dangers of "clean hands but little enduring presence or power."

A Convergence of Goals?

Despite these and other differences, globalization-from-below represents an unexpected convergence of goals among many people the world over. As Primitivo Rodriguez writes, "the globalization of capital, production, and communications has created the conditions in which the peoples of the world can come together across borders and barriers." This provides an opportunity for the convergence of "world visions—cultural experiences and long-held aspirations"—which can lead to "a profound re-evaluation or revolution in our ways of thinking of and relating to ourselves and the universe around us." Here, says Native American writer and curator Lynne Williamson, is the challenge for all of us: "a New World Order which derives from, depends on, revitalizes, and celebrates our separate and different traditions....*This* will be the 'new world' to discover during the next 500 years."

Muto suggests that we can partly see a "new paradigm" emerging out of the people's movements themselves. "There is a striking concurrence of views among those new movements of different origins," including movements that started in the West and the Third World. The worldwide movement for human rights, for example, largely reflects the perspective articulated by Fang Lizhi, the physicist who helped inspire the Chinese democracy movement of 1989, that "human rights are not the property of a particular race or nationality. Every human being is born with the right to live, to find a mate, to speak and think freely. These are fundamental freedoms, and everyone on the face of the earth should have them, regardless of what country he or she lives in."

Cárdenas articulates a similar sense of "ideals without boundaries" shared by "women and men of good faith in every nation, in every continent." They imply "a world of equals, without exploiters and exploited...no one above the others....No one stepped upon or humiliated....No individual or nation constituted as an arbiter of the rest."

The convergence among the various expressions of globalization-from-below is not an accident. It results from the great historical reality that humanity is discovering itself as one world with a common destiny, and simultaneously discovering itself heading toward collective suicide by overstepping the bounds of the planet. Dokun Oyeshola, professor of International Relations at the Obafemi Awolowo University in Ile-Ife, Nigeria, notes that the relationship to nature currently embodied in "development" and "civilization" has polluted water and air, destroyed natural habitats, eroded the soil, and raised global temperatures. He concludes that "our redemption must bring back balance, harmony, and beauty to what has been destroyed in the world—interpersonal, racial, national, and international relationships." He urges us to think of ourselves as "gardeners, caretakers, mothers and fathers, stewards, trustees, priests, co-creators, and friends of a world that, while giving us life and sustenance, also depends increasingly on us in order to continue, both for itself and for us."

Resources

For information on how to participate in an international on-line computer conference continuing the dialogue in this book, contact:
Global Visions
c/o Professor John Brown Childs
Sociology Department
Sevenson 231
University of California Santa Cruz
Santa Cruz, CA 95064
United States

Internet address: jbchilds@cats.ucsc.edu

Part I

New World Order vs. One-World Community: The Forum

The Hierarchs' New World Order—and Ours

Jeremy Brecher

The world surely could use a new order—one that would correspond to the needs of people and planet. That's hardly the "New World Order" dreamed of by superpower leaders, nor the "Old World Order" that preceded it. But what then might it be?

We live in a world where oil spills, satellite news broadcasts, and fleeing refugees stream across national borders, a world in which an entire factory may be nothing but one work station on a global assembly line. The purpose of this book is to stimulate transnational discussion of what kind of world order would meet human and environmental needs, and how such an order might be realized, in a world whose features are no longer cut to the measure of the nation-state.

The "Old World Order"

The Old World Order which characterized the decades following World War II had as its basis the model of sovereign nation-states developed in early modern Europe. Humanity was assumed to be divided into distinct peoples. Each people was entitled to form a nation which in turn was entitled to a monopoly of political authority within a given territory, governing all who lived there and determining the use of natural and human products. Each such nation was assumed to have or to be acquiring clear boundaries and political, economic, military, and cultural institutions permitting relatively independent, self-directed functioning.

This system was based on illusions. The human population was not divided into distinct non-overlapping groups, but rather was composed of peoples who had been mixing for millennia and who owed loyalties to multiple religious, political, ethnic, economic, kin, and other groupings. The result has been continuing conflict.

3

Furthermore, natural and social forces did not form closed systems where actions taken in one nation had little impact on others. Nations were subject to natural, market, ideological, and other transnational forces; weaker nations were subject to pressure from stronger ones; and nations were often caught up in the unintended effects of transnational interaction processes like arms races and wars.

Nonetheless, the nation-state system was reinforced during the 19th and most of the 20th centuries as the boundaries of social institutions came increasingly to coincide with those of nations, bringing reality closer to nationalist doctrine. After the decline of European colonialism, the entire world was organized on the nation-state model.

The Old World Order superimposed three supranational structures over this national structure in the years following World War II. The Cold War defined two relatively stable blocs in political, military, economic, and cultural confrontation. The division between industrialized and formerly colonized nations defined an economically developed First and an underdeveloped Third World. The United Nations provided a weak forum through which international cooperation could be managed when dominant nations wished it.

This Old World Order was marked by tremendous concentrations of power. United States economic, political, and military power predominated everywhere except in the communist "Second World"; the United States consumed the lion's share of global resources. The United Nations, the one institution that might have represented common global interests, was a creature of nation-states and was usually immobilized in the face of their conflicts. Measures embodying the interests of the great majority of the world's people—for example, disarmament and environmental protection—had little chance in this order if they conflicted with powerful national or other special interests.

The Old Order Passeth

The end of Cold-War bipolarism, a result of the breakup of the Second World and the declining economic power of the United States, has been widely noted. Less noted—but of greater long-run significance—is the erosion of the nation-state system itself.

The 1970s and 1980s saw not the emergence of a new hegemon to replace the United States, but rather a multifaceted globalization and fragmentation of power. U.S. economic institutions hemorrhaged into a global economy of transnational corporations, world markets, and an integrated "global factory." Huge industrial complexes oriented toward national markets were replaced by small, easily relocated facilities scattered through a variety of countries and producing for a world market. While the economic center of gravity shifted away from the United States, no other power developed comparable military capacity. Satellite broadcasting made it possible for people everywhere to see events across the world more easily than those in the next town. Meanwhile, hundreds of civil wars and ethnic insurgencies fractured the unity of established nation-states throughout much of the world.

In effect, the boundaries of economic, political, military, and cultural spheres began to decouple or de-align from the borders of nations and superpower spheres of influence and from each other. This deep change underlies many of the dramatic visible changes that mark the end of the Old World Order, such as the end of the Cold War, the decline in dominance of both the United States and the former USSR, and the shift of much production from deindustrializing areas in the First World to "Newly Industrialized Countries" in formerly underdeveloped regions. The result is a world in which the boundaries of nations and of First, Second, and Third worlds have been severely eroded, while inequalities of wealth and power have increased but also dispersed through all nations and regions.

New Orders

Gorbachev's "new thinking" was, in effect, an attempt to create a new world order by replacing the bipolar superpower dominance of the Cold War era with a "concert of nations" based on genuine national sovereignty. It foundered because it did not come to terms with the de-alignments that were undermining the nation-state framework itself, particularly the rise of ethnic nationalist movements within established states and the pull of the global economy and culture.

Bush's New World Order, in contrast, represented a tentative step toward a new form of transnational organization in response to the realities of de-alignment. Its intent, while obscure in Bush's speeches, was apparent in his Gulf War strategy and his international economic policy.

The Gulf War coalition pooled different kinds of power possessed by different entities. The United States provided military equipment and trained personnel. Some Arab countries provided base areas. The emirs, the Japanese, and the Germans provided cash. The Security Council, dominated by the major powers, provided legitimation for the entire effort. While the war drew on nationalist sentiment in the United States and some other countries, its coalition model actually reflected the inability of the United States or any other single nation to function as a hegemonic power on its own.

A somewhat similar coalition of "haves" has functioned in the World Bank and International Monetary Fund, where conservative policymakers backed by the United States and a few wealthy allies have forced poor countries to accept "structural adjustment plans" which open their resources to foreign corporate exploitation and turn their economies into money machines for the benefit of their rich creditors. The U.S. government tried, with ambiguous results, to mobilize a similar coalition in the General Agreement on Tariffs and Trade (GATT) negotiations on world trade in order to break down national protection of environments, cultures, and economies and make the world safe for unregulated transnational corporate activity.

The Bush New World Order, in sum, aimed to create a consortium of powerful political regimes, corporations, and military establishments which would cooperate to preserve their access to the resources of the Earth, the products of past human activity, and the fruits of future labor. It aimed to establish for transnational corporations what conservative "law and order" provides within nations: protection for private property and its owners' rights to aggrandize themselves. Nations which attempted to resist their assigned place in the hierarchy (whether through democratic aspirations like Sandinista Nicaragua or through a desire for domination like Saddam Hussein's Iraq) would simply be starved or bombed into submission at financial, political, human, and ethical costs that the Gulf War indicated were acceptable to the coalition. The predictable consequences were repression of insurgencies and increasing concentration of wealth on a global scale.

Whether such a world order could adjust strains and conflicts among its partners over time the way the Gulf War coalition did during the Gulf War remains open to question. But its larger difficulty was its inability to solve the basic problems facing the world. It didn't address impending ecological catastrophe, the growing gap between rich and poor within and between countries, the proliferation of weapons of mass destruction, or the denial of basic human rights in most parts of the globe. Such a New World Order could not provide security, well-being, or freedom to most of the world's people. Indeed, its goal was not to reduce the domination and exploitation of the Old World Order but, under new conditions, to perpetuate them.

The Limits of National Resistance

Most of the established traditions for resisting and replacing domination accept, indeed celebrate, the nation. They envision a nation-state controlled by its own people, controlling its own resources, able to determine its own character and fate. Externally, this has meant "wars of national liberation" to resist foreign domination, ideally to be followed by a world of sovereign nations living in peace with one another. Internally, it has placed wealth and territory under the authority of the nation.

Even under the Old World Order, the nation-state model of resistance and reconstruction proved difficult to realize. Subordination to outside forces and internal ethnic conflict were more the norm than the exception for most nations. State control of economies and militarized strategies for national independence meant dictatorships more often than empowered populations.

With the de-alignment of economic, political, military, and cultural power from the nation, this model has become even less viable. Globalization of the economy has provided most nations a choice of stagnation in isolation or subordination to foreign economic power. Fragmentation has meant fratricidal conflict over just who constitutes the nation. Given the new military capacities and ability to pool repressive resources manifested by the Gulf coalition, wars of national liberation seem likely to prove an increasingly suicidal vehicle for resistance to domination.

An Alternative World Order

A world order corresponding to the needs of people and planet will need to correct the flaws of the Old World Order based on the nation-state—and the flaws of a New World Order based on a transnational consortium of the rich and powerful. It will need a worldview which recognizes the transnational character of human identities and historical forces, a set of principles for ordering them, and institutional means for implementing those principles.

Worldview: A worldview for such an order needs to accept the premise that the social world is composed not of sovereign entities of any kind but rather of a multiplicity of interpenetrating entities with relative and overlapping boundaries. This might be compared to the paradigm of ecology, in which an ecosystem is seen not as a collection of isolated organisms, but rather as a set of overlapping systems and subsystems.

Such an "ecological" approach starts from a conception of the individual as a member of many groups—kinship, ethnic, religious, political, etc.—whose boundaries do not generally coincide and no one of which can be regarded as sovereign over the others. Individuals possess multiple identities; group boundaries overlap.

Such an approach abandons the fictional notion of sovereign nation-states: that they can and should control their own internal affairs free from outside interference and serve as the sole representatives of their citizens' collective will. Instead, it recognizes the current reality of multiple overlapping transnational power networks. It envisions a multi-level system of regulation cutting across the boundaries of existing nation-states to control the transnational forces that actually shape today's world.

Principles: Within such an "ecological" paradigm it is impossible to define completely separate entities which can be treated as private property or national territory. This means that the people of the world must be seen as inheritors-in-common of the Earth and the products of past human activity as a whole. Such co-inheritance implies a right of all individuals and groups to a share of the governing of life on Earth and the benefits thereof. It also implies a responsibility of all individuals and groups to protect the rights of all co-inheritors and to preserve the earthly environment for present and future.

For people to secure their rights and fulfill their responsibilities, two conditions are necessary:

First, individuals and groups must be free to express themselves, communicate, and organize—to exercise what are now generally termed fundamental human rights. This in turn implies that no group or institution can legitimately suppress the right of others to express themselves or to organize in a particular territory or population.

Second, all people have a right to effectively participate in governing all institutions insofar as they affect common rights and responsibilities. Whereas today, in theory, corporations are responsible to their stockholders, governments to their citizens, and international organizations to their member governments, such power centers should be ultimately subject to governing by the world's people as a whole.

Institutions: While ultimate authority and responsibility over such powerful institutions should be held in common by all people, this whole cannot practically express itself or act directly as a whole. Where all cannot assemble and decide, individuals and groups must be able to delegate to representatives their rights and responsibilities vis-a-vis such institutions. But if power is genuinely to remain the people's, such delegation must be temporary, limited, supervised, and revokable.

This doesn't mean a "world parliament" making every decision in the world. There are many instruments through which rights and responsibilities may be distributed for a limited time and under limited conditions, such as leases, licenses, charters, taxation, profit-sharing, easements, and regulation. These define, in effect, "bundles of rights" which may be assigned to different individuals and institutions at various levels. Protection of the ozone layer may be assigned to a global environmental protection authority; building a local road primarily affects—and therefore requires input from—builders, users, and neighbors. Only ultimate authority need remain with the people as a whole.

Such a system might take existing institutional structures as a provisional starting point, but redefine them as subject to approval by the world's people. It could accept, for example, that there currently exist states, corporations, and international organizations, most performing some kind of social function. It would insist, however, that these institutions not block the organization of self-defined groups and that they accept governing by such groups or their delegated representatives.

In sum, the basis of an Alternative World Order can be the free development of self-defined individuals and groups and their participation in the governing of all powerful social institutions.

From Here to There

This kind of world order, unlike the kind dreamed of by superpower leaders, can only be shaped by the efforts of millions of people— not by the edict of one person or one nation. Indeed, it is implicit in the conjunction of two kinds of efforts that are already under way.

First is the creation and strengthening of self-defined grassroots organizations of underempowered groups and of advocates of underempowered social interests throughout the world. In many instances such self-organization requires a struggle for human rights against the power of states and other authorities to suppress or discriminate against ethnic, political, cultural, religious, class, or other groups.

Second is the establishment of influence, and eventually of control, by such organizations from all over the world over corporations, international organizations, states, and other power centers. Some recent efforts indicate that such groups can indeed be brought together to confront the institutions that affect them:

• A transnational coalition of development, human rights, and environmental organizations holds counter-meetings called the Non-Governmental Organization (NGO) Forum at the annual meetings of the World Bank and the International Monetary Fund (IMF). They have proposed alternative policies and helped organize transnational campaigns. They helped generate the pressure that led the World Bank to modify policies encouraging the destruction of the Brazilian rain forest and to create an environmental department charged, among other responsibilities, with being responsive to the concerns of the nongovernmental environmentalist community.

• A similar coalition of environmentalist, consumer, and farm organizations has held counter-meetings at the various GATT sessions and helped organize the opposition which led to the stalling of the Uruguay Round of GATT in late 1990.

• The "Maquiladora Coalition" brings together religious, environmental, labor, Latino, and women's organizations in Mexico and the United States to pressure transnational corporations to implement a "Maquiladora Code of Conduct" which will ensure a safe environment, safe working conditions, and a fair standard of living in the Mexican border export zones.

• A growing network of citizen groups in Mexico, the United States, and Canada are demanding the abandonment or modification of the North American Free Trade Agreement, which would undermine the environment and local economies.

• A transnational coalition of unions and environmental groups organized a successful campaign to affect the worldwide labor and environmental policies of the BASF corporation.

• The campaign for a free South Africa brought together hundreds of organizations inside and outside South Africa and eventually forced the South African government to come to the bargaining table and begin dismantling apartheid.

• Campaigns for human rights have brought together groups inside and outside of many countries. The acceptance by many countries of outside observers to monitor their elections is one example of the incorporation of outside oversight within national political systems.

Democratization movements within many countries over the past few years provide a possible model for how such efforts might evolve toward a new way of governing powerful institutions. These movements generally started with the development of an opposition which brought together a wide range of excluded and oppressed groups and social interests—such as environmentalists, women, workers, and ethnic groups. Due to pressure from the opposition, from outside forces, and from their own contradictions, ruling groups agreed to negotiations with the opposition, informally began sharing power with it, and eventually accepted—willingly or unwillingly—an institutionalization of representation of the previously excluded groups, normally through some version of parliamentary democracy.

A similar process might enable self-constituted groups to establish the right to participate in the decisionmaking not just of "their own" state, but of any power centers which affect them. Coalitions of such groups, both inside and outside particular institutions, can cooperate to put pressure on those institutions. Under certain conditions existing institutions will be forced to negotiate with these oppositions. In some cases they will have to engage in de facto power sharing. Eventually this may be institutionalized in formal governing systems like those described above for an Alternative World Order.

Implications for Action

For social movement activists, helping construct such a world order generally means not abandoning current struggles but conducting them in a new perspective which encourages transnational linkage of movements. Here are some guidelines:

• Support the right of all people worldwide to organize and define themselves without interference from the authorities. Fight the complicity of your own government in such interference.

• Create and strengthen self-defining grassroots organizations of the disempowered and of advocates of underrepresented social interests.

• Define the goals of such groups in ways that are congruent with the common interests of people and planet.

• Address problems and solutions globally. Make proposals not just for a national energy policy but for a transnational energy regime based on integrating the needs of the global environment with those of people in regions with different energy needs and resources. Seek input from people's groups in other lands.

• Reach out for coalitions with others around the globe. Pursue transnational grassroots mutual aid and solidarity.

• Use such coalitions to pressure institutions to conform to the needs of people and planet. Demand that GATT stop devastating local markets and start ensuring the protection of labor rights and the environment. Demand that the UN Security Council stop authorizing massive bombing of cities and start demilitarizing regional conflicts. Demand that the IMF stop turning poor lands into workhouses for export production and start providing resources for their sustainable development.

A New World Order which meets the needs of people and planet boils down to the self-organization of humanity. People's self-organization across national boundaries is what can produce it.

Capitalist Rivalry and People's Participation

Stephen R. Shalom

Jeremy Brecher says that the U.S. government wants to make the world safe for transnational corporate activity, and by this he apparently means any transnational corporate activity, whether U.S.-based or not. However, the governments of the capitalist countries today continue to represent the interests of their own corporations, just as they have always done. Yes, the U.S. government now has to be concerned about such things as a Japanese firm located in Tennessee since it provides employment, but this doesn't mean policymakers in Washington and Tokyo have identical interests. The U.S. government, for example, still cares less than nil about the well-being of a Japanese firm that may be investing in France.

That governments serve their own corporations is not just a matter of nationalist false consciousness, but a result of the links between corporate power and political office. In the United States, for example, U.S. corporations are major campaign donors, and the corporate elite substantially overlaps with the political elite. On the other hand, foreign firms generally do not bankroll U.S. elections, and U.S. government officials are not recruited from key leaders of foreign corporations.

Information and capital flow readily across national boundaries, and firms pick up and move plants to tap different labor markets, but corporations are far less inclined to move their headquarters to other countries. Top U.S. corporate executives see themselves as American, and they aren't interested in permanently relocating to Paris, let alone Seoul.

This doesn't mean capitalist states don't have some common interests and won't cooperate to serve these interests. They do have a common interest in maintaining a world in which capitalism thrives, though at the same time they are vicious competitors. And this has long been the case. The great powers of the past often cooperated to tame some recalcitrant people (for example, the crushing of the Boxer Rebellion in China), but this did not prevent these same powers from engaging in the fiercest competition, including brutal wars.

Brecher sees the recent Gulf coalition as representing some sort of transnational identity of interests. In my view, the rush to war was precisely a U.S. effort to reassert its dominant position over its capitalist rivals. Other countries may be able to make better cars or VCRs, but war brings out the U.S. comparative advantage, namely, military strength and military technology. Victory brought with it a privileged position for the United States in the Gulf vis-à-vis its competitors: the United States will be the one to get those construction contracts, the arms deals, and the right to maintain a military presence in the region. Indeed, according to Lawrence Kolb, a former Reagan-era Pentagon official, the United States has even been overcharging its allies for the costs of the war and then threatening them if they fail to pay up.

Washington's most important prize in the Gulf War was the ability to affect oil pricing decisions through Saudi Arabia. Some have suggested that Bush went to war in order to keep the price of oil low, a goal shared by all the industrialized capitalist nations. But this has not been the U.S. goal. When Saddam Hussein told U.S. Ambassador April Glaspie just before his troops marched into Kuwait, "Twenty-five dollars a barrel is not a high price," she replied, "We have many Americans who would like to see the price go above $25 because they come from oil-producing states."[1] Glaspie didn't have to mention that George Bush was one of those Americans, and had gone on a mission to Saudi Arabia in 1986 precisely to get the price of oil raised. As business correspondent Louis Uchitelle commented in *The New York Times*,[2] "By virtue of its military victory, the United States is likely to have more influence in the Organization of Petroleum Exporting Countries than any industrial nation has ever exercised." If prices were to drop, Uchitelle noted, "Washington might lean on a reluctant Saudi Arabia to cut production and push prices back up...." While Japan, Germany, and other industrialized nations favor low energy prices, the United States wants the price high enough to maintain profits for its domestic petroleum companies—and high enough to help Washington's competitive position vis-à-vis its economic rivals.

Capitalist rivalry showed itself in many other ways as well. In January 1992, Bush accused West Europeans of hiding behind an "Iron Curtain of protectionism," using language previously reserved for our mortal enemies. "We won the Cold War and we will win the competitive wars," Bush declared.[3] In March, the Pentagon prepared a draft policy statement asserting that the U.S. mission will be to prevent friendly or unfriendly nations from competing with the United States for superpower status. *The New York Times* reported that senior White House officials repudiated the document, calling it a "dumb report" that "in no way or shape represents U.S. policy."[4] In fact, however, the report essentially echoed public statements already enunciated by administration officials even before the Gulf War. Sharp cuts in military spending, Defense Secretary Dick Cheney warned the National Newspaper Association in March 1990, "would give us the defense budget for a second-class power, the budget of an America in decline....There's a point below which we cannot go if we want to remain a superpower." And the commandant of the Marine Corps declared that since the interests of the United States and its allies could be expected to diverge, we had greater need "for forces capable of responding unilaterally."

While capitalist states will no doubt continue to cooperate in pursuit of their common interests, there would seem little reason to expect less intra-capitalist competition than before. The nation-state is far from dead.

Democracy and Diversity in an Alternative World Order

Trying to imagine the basic principles of an alternative world order is an important and long overdue task, and I welcome Brecher's taking the initiative in this regard. His principles, however, need to be clarified or refined if we are to avoid some rather undesirable consequences.

Everyone, says Brecher, has the right to participate in governing all institutions insofar as the institutions affect common rights and responsibilities. Direct participation, Brecher acknowledges, would be impractical, and he suggests a system of representation under which representatives have only limited and temporary authority and are recallable. Even such a world parliament could not possibly deal with every decision that would have to be made in the world, so Brecher proposes a variety of instruments through which rights and responsibilities might be distributed. But these instruments are merely mechanisms for assigning authority from the center; there is no real decentralization of power. So he has licenses and charters operating on a local level, but the only *democratic* decisionmaking body that Brecher's model seems to include is the one-world body. This seems to me dangerous for two reasons. First, because the principle that everyone should decide everything is not just impractical, but inappropriate, and, second, because decentralization has certain important virtues in its own right.

The key principle of socialist democracy, on an international scale as well as on smaller scales, ought to be not that everyone decides everything, but that people ought to participate in decisions in proportion to how much the decisions affect them. On one level, of course, everything affects everyone and so everyone should have a say on everything; but not everything affects everyone equally. Thus, for example, whether English or Chinese is taught as the main language in my local school affects to some degree everyone on the planet, but it obviously affects local folks more than it does the residents of Beijing, so much so that the interest of Beijing residents in the matter probably approaches zero. Therefore, my neighbors and I ought to have the decisive say on the question. On the other hand, many issues dealing with the Earth's resources and environment affect all the world's people (and their progeny) to a substantial degree and in roughly equal amounts, and therefore these issues ought to be decided by everyone. (Brecher refers to this distinction when he talks about the ozone layer and the local road, but he doesn't make explicit that democratic structures are needed at every level, not a parliament on the world level and licenses and charters on the others.) How do we decide which decisions get made at which level? Sometimes there will be disagreement about just how much a decision affects different people, and, if no consensus can be reached, we ultimately will have to let the global community resolve the disagreement. But at least the general principle—participation in proportion to how much one is affected—ought to be clear.

In deciding the proper locus for decisionmaking, another consideration is involved as well. Decentralization is not simply a means of operationalizing the "participation in proportion to how much one is affected" principle. Decentralization—making decisions on lower levels—has other benefits as well. It tends to promote more participation, more individual initiative, more experimentation, and more diversity. These things are desirable in and of themselves, and to encourage them we might want to sacrifice a little of our global authority. The international community will have to protect the planet's environment and ensure minimal standards of democracy and social justice, but often the human and social benefits from decentralizing the decisionmaking for certain decisions will outweigh the costs.

Democracy and diversity: these are at least two of the values that must inform any vision of a better world.

Notes

1. Transcript published in *The New York Times,* 23 September 1990.
2. 5 March 1991.
3. Newark *Star Ledger,* 14 January 1992, p. 1.
4. 11 March 1992.

The Value of Diversity for Global Cooperation

John Brown Childs

*Exercise great patience and goodwill toward each other in
your deliberations. Let the good tidings of Peace and Power
and righteousness be your guide....Cultivate good feelings of
friendship, love, and honor to each other always.*

*—Dekanahwida, 15th century co-founder of the Native
American inter-tribal "Iroquois Confederacy"*[1]

It is to the ongoing creation of Planetary Community that I direct these remarks. To assist in the growth of this community requires grappling with the tremendous diversity of peoples holding many different outlooks, while simultaneously undoing elite-dominated, deeply rooted structures of inequality and subjugation. I believe that locally rooted, culturally grounded diversity is not intrinsically a barrier to a Planetary Community. To the contrary, locally rooted diversity can be fundamental to the growth of egalitarian cooperation rather than domineering forms of world order inequality.

The "alternative world order" that Brecher discusses is actually one of "community," rather than one of "order" with its hierarchical, elite-dominated command systems. But Brecher's "community" is at first glance different from the village, the tribe, the ethnic group, and nation which are the more usual sites to which that term is applied. This globally expansive community is premised on a worldview that, Brecher says, "recognizes the transnational character of human identities."

Can such a view, "Of the planet, By the planet, and For the planet," be anything more than a pipe dream lost in the smoke of pollution, war, and hatred? I believe a Planetary Community with its embracing worldview is both possible, necessary, and currently in development. But we must identify and address countervailing problems that erode the tendency toward this community.

Obviously the world is riddled with conflicts, infused with tremendous inequalities; at the same time it is being shaped by powerful elites that survive through brutal subjugation of whole peoples, classes, and regions. Huge economic empires of multinational corporations mold the destinies of millions of unwilling people. The subordination of women, the virulence of racism, bloody conflict, and the willingness to use the genocidal force of powerful national military machines in the interest of maintaining "geopolitical" domination are harsh realities. What chance does the thin reed of Planetary Community stand in these powerful currents?

Were Planetary Community only an idea, however compassionate, I would have to say it stood no chance at all. However there are also powerful requirements for global survival that work toward the growth of such a community, and some apparent barriers to that growth are not what they seem on the mirage surface presented by the mass media.

Consider "race" and ethnicity. We hear about the very real ethnic/racial conflicts in the former Soviet Union, Yugoslavia, France, Belgium, Northern Ireland, the United States, and elsewhere. Indeed, there are strong indications that increasing inequalities connected to changing industrial/economic realities and fueled by hard-core racism will produce social explosions in many Western nations to rival the difficulties now being faced in the former Soviet Union. Some deride "the new tribalism" and "ethnic separatism" as the source of all social conflict. They point to intensive local identities as barriers to interaction.

But conflict is not intrinsic in terms such as "tribe," which means a group of people who share a common way of life and history. Tribes and local groups do not *per se* stand in the way of a planetary outlook. In North America alone, there are numerous historical examples of inter-tribal alliances and cooperations such as the "Great League of the Iroquois," or Haudenosaunee, founded in the 15th century; the huge pan-tribal alliance created by Tecumseh in the early 1800s to resist white expansion; and the African-American/Seminole alliance that fought some fifty years of guerrilla war against U.S. expansion in Florida in the early 1800s. Rather, it is modern industrial society, which in about 200 years has brought the planet to the brink of destruction, that has much to learn philosophically from indigenous "tribal" peoples who managed to live with, not against, other tribes and the planet for centuries. To be sure, there are also histories of tribal warfare among some peoples. But those are at most just subsets of a long, sad human history in which groups of all sorts fight one another. The most destructive wars using the most horrible scientifically developed weapons in human history have originated in this century not among tribal peoples, but among modern "civilized" industrial nations struggling over power and territory.

The nightmares of imperialism and totalitarianism are historically carried out in the name of a uniformity that subordinates and obliterates diversity in the name of one nation's asserted superiority. Imperialism, lock-step totalitarian systems, the World Wars, and conflict in the former Yugoslavia are not caused by efforts to create "cultural diversity." To the contrary, it is monocultural uniformity, imposed from above, using the barrel of the gun and the power of "cold cash" to obliterate diversity that has wreaked major destruction and suffering in modern history.

Consequently, the growth of Planetary Community requires constant vigilance against claims of monocultural uniformity and the superiority of one nation over another. If we are to be a Planetary Community rather than a New World Order run by the United States and its "consortium" partners, we must rely in part on diversity as a resource. The resilience of local groups can be the elemental stuff from which will grow a real community that can resist the deadening hand of international uniformity used to maintain the power of the few. This said, we still are left to wrestle with the classic dilemma of how to form unity with, rather than against, the real diversity of peoples.

We are flooded with negative examples of the apparent disruptive effects of diversity every day in the media. Some examples are tragically real and must be confronted directly. But we must be very careful not to be lured into the simplistic, indiscriminate, and misleading use of the term "ethnic conflict" as the core source of all current societal tensions. It is to the advantage of powerful national elites in countries such as the United States to construct a new post-Soviet threat to world peace as one of "ethnic conflict." To the contrary, the threat comes more from aggressive European-style nationalism, with various national elites armed to the teeth by international arms merchants, including many Western ones. Of course, if such "nationalism" and the international arms trade are really the issue, then the very role of the United States and its allies would also have to be reexamined given their own nationalistic strivings and profit-oriented arms manufacturers.

The misleading shifting of the source of all crisis to "ethnic conflict" implies that in various parts of the world, two or more groups, each homogenous and culturally distinct from each other, are engaged in "primordial," "intractable," "tribalized" warfare of the most "primitive" kind precisely because they are fundamentally "different." But in many instances, conflict does not arise out of group diversity *per se*. Nor, despite the claims of some partisans, is it simply a continuation of historical memory. Rather conflict often erupts from efforts of powerful state-supported elites and groups to obliterate multiculturalism, and to subordinate or exterminate the communities that make up heterogenous social environments. State-sponsored terror, subordination, oppression, and genocide aimed at particular cultural communities then inevitably produces resistance. Such conflicts are more often the consequences of the damaging impact of oppressive inequality, not of ethnic plurality *per se.*

For example, in Guatemala, at least 100,000 indigenous peoples have been murdered by (U.S. supported) government forces; at least 40,000 have "disappeared," which is to say they have been murdered; 450 villages have been destroyed; and 250,000 people have been turned into refugees because of government "anti-guerrilla" campaigns aimed at the Mayan population along with labor, human-rights, and other activists. Some observers would consider this situation as "ethnic conflict" between the indigenous Mayan people and the Hispano-Eurocentric dominated government and population. But as diverse writers such as Susanne Jonas and Maurice Lemoine point out, the history of Guatemala is one in which, "the (majority) indigenous populations live under all sorts of discrimination and violence."[2] Socially sanctioned anti-indigenous discrimination and violence, not the presence of distinctive cultural groups, is the issue. Salvador Palamino Flores says of similar events in Peru:

> Without respecting the multiplicity of cultures and the concept of multiculturalism, they want us all to be Westernized like they are. But that clashes very sharply with an Indian principle—the way of living of Indian people that is based on plurality.[3]

And as Lynne Williamson points out in her chapter on the situation of Native Americans in North America, written for this book:

> United States government policies of extermination, economic dependence, assimilation, termination of some tribes, and now homogeneity under the guise of economic independence…are always driven by the goal of mainstreaming us until we no longer exist as separate nations or groups.[4]

Remove such inequality and suppression aimed at particular cultural groups; produce a democratic non-oppressive multicultural environment such as that of Switzerland; and "ethnic difference" would no longer be connected to "conflict." Let us not put the "cart of cultural distinctiveness" in front of the "nightmare horse of oppression."

Similarly, Bogdan Denitch points out that the war in Bosnia (usually called "Muslim-dominated Bosnia" in much of the U.S. media) is less "ethnic conflict" and more an effort to impose a nationalist monocultural uniformity by evaporating a complex vital multi-ethnic cosmopolitan society. The blood-drenched term "ethnic cleansing" *does not involve an effort to create multiculturalism, but instead to destroy it.* Denitch points out that the cities have been sites of multicultural interaction and cooperation. And, it is the cities that have been targeted. He says:

> Multi-ethnic Sarajevo was the major source of popular music and culture...The cities where massive intermarriage and denationalization take place, where various national groups mix and make friends, where women enter professions, where the young reject tradition—these cities are the sources of modernity. Being a citizen of Yugoslavia had meant to me being a member of a very heterogenous community.[5]

Consequently, the sources of the tragic situation in the former Yugoslavia today, says Denitch, are not to be found in the very "multi-ethnic" society that is now being systematically destroyed. Instead, roots of destruction entwine their constricting stranglehold around expansive multiculturalism by forcing the creation of new identities that "are so much narrower, more parochial, and less flexible."

And what pushes toward such deadly monocultural narrowness? By definition, an essentially non-oppressive multi-ethnic society does not do so since its very existence is one of pluralistic breadth rather than constriction. Rather, in the former Yugoslavia, the parochialized mono-ethnic version of the nation-state is imposing an "aggressive nationalism [that] is mainly responsible for this unnecessary death." Moreover, while certainly there are "grassroots" elements of average people who participate in pogroms, manipulative national elites are orchestrating much of this disaster in former Yugoslavia and elsewhere. Denitch says:

> The political elites of the states of former Yugoslavia have wrought a massive disaster on their peoples....[They] are not alone. Throughout Eastern Europe and the former Soviet Union destructive over-ambitious bunglers, often uncritically supported by a West relieved to see the last of the communists in power, were able to get more or less popular mandates.[6]

We should note that opinion surveys conducted in the former Czech and Slovak Federated Republic before the break-up there showed that the majority of people opposed the split into two nations. Key nationalist elite gate-keepers succeeded in their aims by refusing to hold a referendum on the subject. The "ethnic" split took place not because of popular opinion but despite it.

I am certainly not an "expert" on the former Yugoslavia, or on Guatemala, or on various other sites of carnage and division around the world. I stand dumbfounded and aghast at the slaughter. I make no claims to fully comprehend or to speak about the depths of human suffering in so many places; about the horrible systematic mass rapes of thousands of Bosnian women; about the brutal blasting of cities such as Sarajevo; or about the genocidal attacks on the Mayan people in Guatemala. But clearly it is not the everyday life of locally-based ethnic diversity from Sarajevo to Guatemala that is the problem. To the contrary, often it is a brutally imposed, state-sanctioned, elite-directed, *mono-ethnic uniformity* combined with purist single-culture nationalism that is the key culprit.

Elite-directed national conflict, rather than multi-ethnic difference, is the wellspring from which flow many tragedies. The dangerous illusion of mono-cultural and racial "purity," coupling in deadly embrace with the bloody nationalism of political elites, produces the offspring of horror.

By contrast, the most positive possibilities for Planetary Community are coming from highly distinctive cultural/occupational/local groups who are increasingly working cooperatively with one another. Many such groups have intersecting concerns about the environment, about corrosive massive poverty, about militarism and elite control, and about the still real specter of nuclear war.

Such group concerns are important for a variety of reasons. They are often grounded in tangible economic and environmental issues that operate at both local and global levels. The felt need to do something about these problems is intense. From the Veracruz Ecology Group in Mexico to "Ecology Club" activists in Poland; from Bhopal to Chernobyl; from nuclear testing sites in the former Soviet Union to the land of the Shoshone in the western United States diverse peoples face the awesome consequences of the world's elites' lust for power and money.

But local groups do not have to give up their distinctive identities in order to address these problems collectively with others at great distance from them. Rather, their strength can flow from their tangible senses of distinctive self and place. We see this powerful sense of self, place, and planetary connectedness among the Kayapo in Brazil; among aboriginal peoples of Australia; among the Inuit and Saami of the Arctic. We see the importance of local diversity in the activities of Love Canal organizers, in the coalitions of the Yakima, Umatilla, and Nez Perce Indian peoples near the Hanford nuclear weapons facility. We see it among women organizers in the Chipko "Embrace-the-Tree movement" in India; among the "Greenbelt movement" activists in Kenya; in the anti-toxic waste-dumping coalition of Chicano and African-American community activists outside Los Angeles; and in the base community movement in the *favelas* of Brazil. Such distinctive local groups often have stamina, knowledge, and resilience because they are grounded in tangible global environmental/economic dilemmas, while simultaneously working from deep cultural, historical, and local rootedness.

So the Planetary Community is being created from below, from a diverse variety of ethnic, cultural, and local contexts that confront globally destructive, international economic elites and forces. Moreover, it is precisely because this community is being created from grounded, distinctively diverse groups that it is not a pipe dream lost in the ozone-thinning sky. Cross-border alliances of indigenous, ethnic, tribal, and other communities—such as the "Unrepresented Nations and Peoples Organization;" the "Circumpolar Conference" cutting across Greenland, Canada, the United States, Russia, and Scandinavia; and the "World Conference of Indigenous Peoples"—work to avoid the historical trap of imposing one monocentric viewpoint which has so bedeviled human existence in recent centuries.

Given that culturally and locally rooted diversity is vital for a nonauthoritarian Planetary Community, it follows that we do not need a New World Order's monocentric, elite-dominated blueprint to shape us. Rather, as Brecher suggests, we need improved and expanded instrumental means for mutual communication and interaction between these diverse groups across national boundaries. It is time to make greater use of the technological and often simple means of communication now available if we are to build bridges among distinctive yet parallel groups.

In his book *A Dying Colonialism*, Frantz Fanon describes the way radio, originally viewed as an instrument of French domination of colonized Algeria, is transformed into a weapon of resistance once revolutionary broadcasts are made by liberation stations.[7] Today, satellite communications, videotapes, audiotapes, and relatively cheap means of duplication are but some of the ways increased activity could open up vast planetary networks of cross-group contact. Information about successes, failures, and common needs can be shared more widely. Such "people-to-people communication" is important precisely because the strength of local groups flows both from their autonomy *and* from their ability to know about and work with similar groups.

Alone, of course, such mutual communication is not sufficient. But it is a necessary aspect in the battle against a monocentric New World Order that maintains the old order of massive inequality and violent suppression. Diversity of grounded tribal, ethnic, neighborhood, labor, environmental, women's, and other local groups is a tremendous asset which, assisted by mutual sharing of information among us, will aid in the ongoing growth of the constructive egalitarian Planetary Community.

Notes

1. Dekanahwida, (Founding statement of the Iroquois Confederacy or the Haudenosaunee), in *Voices of the Wind,* Margot Edmonds and Ella Clark, eds., New York: Facts on File, 1989, pp. 351-357.

2. Jonas, Susanne, *The Battle for Guatemala: Rebels, Death Squads, and U.S. Power,* Boulder, Colorado: Westview Press, 1991; Lemoine, Maurice, "Le Chagrin et l'effroi au Guatemala," *Le Monde Diplomatique,* 22 December 1991, pp. 22-23.

3. Palamino Flores, Salvador, "Keynote Address" in *Proceedings: World Conference of Indigenous Peoples Education,* Vancouver: First Nations House of Learning, 1987, pp. 21-22.

4. Lynne Williamson, "The Great Tree of Peace," in this book.

5. Denitch, Bogdan, "Tragedy in Former Yugoslavia," *Dissent,* Winter 1993, pp. 26-34.

6. Ibid.

7. Fanon, Frantz, *A Dying Colonialism,* trans. Haakon Chevalier, New York: Grove Press, 1965.

Building
an Alternative World Order

What is to be Done?

Juan J. Palacios

The world is nowadays at a decisive turning point, where the powers that be frenetically strive to mold a world structure that assures the preservation of their interests, largely disregarding the social and environmental consequences it might beget, in a vast offensive whose overwhelming force can only be counteracted by the actions of concerned people and organizations committed to a more humane order, one respectful of nature and life on the planet. I would like to add some reflections to the views put forward by Jeremy Brecher about such an order.

A Sense of History

Before thinking about the appropriate strategies to adopt, we should attempt a more thorough characterization of the present world conjuncture, one that permits us to discern its essential features and trends, so that we are able to know better how to act on them. This requires us to place this conjuncture in historical perspective, and thus to understand it as a specific stage of capitalism's secular development. What I intend here is to make more explicit that it is the system we should struggle against, not a particular policy of a given hegemonic nation.

The Present World Conjuncture

From such a perspective, it should be acknowledged that the transition to a new international order is taking place at the end of the 20th century, when the 21st is becoming an imminent reality. The rise of Japan as an economic and technological superpower, followed by other nations in East and Southeast Asia, has led to the emergence of Asia and the Pacific as the most dynamic region in the world. This phenomenon is becoming one of the determining factors in the shaping of the world order that will prevail in the 21st century, which, significantly enough, is already referred to as the Pacific Century.

Now that the Cold War has ended and the collapse of the socialist world has culminated in the final breakdown of the Soviet Union, Japan has become the new ideological enemy for the United States and, in a way, of the West at large. The close interdependence that has developed between the United States and Japan has resulted in growing tensions that may soon result in open confrontation, as George Friedman and Meredith Lebard have argued in their book *The Next War With Japan*. This is a reality in international relations: the more interdependent two countries are, the more potential for conflict develops between them.

Another major feature of the present conjuncture is the evident decline of U.S. hegemony, and thus the absence of a single, undisputed hegemon. Even more, it seems virtually impossible for any nation to become such a hegemon in all respects, as the Gulf War demonstrated in 1991. The end of the Pax Americana is thus another reality at the end of the 20th century. In this respect, the rise of Japan as an economic superpower has led many to think of the possibility of a Pax Nipponica, at least a limited one based on Japan's position as the world's largest financial supplier, as Ezra Vogel, in his book *Japan as Number One*, anticipated as early as 1979.

The solution of the ongoing dispute over who will have an hegemonic position in the new international order will mainly depend on how U.S.-Japan relations evolve in the coming decades. In any event, Japan will be at least the number-two hegemon, a circumstance that should be taken into account for the design of a bottom-up strategy to build a new global order, if we consider that Japanese views of the world are not the same as those held by the United States; after all the two countries hold quite different conceptions of capitalism.

The Underlying Realities

But beneath the apparent restructuring of power relations, what truly characterizes the present international conjuncture is what I have termed underlying realities. The most all-encompassing of these realities is the trend toward global stagnation that began to emerge in the early 1970s and is deepening in the 1990s, giving rise to an exacerbated economic competition among both nations and multinational corporations as investment opportunities have narrowed and profit rates have concomitantly slumped. As a result, world commercial exchange has increasingly turned into what Peter Drucker in his book *The New Realities* terms adversarial trade, that is, trade in which the purpose is not to displace competitors through better and cheaper products, but simply to destroy them. In this hostile environment, Drucker argues, the only way for nations to obtain reciprocity is by grouping with other nations to form multistate economic blocs with sufficient power to face this reality.

This is the major feature of what the CIA termed, in its report entitled *Changemasters*, the new transnational, as opposed to international, economy, in which trade is no longer carried out between nations but between regions, as the nation-state is being undermined by the power of the multistate conglomerates that characterize this new economic order. The consolidation of the European Common Market and the North American Free Trade Agreement treaty are examples of this trend.

From another perspective, the formation of trading blocs, and more generally the process of global regionalization, is nothing more than a response of capital to global stagnation. Proponents hope that trade liberalization in larger regions will bring about the stimulus the world capitalist economy so needs to get out of its present slump; this is particularly the case of the European Community. At the same time, regionalization is a search for collective security before the growing uncertainties of such a stagnant, fiercely competitive global economy.

The other major response of capital to the stalemate of this epoch has been an unprecedented acceleration of the process of globalization, as is now called the expansion to a global scale of the power and operations of the large multinational corporations based in the leading industrialized countries. Globalization has resulted in one of the essential contradictions of this period of transition: that between the formation of regional blocs and the transnationalization of productive operations across national, regional, or even continental borders. Such transnationalization has entailed substantial changes in the international division of labor which, it should be stressed, constitutes the sustaining economic fabric of every world order.

All these underlying realities remind us that we live in a hostile world in which every actor is doing whatever can be done to weather the storm and preserve its own interests. What we have to bear in mind is that those interests oppose any attempt, either top-down or bottom-up, to build a world order based on an institutional system different from that in which they were originated and in which they can be reproduced.

Neoliberalism as the Dominant Ideology

A powerful force that has taken shape in the last decade is the renewed liberalism that the powers that be have imposed as the dominant ideology of the end of the 20th century. More than ever, the principles of free market, free trade, and free enterprise stand now as articles of faith; capitalism is portrayed as the natural order that must be preserved for humankind to prosper and survive. The collapse of actually existing socialism contributed to this view, appearing as proof of the unviability and undesirability of the order inspired in Marxist thought, and indicating the corresponding triumph of capitalism.

The rise of neoliberalism is part of the strategies of large capital and its representatives in advanced nations for breaking out of stagnation, and at the same time for renewing the ideological bases of the triumphant system. The problem is that neoliberal policies and development strategies are already revealing the heavy costs they imply in social and environmental terms. This is occurring both in the United States after Reagan and Bush, and in countries like Mexico and Chile, the Third World nations that most faithfully embraced neoliberal doctrine as inspiration for their development models. Poverty, malnutrition, and a brutal concentration of income and wealth are growing, notably in these two Latin American countries.

The truth is that, inasmuch as it is based on the blind logic of the market, neoliberalism is inconsistent with social, progressive redistribution, and also blind and deaf to ecological considerations. The task of shaping an alternative world order that cares for social and environmental needs will thus require a struggle against this powerful ideology and its corresponding theoretical underpinnings which, in his book *La Contrarrevolución Monetarista* (The Monetarist Counterrevolution), Mexican economist René Villarreal has termed "bastard monetarism."

What is to be Done?

It may be clear from the above discussion that the transition we are going through at this point in history is not a result of the crisis of the nation state, as Jeremy Brecher argues, but a consequence mainly of the collapse of the international order forged after World War II along the path of capitalism's development. This order has now become what Chinese analyst Chen Xiaogong has characterized as a "turbulent détente, an order in which one superpower coexists with several other lesser powers all depending on and struggling against each other." What collapsed was not only the postwar structure of power in a geopolitical sense, but also the international economic and financial edifice engendered by the Bretton Woods agreements of 1944 and the institution of the welfare state, likewise created along the lines of Keynesian doctrine.

Present trends thus point to a multipolar world structure in which the balance of power will hinge on what I would call a shared hegemony. At the same time, we can anticipate a world map composed of regional multistate clusters cut across by an increasingly globalized network of shared production among nations—a structure that will correspond to a highly hierarchical international division of labor. We are therefore still far from the demise of the nation-state. It is both an institution and an actor with which we will be living in the foreseeable future; the reemergence of the ethnic groups and ancient nations that for a long time were oppressed under the Soviet empire and now claim a territory as a matter of historical identity shows how deeply rooted is the concept of the nation-state as the basis for the organization of peoples the world over.

The question is how to go about building another kind of world order, which means going against the powerful trends giving birth to today's. First of all, any initiative in that direction should have a sense of timing. To build a new world order takes decades and even centuries. What is needed, therefore, is a strategy that envisions steps to tackle immediate urgent problems, and at the same time defines the guidelines for actions to induce structural changes in the long run. This requires us to begin by taking rather modest but at the same time more solid and viable actions, instead of devising from the outset global institutions to administer a new order we still do not know how to bring about.

The actions of today's self-organized groups, grassroots and social movements, environmental organizations, and concerned communities can exert pressure for orienting or changing decisions on specific issues, but only up to the point "the powers that be" consider unthreatening to their interests. Moreover, up to now the actions of those groups have mainly dealt with the consequences and effects of capitalism. Although this is a most encouraging starting point, the task of building up an alternative world order requires us to struggle against the capitalist system itself.

One approach is to focus on issues that may result in the imposition of limits to that system, to which end environmental demands have the highest potential. In this sense, bottom-up organizations and movements have pointed to the right target. What is needed, though, is to bear in mind that unrestricted capitalist production is the single most important cause of environmental devastation, as it is guided by the logic of the market which implies a reckless disregard for ecological considerations.

Marx taught us that, in order to survive, capitalism must be in permanent expansion. More recently Paul Sweezy and Harry Magdoff have reminded us in the pages of *Monthly Review* that unlimited growth in a limited environment is a contradiction in terms and ultimately "a recipe for disaster," a disaster that may occur in the next century. They add that if we care about the survival of the human species, we must listen to the ecologists and design a program that permits us to relieve "current suffering" and at the same time to initiate a process of radical reform.

A sound strategy for building up an alternative international order careful of human needs and respectful of the preservation of the natural habitat will have to combine actions to induce or change decisions on immediate issues with others geared to effect a radical reform in the system. In this latter respect, although grassroots and other social movements are multiplying all over the world and are already affecting policies and decisions, the overall strategy could be made more effective with the emergence of a new class or social stratum that the globalization of production and the advances in telecommunications can make possible. Hopefully, it would be a stratum with sufficient leverage to adopt and promote the interest of the masses who will suffer the consequences of the world-order-to-be, but cannot make their voices heard. It would be a plural, transnational class with a world vision favorable to the needs of people and planet, whose views and claims thus combine both economic and environmental demands from grassroots and other bottom-up groups. If it develops, such a class—comprised of workers in multinational corporations, backed by ecologists, intellectuals, and other concerned people—could be a more viable and effective actor and promoter than the rather vague figure Brecher calls "self-organized people."

But instead of making more predictions, I would just say finally that what is definitely imperative both for the emergence of the said hypothetical class, and ultimately for the launching of any progressive offensive to influence the conformation of an alternative world order, is the conception of a new doctrine and a new paradigm that are capable of generating a new ideology that takes up the claims and worries of the masses of individuals of the new order. Only in such a way can major advances be achieved, as these groups organize themselves and thus become a force capable of forcing capital to make things easier for the working class and the planet. In the past, marxism provided such a paradigm for workers and progressive groups. After the fall of real socialism and the corresponding crisis of marxism, a new doctrine is needed as a real and viable alternative to neoliberalism, and thus as a guide for progressive movements that strive to procure more humane living conditions and a better world for our children now and in the imminent Pacific Century.

Peaceful, People-Centered, and Ecologically Sensitive Development

A Mechanism for Promoting a New World Order

Ben E. Aigbokhan

*Everybody will understand that I recommend attacking first
those expenditures whose external impact is the most
harmful because they result in mounting waste beyond
national borders.*

—*Michel Camdessus,
Speech at United Nations Economic and Social Council, 1991.*

The above quotation underscores the growing globalization of the
world economy. Actions or inactions in one part of the world have crucial
repercussions on the other parts. The consumption pattern in one part
has its effects on the other parts. And like the human body, when one
part is ailing it affects the proper functioning of the others.

Arms production, in which industrialized nations seek markets in
the non-industrialized world, and wood and furniture consumption, in
which the former seek the necessary raw materials (timber) from the
latter, are two major examples of expenditures whose external impact is
harmful because of the resulting armament, wars, deforestation, and
poverty in the latter.

Various forms of world order have existed in the past and have not
succeeded in averting wars. Indeed they have tended to engender wars.
Robert McNamara observed that in the past 45 years there have been
some 125 wars and conflicts in the Third World. He went on to state that
because of the diverse reasons countries have for going to war, we must
conclude that in the world of the future, conflicts within and among

nations will not disappear even though the East and West cease to fight their proxy wars in the South. This "inevitability of wars" view is based on the fact that nation-states are still seen—and will continue to be seen—as distinct sovereign entities with few unifying interests cutting across their boundaries that might reduce or eliminate the "inevitability of wars."[1] In contrast to that view, this chapter argues for an Alternative World Order based on inter-country interests sufficient to ensure peace-oriented, people-centered, and ecologically sensitive growth and development.

The New World Order

Jeremy Brecher describes an Old World Order which is based on the model of sovereign nation-states, each building its own political, social, economic, and cultural institutions. That order has been characterized by the Cold War between East and West, the division of the globe into First, Second, and Third worlds, and the struggle to dominate and the fear of domination. In other words, the Old World Order lacked mutual interests strong enough to ensure permanent peaceful co-existence and thereby foster growth of the world economy.

The United Nations was created after World War II to serve as a rallying point for common global interests, but experience has shown that the body is used effectively only when the dominant nation-states wish it—when it is in their own interest. For example, the UN was not used effectively to resolve the Israeli-Palestinian issue or the South African apartheid issue, but was used effectively to prosecute the Gulf War against Saddam Hussein's Iraq. From this emerged what Brecher refers to as the New World Order, based on a coalition of the rich and powerful political regimes, their corporations, and their military establishments, which will cooperate to preserve their access to the resources of the Earth. The rich and powerful political regimes co-opt a few poorer and weaker ones from time to time to execute programs as and when necessary. Again, as experience has shown, these co-opted countries' benefits are often temporary and short-lived. For example, Egypt's reward for being co-opted in the Gulf War was a debt write-off. Such a benefit, however, only touches on a symptom and not a cause of developmental failure in Egypt, as in any other debt-ridden country. Moreover, Brecher has rightly argued that such a coalition seems incapable of solving the impending ecological crisis, the growing gap between the rich and poor within and between countries, and the proliferation of weapons of mass destruction.

An Alternative World Order proposed by Brecher recognizes the transnational character of human identities and historical forces, a set of principles for ordering them, and institutional means for implementing those principles. It posits a social world composed not of sovereign states but of interpenetrating entities with overlapping boundaries. To execute this Alternative World Order, a world parliament of some sort is being proposed in which everybody will participate in decisionmaking.

There is no doubt that there is a need for a new world order with common interests that transcend national boundaries. Fear of domination and fear of loss of national economic and political sovereignty have been barriers to the success of international economic or political associations. Such fears may be allayed if mass participation by disarmament and environmental movements is used to foster such transnational associations.

However, the approach as presently conceived may face some operational difficulties, for at least three reasons. First, the idea of doing away with national identity may be difficult for people to accept. Even within countries, people still like to maintain their ethnic and cultural ties. This does not prevent inter-ethnic interests binding them together. Similarly, retaining national identities may not pose a serious barrier to a new world order conducive to peaceful coexistence with sustainable growth and development, so long as there are inter-boundary interests strong enough to make parties see themselves as having common interests to protect and promote. Second, there is specialization in knowledge, and therefore everyone cannot have adequate knowledge of every issue, even the ones that affect them. So there would still be the need for delegated authority through the electoral process to allow people with adequate knowledge to handle the issues at hand. And third, there are economies of scale in decisionmaking. There can be only one optimum size of decisionmaking body. Below this size or beyond it the process of decisionmaking may not be effective or efficient. This explains why some sort of world parliament may be a rather large size for effective decisionmaking, and also explains why excessive decentralization of decisionmaking may not be desirable either.

In the same vein, international efforts to promote good governance in less developed countries (LDCs) are often resented as external interference in their domestic affairs. If good governance means a system that has political accountability through a credible electoral process with limited periods in office; bureaucratic accountability and transparency, with an effective and politically autonomous system of correcting abuses; and freedom of association, particularly of associations based on the pursuit of political, economic, social, and cultural objectives, few LDCs satisfy these requirements so far. However, an Alternative World Order which is based on the transnational character of human interests is more capable of promoting good governance and eliminating fear of domination or interference. It is in this context that Brecher's effort is a welcome one.

A Workable New World Order

If we recognize that eliminating national identities will be difficult, that there are limits to the size of decisionmaking bodies, and that there is therefore the need for some decentralization, the question becomes how to promote a workable new world order based on increased democratization in developing countries, and on sustainable growth and development of the world economy. In other words, how do we promote unity in diversity? As Brecher himself has advocated, the new world order should be based on the conception of the individual as a member of many groups. By implication, such individuals could be brought together by common interest(s). Identifying interests and concerns which cut across national boundaries, therefore, provides possibilities of evolving such a new world order. These include the growing arms buildup globally, environmental degradation and pollution, and growing mass poverty.

The global arms buildup has been of concern to a growing band of people for some decades now. If we recognize that resources available for human use are limited, and that what is used for one purpose is no longer available for other purposes, such a concern becomes even more understandable. In terms of the ratio of military expenditures to total central government expenditures, the average worldwide in 1972-88 was 16.5%.[2] While the developed countries' average was lower, that of Eastern Europe and developing countries was higher than average. Yet a growing burden of military spending has been found to contribute to developmental failures in many developing countries.[3]

The trend in military spending worldwide has reached such a high proportion that analysts have begun to simulate the level of savings that could be made and the scale of development possibilities that could thereby be stimulated should there be reductions in military spending. For example, Camdessus noted that "with regard to military spending, which might be expected to decline somewhat with a reduction in East-West tensions and the settlement of several regional conflicts, imagine that...all countries were to decide to reduce their military spending to the level of the worldwide average of 4.5% of GDP [Gross Domestic Product] recorded in 1988,…an annual worldwide savings of $140 billion would be generated."[4]

It is the causes of the growing military spending that pose the greatest threat to world peace. Until very recently it was the arms buildup in First and Second worlds that attracted attention. But an equally alarming level of arms buildup was going on in the Third World. According to McNamara, of the top 15 Third World arms importers during 1978-88, who together accounted for about three-quarters of arms imported by the Third World (i.e. three-quarters of $371 billion), 13 have been party to conflicts of many years' duration. In addition, many acquire arms to protect against perceived internal and external threats. This observation underscores the urgent need for a new world order that would transcend national boundaries to promote international security.

McNamara proposes solutions to the growing arms buildup. These include substantial limitations on arms exports from arms-producing nations, the tying of financial aid in developing countries to reductions in military expenditures by these countries, and reducing the demand for arms. This, he reckons, could be achieved by introducing into the system of collective security a guarantee by the Security Council and regional organizations of the territorial integrity of member states.[5]

These proposals, which apparently were influenced by the "inevitability of wars" view mentioned earlier, have little chance of success. First, it seems to be assumed that the principle of "voluntary arms exports restraint" would work to reduce arms buildup. But experience suggests the unlikelihood of this being realized. Second, considering that aid donors are also often the arms exporters, if voluntary export restraint is not likely to work, one is left to wonder how effective the tying of aid to reductions in military spending would be. And third, the breakdown of the Old World Order has largely been due to the ineffectiveness of the United Nations, as presently constituted, as an organ for promoting cross-border interests. Thus, there is the need for a mechanism to promote a new world order.

As with armament, international concern about deforestation in developing countries has been growing in recent years. In the industrial countries this has been partly because of the implications for global warming and partly because of the political influence of the "green movements." In developing countries it has been because of the awareness that rapid deforestation may hinder possibilities for sustainable development, coupled with popular movements by some indigenous groups negatively affected by deforestation processes.

Barraclough and Ghimore estimate that over 200 million people currently depend in large part on tropical forests for their livelihood.[6] Through deforestation Africa has been losing three to five million hectares of tropical forest annually, and over 20 million hectares are lost worldwide annually. At this rate, tropical forests in Africa will disappear within 60 years. In fact, Nigeria, Ghana, the Ivory Coast and Togo are reckoned to have already lost almost all of their tropical forests. Serageldin further estimates that if the current rate of tropical forest conversion continues unabated, the world may lose between 5 and 15% of its total plant and animal species between 1990 and 2020.[7]

Until recently the consequences of deforestation and environmental degradation in developing countries were borne by local populations directly dependent on these resources. But now the burdens have spread to larger numbers of people because trans-boundary pollution of the atmosphere and international waterways and global warming threaten the world ecosystems. The burdens are, however, heaviest for the poor.

In proposing solutions to deforestation in sub-Saharan Africa and, by extension, the world over, Serageldin calls for "a balanced perspective that divides the responsibilities between North and South, and among the different parties—local communities, governments, the private sector development agencies, and international and local non-governmental assistance agencies."[8] Serageldin does not, however, spell out what mechanism or institution would be used to share responsibilities. If the United Nations is to be used, the question remains about the incapability of the United Nations, as currently constituted, to deal with such issues. Besides, how equitably can the United Nations share such responsibilities? For example, of the $625 billion estimated to finance the Global Earth project (the Rio Summit on Environment and Development), developing countries are expected to contribute $500 billion, while developed countries would contribute $125 billion.

From the foregoing it is obvious that issues of disarmament and the environment are of international concern and these provide real possibilities for fostering a new world order. These two issues have a third issue in common, namely concern about people and their future. This is why it is argued in this chapter that a peaceful, people-centered, and ecologically sensitive development strategy provides a great promise for promoting an Alternative World Order of the type advocated by Brecher. The mechanism is briefly presented below.

The disarmament campaign, which initially started in the North, has now spread to the South, following the observation that most of the wars in the past four decades have been fought there. So there are groups in both the North and the South who have interests strong enough, and that transcend national boundaries enough, to make them come together with the aim of organizing to influence world decisionmaking. There are the Campaign for Nuclear Disarmament in the North and peace movements in the various regions of the South, such as the various Peace Research Institutes which are affiliates of the Stockholm International Peace Research Institute. Such movements could come together to form a new world peace movement with the aim of influencing decisionmaking in both North and South. Such a new peace movement would be less likely to be suspected of external interference and would reduce the fear or threat of domination.

Environmental campaign groups have similarly been quite active in the North; these include the Greenpeace and Friends of the Earth movements. In the South, some popular movements of forest-dependent poor people have also been organizing campaigns to defend their interests. An example is the alliance of rubber tappers and indigenous groups in the Brazilian Amazon to resist encroachment on their forest habitat by large-scale commercial farmers, ranchers, and land speculators. Another is the Chipko movement of rural people in Northern India. They, too, organized to save their forests. A third example is the struggle of Penan and other tribal groups in Sarawak, Malaysia, against the destruction of their homelands by commercial loggers. By forming human blockades across logging roads leading into their traditional territories in early 1987, they brought the logging industry to a total standstill for a while.[9]

Thus, popular participation or decisionmaking from below, by which is meant the organized efforts to increase control over resources and regulatory institutions, in given social situations, on the part of groups and movements of those hitherto excluded from such control, can be an effective way of evolving a new world order. But unlike in the past, when most of these movements were one-issue campaign groups, the new movements could combine two or three related issues like disarmament, environment, and poverty. Such an effort could still be accommodated within the optimum size and specialization of knowledge criteria.

The Africa Peace Research Institute (Nigeria Chapter) is already moving in this direction; that is, it is moving from being solely a peace movement, concerned only with disarmament and conflict resolution issues, to an organization concerned with peace, the environment, and development. Membership at the moment is primarily in the middle-level and policymaking class. Mass public education to enlighten local people is being planned, although it is so far hampered by lack of funds. The African Peace Research Institutes could coordinate such a program across the globe until it gains wide acceptance. Other issues could then be introduced from time to time. In due course there would emerge a world of different nationals, united by common global interests, coming together to create the type of Alternative World Order being advocated by this book.

Notes

1. McNamara, R., "Reducing Military Expenditures in the Third World," *Finance and Development,* September 1991, pp. 26-28.
2. Hewitt, D. P., "Military Expenditures in the Developing World," *Finance & Development,* September 1991, pp. 22-25.
3. Aigbokhan, B. E., "Threats to Peace in West Africa," *Peace Review,* Winter 1991/92, pp. 52-54.
4. Camdessus, M., "Global Investment Needs, Savings, and Military Spending," *Finance & Development,* September 1991, p. 28.
5. McNamara, p. 27.
6. Barraclough, S. and Ghimore, K., "The Social Dynamics of Deforestation in Developing Countries: Principal Issues and Research Priorities," United Nations Institute for Social Development Discussion Paper No. 16, (November 1990), p. 11.
7. Serageldin, I., *Saving Africa's Rainforest,* Washington, DC: World Bank, Africa Region, 1990, pp. 1-4.
8. Ibid., pp. 11-12.
9. Barraclough and Ghimore, p. 23.

References

Brecher, J., "Bush's New World Order—and Ours," *Z Magazine,* July-August 1991.
Conable, B., "Development and the Environment: A Global Balance," *Finance & Development* (December 1989), pp. 2-4.

The Making of Global Citizenship
Richard Falk

Citizenship has always been an uneven experience for the peoples of the world. Even within a particular country, it means one thing for privileged classes, the dominant race, religion, and gender, and quite another for those who are economically, socially, politically, and culturally subordinated to varying degrees. Citizenship, in general, expresses membership and the quality of participation in a political community. Its conditions can be specified by law, but its reality is a matter of politics and the rigors of experience. Thus, citizenship can be understood both formally as a status and, more adequately, existentially as a shifting set of attitudes, relationships, and expectations with no necessary territorial delimitation.

This complexity is further compounded by the two sorts of globalization that are impinging on the life experiences of individuals and groups. There is globalization-from-above, reflecting the collaboration between leading states and the main agents of capital formation. This type of globalization disseminates a consumerist ethos and draws into its domain transnational business and political elites. It is the New World Order, whether depicted as a geopolitical project of the U.S. government or as a technological and marketing project of large-scale capital, epitomized by Disney theme parks and franchise capitalism (McDonalds, Hilton, Hertz…).

The second type of globalization is both reactive to these developments and responsive to different impulses and influences. To stress the contrast, it is identified as globalization-from-below, and consists of an array of transnational social forces animated by environmental concerns, human rights, hostility to patriarchy, and a vision of human community based on the unity of diverse cultures seeking an end to poverty, oppression, humiliation, and collective violence. Instead of a New World Order, this type of globalization inclines toward a one-world community premised on a politics of aspiration and desire. This one-world community rests upon the strengthening over time of the institutional forms and activities associated with global civil society.

Globalization-from-below is, in its essence, an expression of the spirit of "democracy without frontiers," mounting a challenge to the homogenizing tendencies of globalization-from-above. At the very least, the construction of global civil society is seeking to extend ideas of moral, legal, and environmental accountability to those now acting on behalf of state, market, and media.

The specific realities of citizenship—as status and experience—take historical shape in relation to this tension between forms of globalization. Different regional currents are also exerting powerful influences on identity, and hence on citizenship: both geographical and economical aggregates and ethno-cultural groupings. As well, more specific, local attachments are expressive of a transfer of loyalty to more immediate circles of community and away from the sovereign state.

The citizenship associated with the New World Order is very much a stratified conception based on beneficiaries and victims, inclusion and exclusion. It presupposes the sustainability of high-growth capitalism. The one-world community is a far more egalitarian conception that makes environmental and cultural sustainability contingent on drastic lifestyle adjustments and the attainment of ecological/equity balances. In this second orientation toward citizenship, the distinction between expediency and utopianism becomes blurred.

The focus here on "global citizenship" is expressive of the dynamics of economic, cultural, and ecological integration that are carrying human experience beyond its modernist phase of state/society relations. The reality of global citizenship is unavoidable, but its form remains contested. It is not yet clear whether it is largely a globalized identity of elites arising from the integration of capital, or whether it represents a growth of human solidarity arising from an extension of democratic principles as a result of the exertions of peoples and their voluntary associations. Both forms of globalization are unfolding before our eyes, but what sorts of balances emerge will reveal the extent to which the so-called New World Order is our destiny for the foreseeable future, or only a disappointing stage that obstructs a move toward fulfilling our normative potential as a species, expressed by the idea of a one-world community.

Forms and Varieties of Global Citizenship

There are at least four dimensions of the extension of citizenship beyond traditional boundaries of nation and state. First of all, the extension of citizenship to its global domain tends to be aspirational in spirit, drawing upon a long tradition of thought and feeling about the ultimate unity of human experience, giving rise to a politics of desire that posits for the planet as a whole a set of conditions of peace and justice and sustainability. The global citizen, then, adheres to a normative perspective—what needs to happen to create a better world.

Secondly, there is a reinforcing set of trends of much more recent origin that comprise the phenomenon of globalization: the tendency toward global integration, especially economic integration. Financial markets are becoming linked, even consolidated, at a rapid rate; capital formation has become more concentrated in response to global forces; and the annual economic summit of the heads of state in the seven leading industrial countries (G-7) is rapidly becoming an expression of the originality of the world system during its present stage of evolution. In other words, events are rapidly globalizing our outlook.

There is, further, a third element: the adoption of a politics of impossibility based on what I would call attitudes of necessity. An expanding consensus of informed people around the world maintains that, unless certain adjustments are made with respect to energy, resources, and environment, the human species will proceed toward extinction. For the sake of human survival, then, some forms of effective global citizenship are required to redesign political choices on the basis of ecological viabilities. This need is neither a matter of aspiration nor of empirically visible tendency.

Finally, there is implicit in this ecological imperative a politics of mobilization. It is expressed by transnational militancy, and centers on the conviction that it is important to make "the impossible" happen by dedicated action motivated by what is necessary and desirable, rather than by calculations of what seems likely. Such activity can alter the horizons of what seems possible to leaders and to the mainstream public. Such a shift helps provide hope, which is needed, especially when the prospects of success seem poor.

From this dynamic of four levels of engagement we can derive a series of overlapping images of what it might mean to be a global citizen at this stage of history. We have, first of all, the global citizen as a type of global reformer: an individual who intellectually perceives a better way of organizing the political life of the planet, and favors a utopian scheme that is presented as a practical mechanism. Typically such a global citizen has been an advocate of world government or of a world state, or a stronger United Nations—accepting some kind of political centralization as indispensable to overcome today's political fragmentation and economic disparities.

A typical expression of this essential idea of global citizenship was presented to me not long ago at a public meeting in the form of a postcard bearing this message to be sent off by as many persons as possible to the United Nations:

> I vote for life and non-violence among the world's peoples and for the scrapping of all nuclear weapons. I vote for the right to water—clean water—food, public health care, a place to live, work and education for all the world's peoples. I vote for love, freedom and peace.

Next to the text was a drawing of an African woman and her unclad infant child looking up expectantly at her. This spirit of global citizenship is almost completely deterritorialized, and is associated with an extension of citizenship as an expression of an affirmation of human unity. It is not a matter of being a formal member and loyal participant in a particular political community, whether city or state. Instead, it is feeling, thinking, and acting for the sake of the human species, and above all for those most vulnerable and disadvantaged. As such, an African baby is an appropriate and powerful symbol of the vulnerability and solidarity of the species as a whole.

This reformist perspective is a very old tradition of thought that locates its origins in the West, recalling Dante's conception of a unified polity in *De Monarchia*. Such visions usually reflect the cultural and political outlook of the political community in which the person making the proposal happens to live. There is an interesting convergence of imperial visions and global reform proposals, and it is hardly accidental that many reformist schemes on a global scale seem to produce global ascendancy for the state, region, or religion of the proponent. Often this kind of vision unconsciously involves a mixture of pragmatism and idealism, implying that a person can promote a better world by enlarging the framework of their own political reality until it encompasses the world. Not surprisingly, then, we find this kind of thinking mainly originating in the United States since the end of World War II, a period roughly corresponding with U.S. ascendancy. The collapse of the Soviet international presence has allowed American versions of a New World Order to gain further prominence and influence.

This idea about making the world better through a set of proposals is basically a rationalist strategy, associated especially with the reactions of a worried and idealistic component of the elite. It seeks to persuade the rest of the elite that its vision of a preferred world order offers a way of conceiving of foreign policy or international politics that is preferable to the conventional wisdom of the realist worldview. Such a style of idealist advocacy seems to surface and be particularly influential after a major war that is perceived to be futile. The most disturbing major war that the world has known in modern times was undoubtedly World War I, an extended, costly, and disillusioning struggle that appeared even to the winners to achieve very little of enduring value. Despite greater losses and devastation, World War II defeated fascism, and was widely appreciated by public opinion as a necessary, and even a worthwhile, war leading by way of victory to the extension of democratic rule.

Hence, after World War II, despite the advent of the atom bomb, there was little mainstream willingness to discuss the abolition of war. In contrast, during the years after World War I there occurred an enormous upsurge of support among elites and in the public for drastic types of global reform. This period represented the high-water mark for world federalists and aroused popular enthusiasm for world government. Such influence was substantially displaced by the geopolitics that transpired during the Cold War, a framework for states and alliances that saw the best path to peace not as a process of growing international institutionalization, but rather as a matter of balancing power through deterrence, thereby creating a kind of stability between two great blocs of opposed states arrayed on either side of an ideological divide.

There is a second image of global citizenship that is much more a reflection of recent trends, especially in the political economy of the world: the global citizen as a man or woman of transnational affairs. The word "man" is empirically appropriate here because of persisting gender dominance in this sphere. A startling 98 percent of those currently engaged in capital/financial operations on a global level are men. An emergent global identity associated with this expanding vista of business operations became manifest during a conversation with a Danish business leader who was seated next to me on a recent plane ride. He was holding forth on the great benefits of the European Economic Community for the continued prosperity of his business ventures. I asked, partly to disrupt his monologue, whether such convictions were making him feel less Danish, more European? He responded with an expression of puzzlement, and said, "Oh no, I'm a global citizen." What he meant, it turned out, was that his friends, his social network, his travels were all global; that he slept in the same kind of hotels whether he was in Tokyo or London or New York; that he talked English everywhere; that there was a global culture of experience, symbols, infrastructure, food, and music that constituted his way of life; and that being European, as distinct from being Danish or global, didn't any longer have any special significance for him. He probably had to remind himself from time to time that he was today in Copenhagen, rather than Paris or Rome, or New York or Tokyo. His sense of being global partly expressed a loss of cultural specificity. He seemed to lack any special attachment to place and community. This deterritorialized and homogenized elite global culture is becoming extremely influential as a social force driving the political and economic systems of the world. It is, in my view, the technocratic context being set for European integration as a foundation for more effective forms of European participation in the world economy.

This second understanding of global citizenship focuses upon the impact on identity of the globalization of economic forces. Such identity has many secondary implications. Its guiding image is that the world is becoming unified around a common business and financial elite. An elite that shares interests and experiences comes to have more in common within its membership than it does with the more rooted, ethnically distinct members of its own particular civil society; the result seems to be a denationalized global elite that is, at the same time, virtually without any sense of global civic responsibility.

The U.S. version of this outlook is somewhat distinctive, asserting that the U.S. segment of this new global elite should take charge of the geopolitical management of the world. The editorial pages of the *Wall Street Journal,* for instance, offer a consistent, if unwitting, voice for this kind of perspective, advocating an American-based unipolarity (as a sequel to the bipolarity of the Cold War) to ensure a successful global economy. The *Journal* interpreted the Gulf War in this light, arguing exultantly that the military victory gave the U.S. leadership renewed confidence to play this global role.

In this view, only the United States possesses the will and capability to reorganize the post-Cold War world and to locate control over geopolitics in the North, safeguarding a global economy that is for the North's benefit. Europe and Japan need to understand their secondary role of providing financial assistance and diplomatic support, a position in some respects similar to what existed during the bipolar period of the Cold War, but now stressing the increasing responsibility of richer states for bearing the costs of U.S. guardianship. It is an interesting feature of the Gulf War that the pledges of financial assistance from the countries of Europe, the Gulf, and Japan apparently gave the United States a profit from the battlefield costs of the Gulf War of anywhere between $7.4 billion (according to the *Newsweek* figures) and $42 billion. If such a financing scheme for geopolitical affairs were to be made an abiding feature of world order, it would reduce current deficits in world trade. As part of the bargain, the United States would be agreeing to provide security for the system as a whole: a kind of geopolitical protection service against emerging challenges, especially those in the South.

A third view of global citizenship focuses on the management of the global order, particularly its environmental dimensions but also its economic dimensions. This view is embodied in the report of the Brundtland Commission of a few years ago, *Our Common Future,* stressing the shared destiny on the Earth of the human species as a whole. The report argues that unprecedented forms of cooperation among states and a heightened sense of urgency by states will be required to ensure the sustainability of industrial civilization, a view now extended in the Agenda 21 document developed for the Earth Summit held in Brazil during June 1992. Only by a massive technical managerial effort, coordinated at a global level through the concerted action of states and international institutions, can diplomacy succeed in meeting the overall environmental challenge. This challenge includes problems of the global commons: the process of deforestation and the threats to climate posed by global warming, energy consumption patterns, and environmentally harmful lifestyles. A separate influential expression of this Brundtland outlook can be found in the annual reports of Worldwatch Institute (a Washington-based environmental think tank). The introduction to its 1989 volume even anticipated, from an environmental perspective, George Bush's use of the phrase "the New World Order." Lester Brown, the President of Worldwatch Institute, who oversaw the preparation of the 1991 report on the state of the world, titled his introductory essay "The New World Order." What Brown meant, quite optimistically I think, is that the ecological agenda was likely to displace the geopolitical agenda as the central preoccupation of post-Cold War politics on a global level, and that this development would alter the way most of us understood international political life.

To some extent, Mikhail Gorbachev had urged a similar direction of global policy between 1986 and 1988, what became known as "new thinking" in Soviet foreign policy. This Soviet turn toward globalism impressively advocated the importance of disarmament, denuclearization, and a stronger United Nations, justified, in part, by their contribution to solving global environmental problems that could no longer be handled by states, even the powerful ones, acting on their own. Global citizenship conceived from this functional perspective is increasingly caught up in the process of making the planet sustainable for current middle-class lifestyles: working to achieve sustainability in a manner that is sufficiently equitable to be accepted and implemented by political elites and their publics in different parts of the world.

A fourth idea about global citizenship is associated with the rise of regional political consciousness, and it is of great historical relevance at the present time, especially in Europe. It is appropriate to take notice of the fact that Europe, the birthplace of the modern territorial state, is moving along a path that twists and turns, but seems on its way to producing the first significant political innovation since the emergence of the modern territorial state in the 17th century. The Euro-federal process is creating a sufficient structure beyond the state so that it becomes necessary, not merely aspirational, to depict a new kind of political community as emergent, although with features that are still far from distinct and complete. Ironically, the birthplace of the state system—the whole line of development of territorial sovereignty and the modern state apparatus and ideology—may also be the locus of its mutation and rebirth, giving rise to a political reality that is intermediate between a territorial state and a globally unified political order. The future of a unified Europe remains uncertain, especially in light of the dissolution of the East/West divide, controversies as to the acceptability of the Maastricht Treaty, and the pressure to incorporate in the years ahead the far less prosperous and developed former communist states of the East. One troublesome possibility is that the consolidation of states at the regional level could eventually produce a militarized European superstate.

There is no doubt that the incentives for European integration have been powerfully reinforced by competition with the United States and Japan for control of shares at the technological frontiers of the world economy. Additional community-building forces have been also at work, and it is these forces, operating closer to the grassroots, that will determine whether this European experiment will develop into something distinctive and benevolent, making this new European reality a positive contribution to the restructuring of the global system. Can Europe, in other words, forge an ideological and normative identity that becomes more than a strategy to gain a bigger piece of the world economic pie? Can Europe become the bearer of values that are directly related to creating a more peaceful and just world?

Whether regionalism in this enlarged and constructive sense can fulfill its normative potential at this time depends heavily on Europe, and on whether European elites and public opinion can move from the dependencies of the Cold War toward establishing more autonomy, especially in relation to security issues, and a more generous outreach toward the Third World. The severe civil strife in Yugoslavia and the rise of xenophobic passions, as well as the difficulties of proceeding directly from the failed paternalism of the communist regimes in Eastern Europe to the cruel rigors of the unfettered market, cast renewed doubt upon the pace and prospects of subsequent stages of European integration, as well as on the likely meaning of "Europe." Additionally, a unifying Europe would undoubtedly, at least in the short run, produce tension with the United States, especially challenging the more militarist postures associated with recent U.S. foreign policy. This relationship between a more unified Europe, not preoccupied with a threat from the East, and the United States could also evolve in a mutually beneficial direction. One positive possibility would be building links at the societal level, an extension of transnational democratic tendencies in both regions, based on shared popular resistance to both militarism directed at the South and to the effects of the globalization of capital with its increasing impulse, expressed in conferences of the G-7 and elsewhere, to manage the life of the planet from above without adequate concern for longer-run sustainability and planetary life quality.

The fifth and final form of global citizenship is associated with the emergence of transnational activism that started to become very important for social movements during the 1980s. With respect to the environmental, human rights, and women's movements, activism on a transnational basis became prominent for the first time in history. This meant that the real arena of politics was no longer understood as acting in opposition within a particular state, nor the relation of society and the state, but that it consisted more and more of acting to promote a certain kind of political consciousness transnationally that could radiate influence in a variety of directions, including bouncing back to the point of origin. Amnesty International and Greenpeace are emblematic of this transnational militancy with an identity, itself evolving and being self-transformed, that can't really be tied very specifically to any one country or even any region but may also be intensely local in its activist concerns. It is certainly not "political" in a conventional sense, nor is it "professional," but it draws its strength from both sources. This grassroots phenomenon of organizing for action at societal levels is also occurring widely in various ways in the South. It is important to appreciate that this transnational, grassroots surge is not, by any means, just a Northern phenomenon. It has as one of its central features a shared conviction that upholding human rights and building political democracy provide the common underpinning, although adapted to diverse circumstances, for the types of transnational developments that are desired.

These networks of transnational activity, conceived both as a project and as a preliminary reality, are producing a new orientation toward political identity and community. Cumulatively, they can be described as rudimentary, generally unacknowledged forms of participation in a new phenomenon, global civil society. These developments include the emergence of institutional construction of arenas of action and allegiance—what many persons are really identifying with—as no longer exclusively bounded by or centered upon the formal relationship that an individual has to his or her own territorial society as embodied in the form of a state. Traditional citizenship is being challenged and remolded by the important activism associated with this transnational political and social evolution. This tendency is not linear. Indeed, backlash is inevitable, as older orientations toward political identity are challenged and more territorially defined interests grow threatened. What is evident, for instance in the recent experience of the United States, is an intense encounter between territorial, statist identities and loyalty and more temporal, global patterns of association, often combined with local engagement. That is, traditional citizenship operates spatially; global citizenship operates temporally, reaching out to a future to-be-created, and making a person a "citizen pilgrim," that is, someone on a journey to "a country" to be established in the future in accordance with more idealistic and normatively rich conceptions of political community.

Global Citizenship in Time and Space

A satisfactory imagery of global citizenship at this stage of social evolution implies a high degree of unevenness and incoherence, which is a reflection of these five intersecting perspectives becoming actual in varying degrees through time and space. It is necessarily a composite construction that appears in many mixtures. Such mixtures will produce many distinct shapes and patterns of global citizenship, depending on the interaction between the personality of an individual and the specifics of her situation. Further, a recovery of a dynamic and positive sense of citizenship, responsive to the varieties of human situation and diversity of cultural values, presupposes a radical reconstruction of the reigning political culture that informs and underlies political behavior in the modern, postmodern West. The extension of citizenship at this time, especially given the globalization of life and capital, depends on building and promoting a much stronger transnational agenda and sense of community, as well as stimulating more widespread participation at the grassroots, thus contributing to globalization-from-below. It also depends on the emergence of a stronger sense of time, of acting in time in relation to unborn generations.

The overall project of global citizenship, then, needs to be understood also as a series of projects associated with One-World Community horizons. These distinct projects are each responding to the overriding challenge to create a political community that doesn't yet exist, premised upon global or species solidarity, co-evolution and co-responsibility, a matter of perceiving a common destiny, yet simultaneously celebrating diverse and plural entrypoints expressive of specific history, tradition, values, dreams.

Global citizenship in its idealistic and aspirational expression, if mechanically superimposed on the present reality of geopolitics, is a purely sentimental, and slightly absurd, notion that will be completely irrelevant to the operating logic and procedures of the New World Order as promoted briefly by George Bush and associates. In contrast, if global citizenship is conceived to be a political project, associated with the possibility of a future political community of global or species scope, then it assumes, it seems to me, a far more constitutive and challenging political character. From this perspective, time partially displaces space as the essence of what the experience of global citizenship means; citizenship thereby becomes an essentially religious and normative undertaking, based on faith in the unseen, salvation in a world to come—not in heaven, but on earth—guided by convictions, beliefs, and values. So conceived, citizenship brings deep satisfaction to adherents arising from their present engagement in such future possibilities, but without the consoling and demeaning illusion that global citizenship can be practiced effectively in the world of today or the deforming persistence of associating citizenship with unthinking patriotism of the sort mobilized by sovereign states during times of war.

The political implications of this line of thinking about global citizenship need to be worked out. In a preliminary way it is possible to suggest a shift in understanding the essence of politics from an axis of feasibility to an axis of aspiration, from politics as "the art of the possible" to politics as "the art of the impossible." Global citizenship of a positive variety implies confidence in the human capacity to exceed realistic horizons, but it also rests upon the highly pragmatic conviction that what is currently taken to be realistic is not sustainable. To strengthen the foundations for a global civil society to which all women and men belong is to be dedicated to the achievement of a functional utopia, a polity that is meant to achieve both what is necessary and what now seems "impossible."

The multicultural foundations of the embracing idea of global citizenship provide some safeguard against any reliance on one more totalizing concept deriving from the West, but perhaps this is not enough protection. The very essence of global civil society is the actuality and affirmation of such diversity, which itself then provides the ethos of the forms of global citizenship that are being most fully endorsed. Such a restructuring of our understanding of global citizenship is highly skeptical of the sort of global perspectives of the transnational business elite that appear, by and large, to give up particularity of traditional citizenship, and yet never acquire a sense of world community and accompanying social responsibility. We must learn to distinguish such a threatening type of globalization of consciousness from hopeful forms arising from feelings of solidarity, concerns about equity and nature, strong impulses to combine local rootedness with planetary awareness, and the underlying belief that the security and sanctity of the human community rests, in the end, on embodying an ethos of nonviolence in political practices at all levels of social organization, from the family to the world.

The media-disseminated postulates of the New World Order encourage a consumerist orientation toward global citizenship—the world as an homogenizing supermarket for those with the purchasing power, while those who lack the financial means are excluded and, to the extent required, suppressed by police, paramilitary, and military means, a pattern already prefigured in the Gulf War. It is not by chance that such an approach was christened as the New World Order.

In contrast, the gropings of global civil society encourage a human rights and democracy orientation toward global citizenship—the world as delightfully heterogeneous, yet inclusive of all creation in an overarching frame of community sentiment, premised on the biological and normative capacity of the human species to organize its collective life on foundations of nonviolence, equity, and sustainability. This reality imaginatively already exists—and hence, politically, a One-World Community is an emergent possibility.

Notes

For additional reflections, see Richard Falk, *Explorations at the Edge of Time: The Prospects for World Order,* Philadelphia, PA: Temple University Press, 1992.

Part II

Globalization-from-Above:
Critiques

The Greening of the Global Reach
Vandana Shiva

The Green movement grew out of local awareness and local efforts to resist environmental damage. The crisis of deforestation in the Himalayas was a concern first voiced by the local peasant women of Garhwa. The crisis of toxic hazards was pointed out by the affected residents of Love Canal.

Over the past two decades, the pattern has been recognized that major environmental threats were caused by globally powerful institutions like multinational corporations and multilateral development banks like the World Bank, which reach every city, village, field, and forest through their worldwide operations.

Now, in the 1990s, the two decades of the Green movement are being erased. The "local" has disappeared from environmental concern. Suddenly, it seems, only "global" environmental problems exist, and their solution, it is taken for granted, can only be "global."

In this chapter we would like to look more closely at what the concept of the "global" hides and what it projects, how it builds power relations around environmental issues, and how it transforms the environmental crisis from being a reason for transformation into a reason for strengthening the status quo.

The "Global" as a Globalized Local

Unlike what the term suggests, the global as it is emerging in the discussions and debates around the UN Conference on Environment and Development (UNCED) is not about universal humanism nor about a planetary consciousness. The life of all people, including the poor of the Third World, and the life of the planet are not at the center of concern in international negotiations on global environmental issues.

The "global" in the dominant discourse is the political space in which the dominant local seeks global control, and frees itself of local, national, and global control. The global in this sense does not represent the universal human interest; it represents a particular local and parochial interest which has been globalized through its reach and control. The G-7, the group of the seven most powerful countries, dictate global affairs, but they remain narrow, local, and parochial in terms of the interests of all the world's communities. The World Bank is not really a bank that serves the interest of all the world's communities. It is a bank where decisions are based on voting weighted by the economic and political power of donors, and in this decisionmaking the communities who pay the real price and are the real donors (such as the tribals of Narmada Valley) have no say. The "global" of today reflects a modern day version of the global reach of the handful of British merchant adventurers who raided and looted large parts of the globe as the East India Company, which then became the British Empire.

Over the past 500 years of colonialism, whenever this global reach has been threatened by resistance, the language of resistance has been co-opted, redefined, and used to legitimate future control.

The independence movement against colonialism revealed the poverty and deprivation caused by the economic drain from the colonies to the centers of economic power. The post-World War II world order, which saw the emergence of independent political states in the South, also saw the emergence of the Bretton Woods institutions like the World Bank and the International Monetary Fund, which took over the language of underdevelopment and poverty, removed their history, and made them the reason for a new bondage based on development financing and debt burdens.

The environmental movement revealed the environmental and social costs generated by maldevelopment, conceived of and financed by agencies like the World Bank. The language of the environment is now being taken over, and being made the reason for a strengthening of "global" institutions like the World Bank, and increasing their global reach.

In addition to the legitimacy derived from co-opting the language of dissent is the legitimacy that comes from a false notion that the globalized "local" is some form of hierarchy that represents geographical and democratic spread, and that lower-order hierarchies should somehow be subservient to it. Operationalizing of undemocratic development projects has been based on a similar false notion of the "national interest," and every local interest has felt morally compelled to make sacrifices for what seemed to be the larger interest. This is the attitude with which each community made way for large dams in post-independence India. It was only during the 1980s, when the different "local" interests met each other nationwide, that they realized that what was being projected as the "national interest" were the electoral interests of a handful of politicians financed by a handful of contractors such as JP and Associates, who benefited from the construction of all dams such as Tehri and the Narmada Valley project. Against the narrow and selfish interests that have been elevated to the status of the "national" interest, the collective struggle of communities engaged in the resistance against large dams started to emerge as the real, though subjugated, national interest.

In a similar way the World Bank's Tropical Forest Action Plan (TFAP) was projected as reflecting a global concern about tropical forests. However, when forest movements formed a worldwide coalition under the World Rainforest Movement, it became clear that TFAP reflected the narrow commercial interests of the World Bank and multinational forestry interests such as Shell and Jaako Poyry, and that the global community best equipped to save tropical forests were forest dwellers themselves and farming communities dependent on forest.

"Global Environment" or "Green Imperialism"

Instead of broadening and widening environmental concern and action, the recent emergence of a focus on "global" environmental problems in fact narrowed the agenda.

The multiple environmental concerns that emerged from the grassroots, including the forest crisis, the water crisis, toxic chemicals, and nuclear hazards, have been marginalized. Thus the Global Environmental Facility (GEF) set up at the World Bank addresses only four environmental issues: a reduction in greenhouse gas emissions; protection of biodiversity; a reduction of pollution of international waters; and a reduction in ozone layer depletion.

The exclusion of other concerns from the global agenda is artificial since, for example, the nuclear industry and chemical industry are globally operating industries, and the problems they generate in every local situation are related to their global reach.

The way "global environmental problems" have been constructed hides the role and responsibility of the globalizing local in the destruction of the environment which supports the subjugated locals. The construction becomes a political tool to free the dominant destructive forces operating worldwide of all responsibility, and to shift the blame and responsibility for all destruction to communities that have no global reach.

Consider the case of ozone depletion. Chlorofluorocarbons (CFCs), which are a primary reason for ozone depletion, are manufactured by a handful of transnationals like Dupont, with specific locally identifiable manufacturing plants. The rational mechanism for the control of CFC production and use is to control the plants run by Dupont. The fact that substances like CFCs are produced by particular companies in particular plants is totally eclipsed when ozone depletion is turned into a "global" environmental problem. Dupont is left scot-free, and the problem is shifted to the future use of refrigerators and air-conditioners by millions in India and China. Through a shift from the present to the future, the North gains a new political space to control the South. The "global" thus creates the moral base for green imperialism.

It also creates the economic base, since through conventions and protocols, the problem is reduced to the transfer of technology and aid. Dupont then becomes essential to the problem it has created; since Dupont has patented CFC substitutes for which a market has to be found, the financial resources that go into the Montreal Protocol Fund for transfer of technology are in effect subsidies for Dupont, and not for the Third World.

Biodiversity is another area in which control has shifted from the South to the North through its identification as a global problem. As in the case of ozone depletion, biodiversity erosion has taken place because of habitat destruction in diversity-rich areas by dams, mines, and highways financed by the World Bank to help transnational corporations, and by substitution of diversity-based agricultural and forest systems by the monoculture of green revolution wheat, rice, and eucalyptus plantations, which are also supported and planned by the World Bank to create markets for the seed and chemical industries.

The most important step in biodiversity conservation is to control the World Bank's planned destruction of biodiversity. Instead, by treating biodiversity as a global resource, the World Bank emerges as a protector of biodiversity through its GEF, and the North demands free access to the South's biodiversity through the biodiversity convention. However, biodiversity is a resource over which local communities and nations have sovereign rights. Globalization becomes a political means to ensure an erosion of these sovereign rights, and a means to shift control over and access to biological resources from the gene-rich South to the gene-poor North. The "global environment" thus emerges as a principal weapon through which the North can gain worldwide access to natural resources and raw materials on the one hand, and can force a worldwide sharing of the environmental costs it has generated while it retains a monopoly on benefits reaped from the destruction on the other.

The motto for the North at UNCED and the other global negotiations seems to be, "What is yours is mine, what is mine is mine."

This lopsided view of a common future is facilitated by the idea of the "global." The construction of the global environment narrows the options for the South, while increasing them for the North. Through its global reach, the North exists in the South. The South, however, exists only within itself, since it has no global reach. Thus the South can only exist locally, while the North exists globally.

Solutions to global environmental problems can come only from the global, i.e., the North. Since the North is abundant in industrial technology and capital, if the North has to provide a solution to environmental problems, they must be reduced to the currency in which the North dominates. The problems of ecology are transformed into a problem of transfer of technology and finance. What is eclipsed from the analysis is that this assumption that the South needs technology and finances from the North is both a major cause of the environmental crisis, and a major reason for the drain of resources from South to North. While the governments of the South demand "new and additional sources of finance" for the environment, they ignore the reverse transfer of $50 billion per year of capital from the poor South to the affluent North. The old order does not change through the environment discussions. It gets more entrenched.

The Problem of False Causality

With the screening out of the role of the globalized local in local environmental destruction worldwide, the multiple facets of destruction are treated as local causes of problems with global impact. Among the main impacts of maldevelopment and colonialism that have occurred simultaneously are the rise of poverty, the increase of environmental degradation, the growth of population, and the polarization and conflict between genders and ethnic communities.

Extraction of surplus and exploitation and destruction of resources have left people without livelihoods. Without access to resources for survival, the poor have been forced to generate economic security through large families. Collapse of social cohesion and economic stability have provided the ground for ethnic conflict.

However, instead of seeing these multifaceted problems as caused by the global domination of certain narrow interests of the

North, they are selectively transformed from consequence to cause. Poverty and population are turned into *causes* of environmental degradation. Diversity is turned into a disease and identified as a cause for ethnic conflict.

False causality is used as a causal explanation for false connections. Thus some UNCED documents have gone to the extent of pointing to population growth as a cause of the explosive growth in toxic chemicals. A problem caused by an irresponsible chemical industry is converted into a problem caused by fertility rates in the poor countries of the South. The 1991 cyclone in Bangladesh was similarly linked causally to babies in Bangladesh.

The "Global" is not Planetary

The image of planet Earth used as a visual in the discourse on global ecology hides the fact that, at the ethical level, the "global" as construct does not symbolize planetary consciousness. The global reach by narrow and selfish interests does not use planetary or Gaian ethics. In fact, it excludes the planet and peoples from the mind, and puts global institutions in their place. The concept of the planet is invoked by the most rapacious and greedy institutions to destroy and kill the cultures which use a planetary consciousness to guide their daily actions in the concrete. The ordinary Indian woman who worships the "tulsi" plant worships the cosmic as symbolized in the plant. The peasants who treat seeds as sacred see in them a connection to the universe. Reflexive categories harmonize balance from planets to plants to people. In most sustainable traditional cultures, the large and the small have been linked so that limits, restraints, and responsibilities are always transparent and cannot be externalized. The large exists in the small, and hence every act has not just global but cosmic implications. Treading gently on the Earth becomes the natural way to be. Demands in a planetary consciousness are made on the self, not on others.

The moral framework of the global reach is the opposite. There are no reflexive relationships. The G-7 can demand a forest convention that imposes international obligations on the Third World to plant trees. However, the Third World cannot demand of the industrialized countries a reduction in use of fossil fuels and energy. All demands are externally dictated, in a one-way direction, North to South. The way the "global" has been structured, the North (as the globalized local) has all rights and no responsibilities, and the South has no rights, all responsibilities. "Global ecology" at this level becomes a moralization of immorality. It is empty of any ethics for planetary living. It is based not on concepts of universal humanity, but on universal bullying.

Democratizing "Global" Institutions

Creating new mechanisms for responding to the global ecological crisis was one of the agenda items of UNCED. Problematizing the "global" through the collective articulation of all local concerns and interests, in all their diversity, is the creative intervention in global/local conflicts as they are emerging.

Democratizing of the "global" is the next step. Since what exists as the global is not the democratic distillation of all local and national concerns worldwide, but is the imposition of a narrow group of interests from a handful of nations on a world scale, democratizing of international interests is essential if genuine democracy is to exist at local and national levels.

The roots of the ecological crisis at the institutional level lie in the alienation of the rights of local communities to have a say in environmental decisions. The reversal of ecological decline involves strengthening local rights.

Every local community, equipped with rights and obligations, constitutes a new global order for environmental care. However, the current trend in global discussions and negotiations is to take rights further upward toward higher non-local centralism in agencies like the World Bank.

Multilateralism in a democratic set-up must mean a lateral expansion of decisionmaking, based on the protection of local community rights where they exist, and the reinstitution of rights where they have been eroded. Two central planks of local environmental rights include:

• the right to information

• the right to prior consent: any activity with potential impact on the local environment should require the consent of the local people.

Basing an environmental order on globally institutionalized local rights also avoids the impossible issue of representability and the terrible mess of international NGO's "selecting" national NGOs to "select" local NGOs to represent "people" at global negotiations.

The "global" must bend to the local, since the local exists with nature, while the "global" exists only in offices of the World Bank and the IMF and the headquarters of multinational corporations. The local is everywhere. The ecological space of global ecology is the integration of all locals. The "global" in global reach is a political space, not an ecological one.

Institutionally, we should not worry about how to get the last tribal person to sit at World Bank decisions in Washington. What we need to ensure is that no World Bank decision about the resources of tribal people is taken without their prior informed consent.

Whether the local as global and the global as local will exist in a way different from the imperialistic order of the last 500 years depends on this process of democratization. The imperialistic category of global is a disempowering one at the local level. Its coercive power comes from removing limits for the forces of domination and destruction and imposing restrictions on the forces of conservation.

The ecological category of global is an empowering one at the local level because it charges every act, every entity, with the largeness of the cosmic and planetary and adds meaning to it. It is also empowering because precisely by embodying the planetary in the local, it creates conditions for local autonomy and local control.

An Earth democracy cannot be realized with global domination by undemocratic structures. It cannot be realized on the basis of an anthropocentrism that excludes the rights of non-human nature. And it cannot be realized if survival of the planet is used to deny the right to survival of those who are poor and marginal today because they have borne the accumulated burden of centuries of subjugation.

Economic Globalization

A New Geography, Composition, and Institutional Framework

Saskia Sassen

There has been a world economy for several centuries. But its geography, composition, and institutional framework have changed over time. The "world economy" never included the entire planet; it always had more or less clearly defined boundaries. And while most major industries were involved, different types of industries dominated in different periods, generating historically distinct economic structures. Finally, the institutional framework through which the world economy coheres has also varied sharply, from the earlier empires through the quasi-empire of the Pax Americana and its collapse in the 1970s. It is from this collapse that we see emerging a new phase of the world economy. There is considerable agreement among specialists that in the mid-1970s new alignments became evident. The main trends can be defined in terms of geography, composition, and institutional framework.

Geography

The geography of the world economy has changed from a North-South axis to a greater intensity in East-West transactions; significant parts of Africa and Latin America became detached from their hitherto strong articulation with world markets in commodities and raw materials. This new geography can be illustrated with foreign direct investment (FDI) flows, which form the major component of international transactions.

There was a time when Latin America was the major recipient region of FDI. But FDI flows to developed countries have grown at an average annual rate of 46% since 1985, reaching an overall value of

US$163 billion in 1989, out of a total worldwide FDI flow of US$196 billion.

FDI flows have become sharply concentrated: the top five recipient countries accounted for 57% of world inflows in the 1980s; the five major exporters of capital (United States, United Kingdom, Japan, France, and Germany) accounted for 70% of total outflows. By the mid-1980s, 75% of all FDI stock, and 84% of FDI stock in services, was in developed countries. For much of the 1980s, the aggregate net flow of financial resources to developing countries was negative. (The bank crisis of 1982 sharply cut loans to developing countries.)

FDI flows can be constituted through many different processes. For the last two decades, the growth in FDI has been embedded in the internationalization of production of goods and services and in the growth of financial flows. The internationalization of production is particularly important in constituting FDI flows into developing countries. Although flows into developing countries were far lower than into developed countries, they were high by historical standards. Since 1985 they have been growing at an annual rate of 22%, up from 3% during 1980-84 and 13% in 1975-79.

This expanded capital flow affects the major developing regions diversely. The share of worldwide flows going to developing countries as a whole fell from 25% to 19% between the early 1980s and the late 1980s. Latin America's share fell from 49% to 38%. Most of the capital instead flowed into East, South, and Southeast Asia, where the annual rate of growth was up to 37% between 1985-89. Southeast Asia's share of the capital flow rose from 37% to 48%. These figures point to the formation of Southeast Asia as a crucial transnational space for production. It has surpassed Latin America and the Caribbean for the first time ever as the largest host region for FDI in developing countries.

Composition

In the 1950s, FDI was concentrated in raw materials, other primary products, and resource-based manufacturing; world trade was the major international flow. Over the past decade there has been a sharp increase in the weight of direct foreign investment in services (mostly in the form of FDI), and in the role played by the international credit markets in international finance and services. Foreign direct investment grew sharply in the 1980s—much more rapidly than world trade and world output. Since 1983, after the slump of 1981-82, global FDI grew at an average of 29% a year, an historic high. This is three times faster than the growth of the export trade, and four times the growth of world output. Since 1985 the gap between the growth rate of exports and that of foreign direct investment has sharply widened.

Many factors have fed the growth of FDI: several developed countries became major capital exporters, most notably Japan; the number of cross-border mergers and acquisitions grew sharply; the service sector and transnational service corporations emerged as major components in the world economy.

Services, which were about 24% of worldwide stock of FDI in the early 1970s, had grown to 50% of stock and 60% of annual flows by the end of the 1980s. The single largest recipient of FDI in services in the 1980s was the European Community—yet another indication of a very distinct geography in world transactions. But service flows have also increased for less developed countries. While there are severe problems of measurement, by the mid-1980s services accounted for an estimated 60% of all international transactions, whereas only a few years before, trade in goods had been the dominant category.

Institutional Framework

Is this development a mere quantitative change or rather a change in the regime of the world economy? Elsewhere I have argued that the ascendance of services and especially international finance produces a new regime with distinct consequences for other industries, especially manufacturing, and for regional development insofar as regions tend to be dominated by particular industries.

We can't take the world economy for granted and assume that because there are international transactions there is a world economy. How did the "world economy" cohere as a system? The breakdown in the early 1970s of the Bretton Woods agreements, which provided for fixed exchange rates, coordinated economic stimulation, and use of the U.S. dollar as the world's reserve currency, robbed the world economy of the institutional framework it had operated under since the end of World War II. This breakdown was clearly linked to the decline of the United States as the single dominant economic and military power in the world. Japanese and European multinationals and banks became major competitors with U.S. firms.

The central role played by transnational corporations (TNCs) in the system that emerged can be seen in the fact that they accounted for 80% of international trade in the United States in the late 1980s; further, more than a third of U.S. "international trade" was actually intra-firm trade.

Almost all FDI and a large share of technology transfers were undertaken by TNCs. Furthermore, while the financial credit markets, which grew explosively in the 1980s, helped pay for the huge government deficits, to a disproportionate extent they served the needs of TNCs.

TNCs also emerged as a source for financial flows to developing countries, both directly through inflows of FDI and indirectly through the stimulus of FDI on other forms of financial flows. The bank crisis of 1982 sharply cut bank loans to developing countries, to the point that for much of the 1980s the aggregate net flow of financial resources to developing countries was negative, consisting mostly of interest payments to U.S. banks. TNCs largely replaced the banks. When all is said and done, TNCs are strategic organizers of the world economy. Their role also points to the growing importance of internationalization in the production of goods and services.

International credit markets have emerged as another crucial institution organizing the world economy. The central role of markets in international finance, a key component of the world economy today, was in part brought about by the so-called Third World bank crisis formally declared in 1982. This crisis—actually a crisis for the major transnational banks in the United States—combined with financial deregulation, created a space into which small, highly competitive financial firms could move, launching a whole new era in the 1980s in terms of speculation, innovation, and levels of profitability. The result was a highly unstable period, but one with almost inconceivably high levels of profits which fed a massive expansion in the volume of international transactions. Deregulation was a key mechanism facilitating this type of growth, a growth centered in internationalization and in speculation. Markets provide an institutional framework organizing these massive financial flows.

The formation of transnational trading blocs is yet another development that contributes to the new institutional framework. The two major blocs are the North American Free Trade Agreement and the European Community. (The Asian bloc in Japan's zone of influence is far less structured.) The specifics vary considerably, but both blocs greatly enhance the capability of capital to move across borders. These blocs represent the formalization of capital as a transnational category.

Some Consequences

One consequence of the extremely high level of profitability in the financial industry was the devaluing of manufacturing as a sector—

though not necessarily all branches. Deregulation made finance so profitable that it took investment away from manufacturing. Finance allows superprofits by maximizing the circulation of money (e.g., securitization, multiple transactions over a short period of time, selling debts, etc.) in a way that manufacturing does not. One can bundle a large number of mortgages and sell the bundle many times, even though the number of houses involved stays the same. This option is basically not available in manufacturing, in which a product is made and sold; once it enters the realm of circulation it enters other sectors of the economy, and it is to these that the profits from subsequent sales accrue. Furthermore, finance offers the possibility of superprofits without much of a "labor question." The non-professional workforce in finance and in services generally is in a far more subordinate position than the workforce in major mechanized factories, where the shop floor is a terrain for contestation and workers' struggles.

The possibility of superprofits in finance engenders a distortion in the valuation of different sectors of the economy. It devalues manufacturing, which can't produce such superprofits. It can also strengthen the idea that manufacturing needs to be "more" profitable, which in turn can justify the lowering of wages and the extraction of give-backs from workers. Another consequence, more difficult to specify but with strong political implications, is the devaluation not only of manufacturing but of all "local," place-bound activities. The glamour of the global has the effect of depreciating the local.

The developments of the 1980s represent a massive assault on working-class people. This assault is evident in objective conditions: the decline in earnings among the lower third or even bottom half of the earnings distribution in most major developed economies, and now even in Japan; the declining power of unions; the expulsion of growing numbers from the "mainstream economy" (i.e., permanent unemployment). And it is evident in less-developed countries in the form of massive increases in poverty, hunger, and unemployment. Yet the forms of growth that have pushed matters to this desperate condition have their own limitations, as evidenced by the financial and real-estate crisis in many countries. In the United States these limits can be seen in infrastructure breakdowns produced by inadequate investment—due to the greater profitability of speculative financial investments and to the enormous national debt.

Indeed, much of the financial growth of the 1980s was based on the growing debt: deregulation and financial innovation made it possible to make superprofits on the sale of public and private debt to an extent and with kinds of debt hitherto unknown. But making money by accelerating the circulation of debt does not necessarily contribute to strengthening the material base of an economy, be that infrastructure or manufacturing. If the profits made from the accelerated circulation of debt are not at some point taken out of this circuit and redirected to manufacturing and infrastructure, not much happens economically— even when a lot may be happening financially.

References

Sassen, S., *The Global City: New York, London, Tokyo,* Princeton: Princeton University Press, 1991.

—, *The Mobility of Labor and Capital,* Cambridge, UK: Cambridge University Press, 1988.

—, United Nations Centre on Transnational Corporations, *World Investment Report: The Triad in Foreign Direct Investment,* ST/CTC/118, Preliminary Report, July 1991.

Latin America in the New World Order

Xabier Gorostiaga

The depth and speed of the changes throughout the world make the 1990s very strategic. The structural and all-encompassing nature of these changes have the character of a "fourth long wave" in the cycles described by the Soviet economist Kondratief.

We are also experiencing a crucible of Copernican changes, greater than those seen in the 1914-1917 period. The 20th century started late, in 1914, with the great confrontation between capitalism and socialism, and ended early in 1989, with the toppling of the Berlin Wall and the end of the Cold War. The 21st century has begun with a confrontation between North and South, between capital and labor. While this is a long-standing confrontation, it is entering a new phase with qualitatively different parameters.

1992 is a symbolic year. The "discovery" of Latin America cannot be celebrated, since the continent had its own identity and civilization when the Spaniards arrived. What was discovered in 1492 was universal history and the globe as one totality. In the 1990s humanity itself is being discovered as one world, an inseparable unity, a communal home linked to a common destiny. That destiny is the product of a technological revolution, a revolution in information, social communication, and transportation, and also of a growing consciousness of the threat of collective suicide for having overstepped the bounds of the planet.

In addition to symbolism, 1992 represents a tremendous challenge for Latin America's self-discovery and self-construction: to overcome these last 500 hidden years. This challenge, however, comes in "times of cholera,"[1] which reflect the depth of the economic and political crises facing Latin America. On a global level, we are also witness to the massive exodus of the Kurdish people, the ecological disaster in Bangladesh, the civil war in Yugoslavia, and the disintegration of the Soviet Union.

This speech was delivered to the Conference of the Latin America Sociology Association, Havana, Cuba, May 1991.

Persistent and growing starvation in Africa surpasses all these other human tragedies in drama, all at a moment in which both "the end of history" and the "New World Order" are being irresponsibly proclaimed.

In this chapter, we hope to underscore the contradictory, dialectical, and global character of the changes taking place. Latin American intellectuals move between hope and desperation, anguish and rage, while the people are using their ingenuity to survive increasing impoverishment.

In the first part of the chapter we analyze the structural causes of this new crossroads in the broadest framework of the restructuring of capital and the New World Order proclaimed in the wake of the Gulf War. The second part assesses the impact of these changes in Latin America and the Caribbean in the context of the trilateral mega-markets and the U.S. recession. Finally, we indicate some characteristics of the dialectic between increasing democracy and economic submission, both of which are contributing to the crisis of ungovernability and political weariness that affects both the Left and Right throughout Latin America.

Far-Reaching Structural Changes

We agree with historian Paul Kennedy that never before in history has there been such a concentration and centralization of capital in so few nations and in the hands of so few people. The countries that form the Group of Seven, with their 800 million inhabitants, control more technological, economic, informatics, and military power than the rest of the approximately four billion people who live in Asia, Africa, Eastern Europe, and Latin America. This concentration of capital corresponds to the character of the new technological revolution, in which the cycle of capital accumulation depends less and less on intensive use of natural resources, labor, or even of productive capital, and more on an accumulation of technology based on the intensive use of knowledge. The concentration and centralization of technological knowledge is more intense and monopolistic than other forms of capital, and only increases the gap between North and South.

The repercussions of this situation have led to the growing "de-materialization" of production, in which less and less raw material is required per product produced. Over the last 20 years, the Japanese production process has reduced by a third the amount of raw materials used per product. Even more significant is the accelerated rhythm of this reduction. In the 1965-76 period, raw material use shrank 0.6% annually; since 1980, the annual reduction has been 3%, nearly a six-fold drop.

This de-materialization has resulted in a tendency toward lower real prices for the 33 principal raw materials, the majority of which are the South's export products. This price deterioration is even more pronounced in recent years. Automation of production also means that labor loses value relative to capital, in both the North and South. Both processes lead to a permanent structural deterioration of value relative to what are supposedly the South's comparative advantages in production and world trade.

Those phenomena coincide with the transnationalization of systems of production, financing, and marketing, which for the first time permits a truly global market.

The new areas of expansion of global accumulation for the end of the century—such as space, sea, and energy—are completely subordinated to the control of economic, technological, and military power, which will provoke even greater concentration and centralization, and thus, a greater gap and asymmetry between North and South.

The revolution in telecommunications, transportation, and informatics has produced management innovations that have further facilitated mergers of capital and technology, whereby private business in Latin America and the South in general is increasingly incorporated in a dependent way into the logic of centralized capital. National business, both private and state-run, is increasingly marginalized and in an asymmetric position vis-à-vis transnational industry, and thus more and more isolated from the logic of the domestic market and the survival of the large impoverished majority.

This situation is even more serious if we consider that in the same decade the net financial transfers from the South to the North were the equivalent of ten Marshall Plans. In the case of Latin America, according to the most recent Latin American Economic System (SELA) report, foreign debt-service payments alone were 80% more than the total amount of foreign investment in Latin America. If we include Latin American capital in the North (on the order of $160 billion) and the deterioration in the terms of trade (some $100 billion), Latin America's financial and productive debacle in the 1980s could be compared to the worst years of colonial pillage.

We have described this structural phenomenon as an avalanche of North against South, of capital against labor. Never before in history, not even in colonial times, has such an extreme bipolarization of the world existed. This bipolarization, from the South's perspective, is the fundamental element of the structural changes defining the end of this century.

Worldwide Political Changes

Four fundamental elements define the political characteristics of the 1990s:

The profound crisis in Eastern Europe. This has had dramatic repercussions throughout the world, touching off a new historic phase with the end of the Cold War. From a Third World perspective, the evaluation of these changes is very complex. One concern from the Latin American experience is whether or not there really ever was socialism—understood as a social, economic, and political alternative to capitalism—in the Eastern bloc. The majority of the Eastern European countries never developed a socialism indigenous to their own countries, instead forming a defensive and imposed military alliance. The negative impact of this militaristic and statist socialism was tremendous in Latin America. Dogmatism, top-down organizing styles, and statism imported from the Eastern European experience affected all the Communist parties and the majority of the Latin American Left. Nevertheless, the Socialist bloc served as a counterbalance of sorts that permitted a geopolitical space and a rear guard of support for changes in the South.

The collapse of Eastern Europe means the loss of a paradigm, of that economic and geopolitical counterbalance. At the same time, it potentially opens ideological and practical space for new experiences in a world leaning toward resolving conflicts by negotiation and the use of international law.

"Real" or "state" socialism, which was successful in toppling feudalism as well as in creating an important industrial base, collapsed definitively in the face of the technological revolution and the consumer society. The crisis of democracy is, however, the political root of this collapse.

The majority of Eastern Europe is heading toward a rapid Latin Americanization, and could easily be transformed into an area of natural resources and cheap labor for further development in Western Europe and the rest of the North.

In the coming years, Eastern Europe will absorb Europe's political attention and much of its available financial resources, affecting both politically and economically the attention needed by the South. The impact on the South of the changes in Eastern Europe, however, could be very different over time from what they have been to date. The direct relationship between the South and the former Eastern bloc, transformed by its crisis, could become an international source of creativity and complementarity. For this to happen, the complexities and isolation facing both civil societies will have to be overcome.

European unity. Hegemonized by German unification, a new European unity has changed the correlation of international forces. A united Europe could become the productive, financial, and commercial center of the world, together with Japan and the Pacific nations. This would leave the United States in an increasingly vulnerable position, and could lead to a new divvying up of world "spheres of influence." It would also open the possibility for the countries of the South to take advantage of new spaces and contradictions in the system.

Emergence of the Pacific basin bloc. As the century comes to a close, Japan and Southeast Asia are emerging as a preeminent industrial, financial, and technological power bloc. Japan, however, though an economic giant, is diminutive in political stature. It has not been able to play a foreign policy role corresponding to its economic power. From the perspective of Latin America and the South, Japan's history, culture, race, and religion are seen as very different from those of the North. The Japanese are not white, Western, or Christian. But the structural forces of the market and the different institutions of the Group of Seven tend to draw Japan into the northern orbit, thus increasing the avalanche of North against South and capital against labor.

The loss of U.S. economic hegemony. This phenomenon coincides with the three described above, but has its own clear economic roots. The United States has been unable to overcome its fiscal and commercial deficits and is saddled by a gargantuan military budget. Its tendency to base the last decade's growth on a rapidly increasing debt has transformed the only country whose national currency functioned as an international reserve into the most indebted nation on the face of the Earth.

Its loss in technological competitiveness and productivity means that the United States will not be able to maintain its political hegemony unless it is based fundamentally in military and ideological power. This, in turn, requires a military budget of about $300 billion annually, and control over some two-thirds of all media images produced in the world. The financial instability of October 1987 and the more recent Savings and Loan crisis, along with the growing deterioration in the U.S. productive and social infrastructure, indicates that the debt, deficits, and military budget are simply no longer sustainable under these conditions.

The United States, Europe, and Japan comprise a "neo-trilateralism," hegemonized by the Group of Seven, with a constellation of world institutions organized under its control (the International Monetary Fund

and World Bank). The United Nations itself, with its financial dependence and the veto power that the key economic powers hold in the
Security Council, still maintains a framework in which the majority of the
member countries are unable to benefit from equitable and democratic
participation.

The threat to the South is increased by the alliance of geo-economic
interests shared by the countries in the Group of Seven, which are
incapable of attending to the cultural, religious, and national characteristics of the many different peoples of the South, increasingly impoverished and marginalized. The proposal on the table from the North is
integration into "market culture," with a liberalization of trade, finances,
and privatization which reduces state autonomy. This assumes that
market forces will be able to overcome poverty and achieve political and
democratic stability in an increasingly unified world.

A Crisis of Civilization

Five hundred years ago, the world emerged as one geographic and
historic unit. Now the world's population is recognized as one inseparable, although dramatically divided, entity. The trilateral North, which
revolves around the Group of Seven, has increased and centralized
power in all possible forms. The restructuring of the capitalist system
tends to reinforce this polarization and asymmetry given that there is no
longer the countervailing weight of the Soviet Union. The increasing
division of the world, between a North of few people and many resources and a South with many people and few resources, is the axis of
the current crisis. It is true that the terms "North" and "South" simplify the
world's problems, but they also allow us to underline the dominant
contradiction.

The current model of society in the North—its style of development
and lifestyle—cannot be reproduced throughout the world because it
has definite ecological and population limits and carries within it many
structural contradictions. One such contradiction is between the model's
requirement for progressive accumulation—with its growing concentration of capital, technology, and power in the North—and the excluded
majorities in the South who demand not only survival but also a standard
of living conducive to peace and democracy.

The crisis is not only one of distribution and equity, it is a crisis of
values and the direction humanity is taking. For this reason we can call
it a crisis of civilization. Society worldwide is neither sustainable nor
stable under these conditions. Democracy is not possible for the major-

ity of the world's population, and this fact is leading to increasing ungovernability in many nations of the world. Samuel Huntington, the ideologue of the Trilateral Commission in the 1970s, called the increase in Third World demands for democracy a threat. "Guiding" democratic processes in the South has become an imperial necessity if the North wants to maintain its current privileges. What we could call Low Intensity Democracy in Latin America is a structural product of the inability of the material base to sustain even these incipient processes of democratization.

To lend legitimacy to this situation, there is an attempt underway to ideologize the North-South confrontation, presenting the South as the new enemy, in the wake of the demise of the "evil empire." The South is portrayed as a den of evil goings-on, a dangerous place for citizens from the North. In this vision, the threats of drugs, immigration, and political instability, along with regional conflicts, all come from the South.

The objective structural gap between North and South is widened with this subjective ideologization, which has deep and racist roots. Instead of confronting the causes of the crisis, this ideological view looks at the consequences, and seeks to lay blame there.

Latin America: Harvest of the 1980s

The so-called "lost decade" was a complex and dialectical one. Latin America's competitive capacity in the 1990s is substantially lower than it was in the 1980s. Losses in foreign trade and in foreign investment, thoroughgoing decapitalization and disinvestment—both productive and social—as well as other well-known indices from this "lost decade," demonstrate profound and structural economic deterioration throughout Latin America. Most of the continent, with the possible exception of Mexico, Chile, and, in a certain sense, Brazil, Colombia, and Venezuela, is simply not an attractive panorama to capital. The appearance of cholera in "the times of adjustment" symbolizes Latin America's growing "Africanization" and economic marginalization. The region also experienced political marginalization as the North's attention swerved to the Middle East conflict and the strategic interests involved there, as well as to the disintegration of the Soviet Union.

The "lost decade," however, is much more complex. Latin American society is qualitatively different than it was at the beginning of the 1980s. The "lost decade" coincides with, and is in part a cause of, the "explosion of Latin American democracy" in the 1980s. Electoral democratization is nothing more than a reflection of a radical and profound democracy that has touched different areas of civil society. Decades of struggle against oligarchies, dictatorships, and militarism have gelled in this revolution of civil society.

This complex dialectic of economic crisis and revolution in civil society is the defining characteristic of the 1980s. The democratic participation of the organized and mobilized majorities in their own civic institutions has created new historical subjects that demand participation in the economy, politics, religion, and culture.

This dynamic of civil society has obvious exceptions, including Guatemala, Argentina, Panama, and Peru. The culture of terror imposed by military repression in the first two cases, the U.S. military occupation of Panama, and the economic collapse of Peru explain the disintegration of civil society in these nations. This contradictory dynamic leads to a state of ungovernability, in which the demands that arise as part of the advance of democracy find no material base to sustain them. This ungovernability is expressed in the rapid loss of prestige of the neoliberal political leadership that has controlled the majority of electoral democracies since the mid-1980s. Menem in Argentina, Collor de Mello in Brazil, Fujimori in Peru, Cristiani in El Salvador, and Callejas in Honduras are examples of a broader phenomenon so starkly expressed in the ungovernability of Nicaragua and Panama. In neither of those countries has the U.S.-backed neoliberal project brought political stability or economic recovery.

Ungovernability is creating a society of beggars and delinquents who seek individual survival at any cost. This unorganized mass is an important challenge for alternative projects in Latin America. It is a group easily co-opted by escapist religions, drugs, and growing migration out of Latin America, as well as by violent ultra-leftism unconnected to viable proposals. Between hope and disaster: that is how this dialectic of sentiments could be characterized. In another historical moment, Pablo Neruda eloquently declared a similar feeling: They can cut all the flowers, but they will never stop the spring.

Debt, Neoliberal Adjustment, and the Initiative for the Americas

The continuing debt crisis and the structural adjustment processes underway allow us to visualize the North's project to restructure Latin American capitalism and reinsert the continent into the world capitalist market. Debt has substituted for the direct investment of the 1970s as a mechanism to extract net financial transfers out of Latin America. It puts the state and even private enterprise into a submissive position with its denationalizing effect. Latin American attempts to renegotiate the debt individually were unable to achieve equitable terms. The International Monetary Fund, the World Bank, USAID, and, more recently, the Interamerican Development Bank have imposed overlapping conditions on national governments and enterprises, such that the adjustment policies linked to these conditions have severely weakened Latin America's negotiating capacity. It is in this context that President Bush's Enterprise for the Americas Initiative must be understood.

SELA's cogent April 1991 analysis of the plan states, "The Bush Initiative for the Americas does not propose a strategy for the development of the region, but rather constitutes a mechanism to accelerate the economic reforms underway, whose principal elements have been promoted by multilateral financial institutions, with the support of the U.S. government...It responds to economic needs and concrete strategies of the United States."

The Enterprise for the Americas plan is a product of the need for a macroeconomic readjustment of the U.S. economy in light of its profound recession and its lack of international competitiveness. The United States needs the creation of a hemispheric "mega-market" from which to confront both a united Europe with its new zone of economic and political influence in Eastern Europe, and the mega-market of Japan and the Pacific nations.

The extension of a free market from Alaska to Patagonia would permit the United States to share the costs of its own adjustment with Canada and Latin America. At the same time, it would increase U.S. negotiating power in the debates on the new global trade agreements now taking place in the Uruguay Round GATT talks. Given the possibility of failure in reaching new agreements, the United States needs to broaden its competitive capacity to take on trade agreements—both bilateral and multilateral—with Europe and Japan.

Debt, trade, and investment—the three pillars of the Enterprise for the Americas plan—bring with them strict conditions. This is already evident in relation to market mechanisms which have not been used for debt reduction; in official negotiations, financial organizations refuse to accept the real, substantially reduced, market price of the debt as set by the secondary market. By the same logic, conditions for the incorporation of U.S. investment in Latin America will be linked to the acceptance of conditions regarding the debt and the non-reciprocal and asymmetrical use of the market, which will never extend to a free flow of the

Figure 1
Total US Debt (in $ billions)

Debt:	1980	1990
Federal	914	3,200
State	316	850
Business	829	2,100
Consumer	1,300	3,000
Total	3,400	9,150
Gross Domestic Product	2,732	5,300
Foreign debt	+180	-800
Debt service/budget	13%	20%
Savings	7%	4%

Source: US Commerce Department

workforce between the United States and Latin America, even in the case of Mexico.

The plan should be analyzed first from the perspective of the recession and the need for a macroeconomic adjustment in the United States. It will permit the United States to face, in better conditions, its structural indebtedness and loss of international competitiveness, and expand its market toward a zone of privileged influence to increase its strategic security and its continental supply of natural resources, particularly petroleum. This will allow the United States to maintain its geo-strategic hegemony based on a geoeconomic competitiveness that it currently lacks.

The total U.S. debt, shown in Figure 1, reflects the largely fictitious nature of the U.S. economy, which depends on the international transfers superior to $100 billion and on a progressive indebtedness of the state, private business, and consumers.

In one short decade, the United States went from being the world's largest international creditor to being its greatest debtor, almost doubling its budget for debt servicing and reducing the country's savings by nearly half. That has created an imminently unstable situation. The United States simply cannot continue to consume 25% of the world's energy, 50% of which is imported. It cannot continue to maintain gasoline taxes six times less than those of Japan, Germany, Italy, and France. If the United States were to increase its gasoline tax to the level of its economic competitors, it could increase its income by $180 billion annually. This squandering of energy explains the decision to get involved militarily in the Persian Gulf.

In spite of this energy subsidy, U.S. productivity, measured by per-capita GDP, by 1988 was fourth among the world's 22 most indus-trialized nations. If this trend continues, the United States will drop to thirteenth in world productivity by the year 2030. The fundamental

Figure 2
US Competitiveness in the International Market

	1980	1990
Optic Fibers	73%	42%
Conductors	60%	36%
Agricultural machinery	18%	7%
Petroleum dependence	12%	36%

Source: *Newsweek,* April 1, 1991.

reason for this decline in U.S. productivity is that the rate of savings in the United States is half that of its industrial competitors and a quarter that of Japan. The reduction in U.S. savings, moreover, contradicts a basic tenet of neoliberal policy, which holds that a concentration of income allows for an increase in savings and investment. In the U.S., the concentration of income in the hands of the wealthiest top 10% of the population increased by 4% between 1980 and 1990, making that group's share of the Gross Domestic Product (GDP) 27%. In the same decade, however, savings fell from 7% to 4%.

U.S. military spending as a percentage of GDP is four times greater than that of other industrialized countries, while its non-military spending, including infrastructure and social spending, is 45% lower. Maintaining such a high military budget and dedicating two-thirds of all funds to high-level military technology increases the competitive gap in terms of civil technology, particularly with Japan and Germany, which do not have such high spending levels for military technology.

The United States' loss of international competitiveness is also notable. Figure 2 shows an almost 50% decline for the key areas of U.S. technology in the same decade that its petroleum dependency tripled. In 1990, the United States held a technological lead in only a few areas, primarily biotechnology and industrial design.

This loss of competitiveness corresponds to a reduction in the investment rate, funds dedicated to research, productivity, and infrastructure, and even in the loss of its own internal market, which shows a growing propensity for imports. The U.S. consumer is losing confidence in U.S. products, particularly vis-à-vis Japanese and European design and technology. U.S. consumer confidence in domestic products has dropped 54% since 1980, which has begun to have international repercussions. In 1990, Japan withdrew more than $30 billion from the U.S. market.

This analysis could be expanded with other data illustrating the irrevocable need for a structural adjustment in the U.S. economy. The topic has touched off sharp debates in Congress, and even President

Bush had to break his key campaign promise to not raise taxes. The fact is that the United States needs an adjustment even stricter than those imposed in Latin America. Furthermore, the distortions in the U.S. economy have multiple effects on world financial markets, interest rates, stock market fluctuations, and speculation. The international institutions established to guarantee world financial stability, however, are unable to deal with one of the most fundamental distortions of the modern economy.

For Latin America, having a neighbor and key market in a structural recession and with imbalances as great as those outlined above means having a permanently destabilizing factor in its own economies. The Bush plan cannot be analyzed independent of the economy's need for a readjustment and the urgency of increasing U.S. geoeconomic competitiveness vis-à-vis the mega-markets of Europe and Japan.

Those Latin Americans who believe that the Enterprise for the Americas Initiative could serve as an element of growth and stability much like the motor force of growth that the U.S. economy was in the 1960s, when the United States was the world leader in technology, investment, and productivity, need to rethink their relation with the United States in this context. The U.S. military monopoly, coupled with the multipolar economic situation, does not lead to stability. As Professor Paul Kennedy maintains, empires in decline tend to be more militarily aggressive to compensate for their economic weakness.

Three Alternatives to the Enterprise for the Americas Initiative

1) Negotiate better terms with the United States to overcome the lack of reciprocity and the asymmetry that the SELA analysis so clearly shows. This position assumes as a given that the Initiative is the only way out of Latin America's economic crisis.

2) Strengthen the mechanisms of subregional integration in Latin America, integrating the continent through subregional common markets (Merco-Sur, Andean Pact, Central America-Caribbean, with a special relation with Mexico, Colombia, and Venezuela). This integration would permit the complementarity necessary to deal with the U.S. and Canadian markets. This second alternative seeks to obtain more positive results for Latin America from the Initiative by diversifying its linkage to the United States through its own integration and by opening new relations with Europe and the Pacific nations.

3) Put forth an alternative vision and proposal for Latin American society. The thrust of this proposal would be to resolve the causes of the economic crisis and respond to the accumulated demands of emerging civil society. It would seek to create the material base for maintaining and deepening participatory democracy. This alternative springs from a vision of society that has been called "the logic of the majority" and aims to overcome the historical exploitation of work, nature, and sovereignty. The crisis of civilization dehumanizes both victors and vanquished in the market and thus calls for a reconstitution of equity and symmetry, both necessary to an authentically free market.

This alternative offers a medium- to long-term solution that reinforces the Latin American vision of the second proposal. For the 1990s, the most viable route is to advance and deepen Latin American integration and diversification in a context of reciprocity and symmetry. Bold pragmatism, however, requires having a vision of a society that goes beyond strict market mechanisms. The Latin American agenda must not reduce itself to the agenda of the United States.

This third alternative implies some strategic priorities.

1) Develop a strategy of survival and appropriate technology based on the accumulated experience of the popular Latin American economies in which the majority of the population is barely surviving.

2) Make significant investments in human capital, converting the poor into productive agents so that they can overcome their poverty. In classical terms this would be what Adam Smith called the "wealth of nations."

3) Recognize local production as the economic arena of the great majority of Latin Americans, which should be integrated into the internal market and expanded to subregional projects in order to guarantee food self-sufficiency and competitive exports for the popular sectors.

4) Selectively connect with the international market, rather than provide an absolute opening. This is important until such time as conditions of greater symmetry and competitiveness can be achieved.

5) Design special policies for the informal sector, both urban and peasant, that would allow for the creation of an internal market with enough demand to stimulate both agro-industrialization and manufacturing. Without the incorporation of the informal sectors, national industry will be elitist and totally dependent on its transnational counterpart. This requires regionalizing this proposal throughout Latin America.

6) Make the state—that ambiguous, yet initially essential, entity—increasingly unnecessary as the transition to civil society is effected. State power should be decentralized to civil institutions. Use the state to create

the social framework that would strengthen the growth of popular organizations and increase their negotiating capacity at both the regional and international levels.

7) Internationalize the work, technology, institutions, and financing of popular organizations required by the transnationalization of capital in the world market. Such internationalization is aimed at democratizing the market at a national, Latin American, and international level.

The popular alternative starts from the premise that a monopolistic market produces an asymmetrical "economic Darwinism" in which state equilibrium disappears, given that the market progressively substitutes for the state and the weakest are absorbed by capital concentration.

8) Democratize the international institutions, in particular the International Monetary Fund and the International Development Bank. This democratization is key to establishing equity in international relations. Like the United Nations, these institutions emerged during the Cold War and respond to the interests of the North. The international network of non-governmental organizations (NGOs) could play an important role in opening a space for representation of the South. An analysis of the Mexican and Canadian experiences could be very instructive for the rest of Latin America. Initial evaluations indicate that the "fast track"—rapid negotiation—is not permitting Mexico to negotiate in equitable, reciprocal, or symmetrical conditions. Moreover, Mexico's free trade agreement is essentially an agreement of free investment with full supranational guarantees. In other words, trade is not subject to any legal changes that could take place in Mexico in the future. This avoids controls in both the United States and Mexico, while the cheap and abundant Mexican labor force reduces the negotiating capacity of its U.S. counterpart.

The social pact that permitted political stability in Mexico after its revolution has been broken with the latest electoral fraud that brought Salinas de Gortari to power. His policies have meant a drastic reduction in salaries—from 40% of the GDP in 1976 to 23% in 1990. Super-exploitation of labor, natural resources, and sovereignty, all in the context of a so-called free market, could soon be the rule throughout the continent if the balance proposed in the second and third alternatives is not achieved.

The Revolution of Civil Society

The ungovernability that will likely continue to characterize the 1990s implies the lack of a material base for the emergence of civil society through the innumerable organizational forms of the masses and the emergence of new historical subjects. The dominant characteristics of this new civil society have been hidden by the economic realities of the "lost decade" and the cynical proclamation of the "end of history."

The majority of Latin American societies are qualitatively different in the 1990s. They have overcome the old oligarchic, dictatorial, and military models. A broad demilitarization process is underway, even in areas of great conflict, such as Central America. In most of Latin America, the military is being progressively subordinated to civil society. In the face of pressures from civil society, authoritarian governments and military dictatorships have opened up to electoral processes and democracies, although these are still supervised and restricted. Nevertheless, submissive and asymmetrical stagnation, dependence, and transnationalized insertion are the legacy of the 1980s. The harvest of the 1980s also clears up any ambiguity about foreign cooperation and the international market as motors of growth and development.

In very telescopic fashion, we describe below some elements evolving in civil society. This takes us into the realm of hypotheses and suggestions, some provocative, which call for creativity and political honesty. If the proposals are not painful, there will be no solution to the crisis.

Fiscal crisis and state disintegration. The debt, adjustment plans, and generalized economic recession have weakened and in many countries (including Peru, Argentina, Haiti, and Panama) completely destroyed the state's regulatory capacity. In its role as economic promoter and regulator, the state has become a factor of economic deregulation. The indiscriminate opening to the international market has provoked what has been characterized as transnationalized, submissive, and asymmetrical insertion.

Emergence of new popular movements. These are the products of increasing impoverishment, social polarization, and the weakening of traditional political parties, both of the Right and the Left. The struggle for survival has spurred reorganization in both the informal sector and the peasantry. Neither the state nor the political parties offer channels of action for this emerging social phenomenon, since neither comprehend it theoretically or in practical terms. The Lavalas movement that brought Jean-Bertrand Aristide to power in Haiti symbolizes such popular forces.

The coming together of a new Latin American Left. In many senses, this left is returning to the historic vision shared by Latin Americans from the late 19th and early 20th centuries, including Martí, Mariátegui, Haya de la Torre, Sandino, Zapata, Recabarren, and others.

This also corresponds to what was being synthesized in the same era by Gramsci. Undoubtedly, this new Left has been affected by both the crisis of socialism in the East and the stagnation of the Latin American Left. Again today, alongside the confusion and initial loss of spirit, a strong and creative movement is restating the issues and demands in a new historic framework, making way for what has been called "socialism of the majority," "creole socialism," and "Third World socialism"—all of them part of a search for socialism within civil society. Lula's Workers' Party in Brazil and Cárdenas—more specifically than his Party of the Democratic Revolution itself—in Mexico reflect similar dynamics. Lula, Aristide, and Cárdenas symbolize this phenomenon, which also has peculiar expressions in Colombia's M-19 and Uruguay's United Front. The profound political restructuring of El Salvador's FMLN and Nicaragua's FSLN in their revolutionary processes would seem to indicate the existence of a conscious awareness of this phenomenon, which implies new understanding of the tasks of the party in relation to civil society, the state, and the armed forces.

In the innumerable encounters that have taken place among these new emerging forces, there are some fundamental points of agreement. This common profile permits a clear insight into the character of this new political leadership that is filling the void left by the traditional and neotraditional parties across the political spectrum.

The radicalizing nature of democracy as culture, method, style, and political project. For the first time, the Left has taken up democracy as a banner of struggle interwoven with the rest of its demands. The goal is to bring participatory democracy to all levels of society, respecting the independence and autonomy of different movements and transforming the top-down styles and ideological rigidity that characterized past actions.

A new political language. "Forbidden to forbid" was Lula's slogan at the Workers' Party Congress. "A President in the opposition" was Aristide's pledge to the peasant movement in Haiti. These are only a few indications of a new language accompanied by a new pedagogy that respects popular rhythms and consciousness.

There is a rejection of the Left's political language, as there is of the oligarchic language Vargas Llosa used in his campaign. Collor de Mello, Fujimori, and Menem himself have tried to create a new language, ultimately failing since they did not also change the content.

It is important to make reference here to the massive invasion of the fundamentalist evangelical movement in Latin America. The "sects" indicate the need to take stock of liberation theology itself, along with the pedagogy and practice used in the Christian base communities, in the face of these expressions of popular religiosity that have become escapist movements and serve as a political base for the rightwing. The advance of the fundamentalist evangelical movement points to a serious weakness and even a certain failure on the part of liberation theology. It is clear that funding for these movements comes from the United States and that the CIA has politically infiltrated them. Nevertheless, popular religiosity, in which the culture and consciousness of the impoverished masses is primarily expressed, was never taken up adequately by liberation theology. Its theological discourse was excessively abstract, theoretical, and politicized. In addition, it did not leave sufficient space for celebration, for joy, for letting go, for the spontaneous participation of a people exhausted by the struggle for survival.

New, not exclusively economic, demands. These demands seek a new project of society, new values, and a new civilization. They come essentially from the new historical subjects—women, indigenous peoples, youth—as well as from growing awareness of the deepening ecological crisis. The topics of "gender" and "political machismo" open great potential for rectification, creativity, and popular mobilization. The demands of women and of different ethnic groups, as well as those calling for environmental protection, are the most radical, alternative, and international ones. The technological and neoliberal paradigm is weaponless against these demands, which have long been a challenge either rejected or given short shrift by the traditional Left.

New *concertación* and new alliances. The change in the correlation of forces within each country, resulting from the prolongation and extent of the crisis, is leading to unprecedented rapprochements between some sectors of society. At the same time, society's most extreme and ideologized groups are being polarized. *Concertación*, which at first glance could be seen as a centrist position, a third way, is an ambiguous and fluctuating movement. It has components of exhaustion and confusion, as well as of aspirations and demands unsatisfied by politicians from either the Right or the Left. It is not a third way that denies the Right and Left; it is a search for consensus, for a common denominator that would permit a national project hegemonized by the popular majorities.

The economic *concertación* taking place in most Latin American countries has pushed ideology and even medium-term political interests off to one side, seeking instead stability and security. "Politics is the art of the possible," declared one of the more lucid modern thinkers. Politics in the 1990s needs this art, not in order to renounce values and principles, but rather to deepen and purify them, adapting them to new conditions.

Non-organized sectors. Setting up links with these groups is a priority task and one of the most difficult to achieve. The widening of the cultural and political gap between organized groups and the growing unorganized masses demands new styles and leadership. For many among the unorganized, political messages and politicians are increasingly seen as old and worn out. Ethical standards are determinant in the culture of the unorganized. They involve a language with more to say to a culture threatened by desperation and with no hope for the future.

The crisis of management and the problem of efficiency. In the era of the technical revolution, efficiency and management are two paradigms of today's world, but they have not been the most outstanding characteristics of the parties and groups with popular objectives. Reversing both the lack of credibility in the Left's efficiency and the mythology of the private sector's efficiency is another of the challenges of this decade.

The crisis in management is also a crisis of the rhythm and speed with which new technologies are imposed. The changes produced by consumer society have put supply in direct communication with demand, at least in the manipulated imagination of media images.

It is also a crisis of the communication media. Brzezinski correctly declared that, in addition to military hegemony, the United States exercises media hegemony, given that four of every five messages or images produced in the world are controlled by the United States.

At the same time, the revolution in management implies the de-ideologization of this science, generally seen as bourgeois. It must be appropriated as a contribution to the socialization of available resources. The efficient and complementary linking of the macro and micro is one of the greatest contributions of technical management and is an economic, political, and even military necessity.

Negotiation and alliances as political forces. The end of the East-West conflict and the new "culture of peace and tolerance," after decades of polarized ideological alliances, turn negotiation and alliances into priority instruments, both for co-opting the enemy and for achieving hegemony over the pluralism and diversity of civil society. The ideological alliance that divided the world into two poles has left a void in values for the creation of a new world order. A truly global world requires an alliance of common values able to link together 21st-century civilization. It is an alliance of common material interests in the face of shared threats (ecological crisis, security and disarmament, regional crises, etc.) Without this alliance, imposed political power will determine the future within the very same parameters that have brought us to civilization's current crisis.

Popular Agenda for the 1990s

The 1990s is a complex decade, ushered in with the Sandinista defeat, the growing disintegration of socialism in Eastern Europe, the division of the South exacerbated by the Gulf crisis, and the current incongruencies of the Movement of Nonaligned Nations. Pax Americana implies a defeat for the "wretched of the Earth" and the formation of a new trilateralism coordinated with the Group of Seven.

The United States has overcome "the Vietnam syndrome" with the Persian Gulf victory, and consolidated the already strong coalition in U.S. economic, political, and ideological power circles. The alliance of the three big U.S. lobbies—petroleum, military, and pro-Israel—around the Gulf crisis exceeds in strength the alliance around the Committee on the Present Danger that brought the New Right and Reagan to power. The ideological roots of the Truman Doctrine in the 1940s and the National Security Council's foreign policy formulated in the 1950s (known as NSC 68) have also been strengthened with the Gulf victory. There is even talk of establishing a special alliance between the United States and Japan, which Brzezinski refers to as "Ameripon."

At the same time, the international counterweights are disappearing—first of all in the East, but also in the nonaligned movement and the international organizations. The last is particularly true for the United Nations, which has been virtually paralyzed by the veto power wielded by the five big Cold War powers.

From the perspective of the Southern countries, this avalanche is a threat comparable to 1930s fascism in Europe. Confronting it will require a broad alliance within each country as well as internationally, including with the new historical subjects of the North, who, though minorities, are increasingly conscious that this crisis of civilization affects both North and South.

What is still needed is a rethinking of the global theory of socialism or of non-capitalist alternatives. The long-standing debate about socialism in one country is again demonstrating that it cannot survive, something Lenin realized at the beginning of the century when socialism did not expand throughout Europe. The lack of a global project of change and of an accumulation of forces will make any alternative project in one single country impossible, or at least extraordinarily costly.

The transnationalization of labor and the South. International social subjects are sending out calls in different forms, in all parts of the world, through political, religious, union, and NGO forums, and for the first time, they have begun to link up internationally. Examples include the Japan-Asian People's Plan 21, which brings together hundreds of Japanese and Pacific organizations; the Third World Network; and the Forum for People's Economics, which draws in numerous groups of researchers from the North and South and is working on economic alternatives to neoliberal economies.

The network of NGOs and the South, as well as the political parties that have organized around a "socialism of the future" project that includes, for the first time, diverse tendencies from the European left (communists, Trotskyists, socialists—the "casa comun of socialism") originated in a meeting between Mikhail Gorbachev, Willy Brandt, and Ernest Mandel organized by the Polish philosopher Adam Schaft. This network is trying to put to one side the historical differences within the Left and create an "ecumenical humanism." Although this project has not produced more than a few relatively small ideas with relation to the South, the significance of these examples is the growing tendency toward a transnationalization of non-capitalist alternatives whose dominant logic is that of the majorities.

Be that as it may, there is no room in this new single world for "anti" revolutions; there must be "pro" projects and proposals. Anti-imperialism and non-capitalism should be rethought within the sweeping global changes taking place and within, as well, a culture of peace and democracy, where any form of imperialism loses legitimacy and remains isolated as an "enemy of humanity."

The appropriate context for such an effort, which could well include broad sectors of the North, would be the formulation of an international agenda for the 1990s. This requires beginning a country-by-country process of popular agendas in Latin America to find the cumulative synthesis and consensus in all forums dealing with the problem of the New World Order. What is needed is an assertive and creative attitude, going beyond "protest without proposal" to instead present "the proposals with protest" that need to be put forth now.

Notes

1. A play on words in Spanish, since the word *cólera* refers both to the epidemic disease now sweeping Latin America and also means rage or extreme anger. Also a reference to Gabriel García Marquez' bestselling novel, *Love in the Time of Cholera.*

Glasnost

The New World Order and Post-colonialism in Africa

Siba N'Zatioula Grovogui

The defeat of Nazism in the aftermath of World War II brought about a New World Order. The former Allied Powers, however, now divided by the Cold War, soon split over its purpose, and in particular over the international organization which embodied it—the United Nations. Likewise, the majority of Third World countries disagreed with the developed countries of the North over the goals of the new order. Given these divisions, the dissolution of the Soviet Union in late 1991 and the subsequent end of the Cold War are unlikely to produce agreement about the flaws of the present system or a cooperative climate in which to design a post-Cold War order.

For many Western intellectuals and policymakers, the failure of the postwar order was due to the antagonisms of the Cold War. East-West rivalry prevented the West from completely dominating the different organs of the UN. Many in the Third World, however, believe the makers of the new order betrayed their proclaimed universalist ideals of internationalism, interdependence, and national equality by obstructing the full self-determination of former colonies and maintaining their own hegemony through the UN Security Council and other mechanisms of the UN system.

Many in Africa see current Western proposals for a New World Order as predicated on principles which assume the same inequitable power structures. This chapter maintains that hegemonic behavior, the lack of equal participation, and the failure to fully implement self-determination account for the deficiencies in the UN system. It argues that the new storm of democracy sweeping across Africa is not a vindication of Western objectives. Rather, various democracy movements which had long been suppressed by both ideological camps during the Cold War have benefited from the current transition period. In fact, some of the imperatives of reform in Africa, and in the Third World more generally, conflict with the Western desire to control the new international regime. Such is the case with the call for equal national participation in global affairs. The success of the forthcoming order will depend on the desire of current powers to respect international diversity, cultural pluralism, the equality of national interests, and greater democracy in global decisionmaking. Global security and international peace will be obtained only if the end of the Cold War emboldens decisionmakers, politicians, and theorists to experiment with new intellectual tools and approaches to questions of identity, democracy, pluralism, cooperation, and global responsibility.

Globalism, Antagonism, and International Cooperation

An international order is a juridico-political system defined by the ideals, legal principles, and political norms which organize intercommunal relations. Ideally the juridico-political regime has an internal logic which is consistent with the aspirations of the constituent communities. The latter collectively generate the ideals and principles of the regime. The world envisioned for the post-World War II era was expressed in the 1942 *Declaration by United Nations:* one of independent nations, free of oppression and domination, free to exercise their religions, in dignity and justice, yet collectively committed to maintaining international peace and development.[1]

While the UN Charter does refer to the equality of nations and the right of peoples to self-determination, little was included either to enforce national equality and decolonization, or to mandate multilateral participation on issues of global concern. In fact, during various wartime meetings the Allied Powers had already begun to discuss the postwar global agenda in terms of East-West influence. International security, cooperation, and the rights of less powerful nations, particularly in the developing world, were subordinated to the self-defined "national interests" and "security" of the capitalist and communist blocs.

The Allied Powers divided UN authority between the Security Council (S.C.), the General Assembly (G.A.), and lesser organs. They created a weak G.A. even though that organ represented the majority of nations. According to the UN Charter, its decisions are only non-binding recommendations. In contrast, the principal Allied Powers (the United States, Great Britain, France, and the Soviet Union) concentrated power in their own hands by constituting themselves permanent members of the S.C., giving themselves virtual executive power in issues of international security. The permanent members possess veto power [2] over S.C. resolutions, which are binding on all UN members. However, they have repeatedly betrayed their international responsibility by vetoing resolutions that conflict with their national interests.[3]

Ironically, however, the veto power prevented the Cold War adversaries from making an international order solely responsive to the requirements of their respective political economies. In fact, each rival power had the procedural instruments with which to block any international process too favorable to the other. The stalemate caused by the veto was the most significant obstacle to their hegemony.

The end of the Cold War has brought about a realignment within the Security Council which assures Western powers of the cooperation of the Soviet Union (now Russia) during international conflicts or crises. The willingness of Russia and other permanent members to work together under a unified Western leadership during international conflicts was demonstrated during the Persian Gulf crisis.

Self-determination and Hegemony in the Old New Order

While the Cold War's end has suppressed the ideological rivalry which in the past atrophied the Security Council, it has not altered imperialism, particularly toward the formerly colonized. In the 1950s, many Africans were encouraged by the UN Charter's promises. They agitated for national independence, the restructuring of international relations, and for new international norms which respected identity and equal participation in decisionmaking. The nationalists requested fundamental concessions from the makers of the postwar world order, their former colonial masters. These concessions included the fulfillment of the promise to built a world free from discrimination and racial oppression.

Many in Africa thought that the postwar order would usher in a political and cultural renaissance. In their enthusiasm for a new order, African and other Third World elites envisioned new juridical propositions that would confirm interdependence and cooperation. A hierarchical order dominated by a few powers was inconsistent with the spirit they envisioned of self-determination, equal rights, and equal protection from hunger, disease, and illiteracy.

African and other Third World leaders also fought to preserve their national assets and natural resources. They demanded negotiated pricing mechanisms in a more equitable international economic order. It was in this context that the debates over the New International Economic Order and the Law of the Sea took place. African and Third World enthusiasm was short-lived. The formerly colonized were excluded from most postwar international discussions. The similarities between the old and the new order became apparent to the majority of then colonial peoples as the postwar order emerged and the mechanisms of international law were set in motion. Africans who petitioned the Security Council or the UN's Trusteeship Council discovered the inequities inherent in their procedures. They realized that the juridical questions and legal concerns most crucial to their cultural and political affirmation had been muted by assumptions and procedures that had little bearing on their own individual or collective experiences.

One such issue was the validity of agreements entered into by African officials who had been appointed during the colonial era. The colonial powers who controlled the UN privileged Western traditions of state succession over African ones, obscuring the fact that colonial officials had often transgressed African customs and rules in making official appointments. The permanent members of the Security Council paid little attention to questions of the damages due to individuals and collectivities as a result of colonial exploitation. For instance, the expropriation of lands in South West Africa, Tanganyika, the Cameroons, Togo, and Algeria was disregarded, although petitioners justified their claims with Western notions of torts and compensation.

The colonial powers used their domination of the UN to exclude such African concerns as the debt incurred by colonial powers; the rights to resources beyond the boundaries of nation-states, whether on the sea bed, in the air, or in space, and the right to bear arms in self-defense or for national liberation.

Western imperialism and hegemony have been the targets of African intellectuals, who have viewed them as the main obstacles to their self-determination. For this reason, African nationalists are generally disregarded in official Western discourse. In fact, such discourse rarely refers to Western obstructions and rejections of alternative proposals for a New World Order. Likewise, little is said in professional circles about the consequences of direct Western involvement in manipulating the processes of decolonization and their role in post-independence destabilization. Yet, the manipulation or obstruction of popular will and the elimination of unwanted potential—or even elected—leaders produced grave consequences for African politics. By the end of the first decade of independence, only three kinds of leaders had been able to survive in Africa: the shrewdest, those who survived political intrigues (Gamal Abdel Nasser, Sekou Toure, Julius Nyerere, Kenneth Kaunda); the collaborators, those who opted for nco-colonial solutions (Leopold Sedar Senghor, Felix Houphouet-Boigny, Jomo Kenyatta, etc.); and the coupmakers, who took their cues from foreign intelligence services (Mobutu Sese Seko, Gnasimgbe Eyadema, Jean Bedel Bokassa).

Cold War Attitudes for a Post-Cold War Era

The mindset that dominated the Cold War era remains central to the proponents of today's New World Order. Throughout the postwar era, policymakers used anticommunist rhetoric to obscure their political and ideological hostility to any breach in Western hegemony—in particular, challenges to the intellectual codes that guided international relations. These politicians, scholars, and other professionals justified their resistance to national independence, as well as their support for wars of destabilization and political interference in Third World countries, by pointing to the ongoing struggle against communism.

However, the intellectual propositions and scientific traditions used to justify Western superiority and hegemony transcend the Cold War. Throughout the imperialist era, social scientists and politicians helped popularize many racial myths and stereotypes in order to justify official hostility to African self-determination and full participation in international relations. The result has been continued Western interference in Africa and other parts of the Third World, and the absence of necessary dialogue toward the restructuring of international relations.

Consider these propositions which recently appeared in the *International Herald Tribune,* "Why is Africa Overwhelmed While East Asia Overcomes?" in which Keith B. Richburg quotes various authorities on the present African crisis. Pauline Baker of the Aspen Institute attributes "Africa's poor record of economic development" to a combination of "bad luck, bad environment, bad policy, bad government and bad faith." She then adds that various African cultures are incompatible with economic progress. Richburg also insists that Africa has produced bad managers, "dictators, tyrants and buffoons," who have run their countries' economies to the ground. This view is supported by Herman J. Cohen, the U.S. Assistant Secretary of State for African Affairs. Cohen states that East Asia, in contrast to Africa, "did all the right things."

Typically, the dominant Africanist discourse in the West is grounded in half-truths. It not only downplays the external factors of the African crisis, it also fails to recognize the specificities of African struggle for political and economic reforms. Most specialists ignore African, and Third World, demands for a restructuring of the international order, in particular for greater collective participation in determining the global political and economic agenda.

The single-party system dominated African politics during the first two decades of independence; the dominant ideology was that multi-party competition was not suitable to African countries, which regrouped disparate ethnic populations. It was believed that the primary task of African leaders was to build new nations based on common cultural and political grounds. The 1963 military coup in Togo and the Nigerian civil war of the 1960s and '70s provided evidence that fledgling African democracies were indeed vulnerable to political and ethnic factionalism. In response to the perceived dangers of destabilization, academics and politicians alike proposed development schemes that stressed national unity, political integration, and a significant managerial role for the state. African states were to become the primary agents of development, which would lead to a high degree of centralization. Besides drafting investment codes and trade and banking laws, governments were to build schools and hospitals, bridges and soccer fields. Each African state was expected to distribute the spoils of independence to its constituent groups.

African leaders themselves viewed the single-party state as the answer to the evils of fragmentation inherent in multiparty or multi-ethnic competitions. They perceived authoritarian rule and absolute power to be prerequisites for effective management and stability. They implemented single-party systems—with disappointing results. Out of centralization grew clientism, favoritism, nepotism, and corruption. In nearly all African countries, economic centralization and political repression coexisted. No sooner did African countries become independent than heads of state and government began to use national unity as a pretext for stamping out criticism and opposition.

From the mid-1970s, Africa began a serious economic decline that undermined the capacity of single-party states to deliver the prosperity they had promised. The middle classes, consisting of the urban elite, small businesspeople, intellectuals, and wealthy farmers, began to demand political and economic reforms, in particular the restoration of civil liberties. These demands were also supported by militant students and trade unionists. Not surprisingly, authoritarian and autocratic rulers of all ideological persuasions were unable to satisfy these demands. Instead, they responded with intensified repression, interdiction of political opposition, and increased human rights abuses. The persistent suppression of political protest was ignored by the wider international community during this era of Cold War posturing, as each bloc sought to justify the repressive actions—and crimes—of its despotic clients.

The economic situation worsened in the 1980s, reaching crisis proportions. Many African countries, even those that grew moderately during the 1970s, were saddled with debts they were unable to repay. More significantly, few were able to find funds to invest in production. In this growing crisis, social services, such as healthcare and education, suffered the most severe cuts. The crisis was compounded because lender countries and international financial institutions were preoccupied with their own financial health. Their own problems led to the World Bank and the International Monetary Fund (IMF) to mandate economic restructuring and austerity measures so Africans could repay their debts. Governments were obligated to freeze hiring, privatize state-controlled industries, and streamline social and other expenditures. The implementation of these measures created social tensions, not only because the most vulnerable were made to bear the brunt of the austerity cut-backs, but because at the same time government officials failed to curtail their own lavish lifestyles. Labor unions and student groups, specifically, resented the fact that the lay-offs of so-called redundant government employees affected only those who had no patrons in government.

The IMF/World Bank-imposed economic measures combined with the political climate created by events in Eastern Europe to stimulate the current democracy movement. The IMF measures in particular exposed the weaknesses of existing African regimes; the end of the Cold War removed the pretext for internal repression often used by dictators and patriarchs on the one hand, and foreign support for discredited regimes on the other. However, the impacts of IMF conditionalities and Eastern European events on the reform process in Africa should not be exaggerated. For the majority of students in the Cote d'Ivoire and Zaire, or the bulk of workers in Benin, Zambia, and Kenya, or many women in Niger and Nigeria, the most important concern is how to wrest power from the likes of Mussa Traore, Daniel Arap Moi, Mathieu Kereku, Paul Biya, Gnassingbe Eyadema, civilians and military, friends of the West or the East, who have all failed to submit to popular sovereignty.

A Second Independence in Africa

Today's fervor for decentralization and democracy has enabled African peoples to assert the rights and authority of which they were deprived at independence. At that time, African leaders wrested the reins of power from the people by means of consultations and negotiations in Paris or London. The majority of Africans were excluded from this process. The negotiations themselves involved the protection of property rights and political privileges which meant little to the majority of Africans. In most African countries, even those where independence was obtained through wars of liberation, there was no real popular consultation concerning national institutions nor negotiation about post-independence priorities. Few African peasants—the majority in all countries—understood the nature of the modern state or their rights in it. Instead, they witnessed the vanishing of their political and civil liberties, the confiscation of their lands, the plundering of their natural resources, and the appropriation by public officials of the public treasury.

The goal of the present democracy movement is to correct that anomaly. Across the continent, the process for achieving this objective has varied. The central African republic of Gabon was one of the first to be struck by popular discontent and the call for change. In 1989, its president, Omar Bongo, was pressured by students and trade unionists into multiparty consultations and an agreement with the opposition to hold the first pluralist national elections to select a new national assembly. The Cote d'Ivoire, Burkina Faso, and other countries followed suit, holding multiparty elections which gave representation to opposition parties in popularly elected legislative bodies. The most dramatic outcome of multiparty elections to date has been the defeat of the president of the island of Cape Verde, Aristide Pereira, and Zambia's Kenneth Kaunda. Both are uncontested leaders of the nationalist movements which resulted in independence, and both bowed to popular will relatively gracefully.

In Francophone Africa, opposition parties were emboldened by a 1988 declaration by French President Mitterand indicating that he was no longer committed to defending African dictators. At the 1989 Francophone Summit at La Baule, Mitterand went further by tying French aid to democratic reform. No longer afraid of French intervention to maintain former clients, opposition parties in Togo, Benin, Mali, Niger, and the Congo have made radical demands for restructuring society through national conferences, followed by popular referenda to ratify the results.

The national conferences resulted from the realization that political power and authority in the African state had been flawed from the outset. Paternalists and authoritarians, dictators and soldiers had suspended the political rights of the majority; orders rather than negotiation dominated political life; civil society lost its capacity to function independently of the state; constitutional rights had become meaningless; and political consultation was only an illusion.

The promise of national conferences has brought together many Africans, within truly representative national gatherings, to decide future relations within their states. In the countries where such conferences have taken place, representatives of political parties, various elements of civil society, regional and religious leaders, and the military have drafted new social contracts. In general, the conferences represent the first opportunity that Africans have had to negotiate power, to draw the boundaries of political authority within the state, and to set the priorities of their nations.

The stakes invested in political reform have risen so high that, for the majority of opposition parties, failure is inconceivable. The protesters and reformers have been eager to understand how their own states have been managed. Protesters everywhere in Africa wonder why the restructuring policies and austerity measures forced upon them by the IMF and the World Bank have not included the recovery of the public funds embezzled by Mussa Traore, Hissen Habre, Lansana Conte, and the like, which would relieve them of more than half their debt burden.[5]

The Western Solution: Perestroika without Glasnost

While Africans have come to the conclusion that they need new thinking and restructuring at home, Africanists—especially those who advise on policy—and Western policymakers have not overcome past patterns. Their euphoria over the near-reality of perestroika in Eastern Europe has not contributed to a better understanding of the global international crisis. In the United States, as in Western Europe, scholars, journalists and politicians are observing this phenomenon within old intellectual paradigms. The dominant attitude is that the West won, the communists lost, and Africa should take note.

Indeed, Africans can learn from events in Eastern Europe and elsewhere. However, the lessons should be grounded in their own experiences. For instance, there is abundant evidence that the countries that adopted central planning failed to improve the lot of their peoples. However, those African countries with so-called free market economies did not necessarily succeed. One of the ironies of recent developments in Africa is that the old clients of the West are the most reluctant to implement democracy. The leader of the West African state of Guinea, Lansana Conte, the Cameroonean president, Paul Biya, and the Malawian president Kamazu Banda, have all resisted opposition calls for reform. They all fear the propensity of national debates to review past activities—including mismanagement of public funds, human rights abuses, and nepotism—as a prerequisite to a clean beginning.

Unfortunately, the Western response to the reform movement in Africa shows that the ideological and intellectual temperament which marked the Cold War has outlasted it. Western ideologues hostile to African emancipation once represented African demands as "anti-Western"; they now must find new justifications for their blindness to the political and cultural transformation taking root in Africa and elsewhere in the Third World.

The imposition of Western liberal models of democratization on Africa has obscured the experiences of the subjugated masses. Few Western analysts have explored the issues invoked by current African reformers and protesters. In fact, many still reduce democracy to the ballot box and self-determination to majority rule, however manipulated their processes. These intellectual paradigms have caused many unwarranted misgivings about the ongoing struggle in Africa, especially in countries beset by alienation or violence.

In Zimbabwe, for instance, the Lancaster House Agreement that preceded independence in 1980 forced the nationalists to abandon their plans for land redistribution which, coupled with better pricing policy and assistance to the poor, could have helped many peasants move beyond subsistence agriculture. Instead, the mere resignation of the white minority prime minister, Ian Smith, and the advent of majority rule was heralded as a triumph of "Western-style" democracy. When, in early 1990, Zimbabwe was on the verge of a social crisis, few Western scholars were willing to risk an examination of the reasons behind attacks on white farmers who not long before had expropriated ex-combatants' lands. Such an examination would involve not only a critique of the Lancaster negotiations but also of the deceptive means (including broken promises to finance land redistribution) used by Britain to broker the negotiations between white settlers and African nationalists.

African reformers desire democracy and political transformations, but their history differs from Western or Eastern Europe. Students, the children of destitute and landless freedom fighters in Algeria, Namibia, Zimbabwe, and elsewhere, have their own indigenous agendas. Political alienation and loss of faith in legal procedures, which fan violence in many countries, reflect inequalities and constraints which were not adequately addressed during and after decolonization. The underlying problems of decolonization have been exacerbated in Southern Africa by economic disparities and racial injustice, but they are increasingly felt elsewhere in Africa.

The gap between the masses of Africa and Western ideologues and policymakers is even wider with respect to the proposed solutions for the current economic crisis. Recent IMF restructuring policies and their accompanying austerity measures, for example, have been designed by Western experts without the participation of Africans, and implemented without popular consultations. (No wonder military regimes, autocrats and dictators have been most successful at implementing the IMF policies.) The resulting decrease in real living standards and increased poverty and unemployment have compounded the sociopolitical and economic crisis in Africa. In most cases, students and workers under military dictators and authoritarian rulers have reacted with violent disapproval. Popular responses to IMF measures have ranged from violent street demonstrations and university protests, through alternative African-initiated austerity programs, to popular demands for national sacrifice.

Some African leaders understood the need to live within their nations' means long before the IMF intrusion. Thomas Sankara, late president of Burkina Faso, shifted the weight of austerity from the rural masses to the politically powerful and wealthy middle class. Cabinet ministers and other state officials were asked to exchange expensive chauffeur-driven official cars for Renault 4s, to travel fourth class on international airlines, and to save on hotels during official travel.

During the 1991 National Conference in Niger, the participants insisted that African peoples be consulted on major economic policies. Instead of the normally stipulated massive layoffs, conference participants opted for what they termed the "national effort"—a 10% cut in the gross earnings of all public employees—to retain the 10% of the workforce which would have been laid off from the government payroll to reduce the budget in accordance with the demands of international donors. Significantly, the "national effort" avoided the drastic social effects which would have resulted from the standard IMF structural adjustment policies.

Despite such optimistic examples, most Africans are aware of the limits of such efforts in repaying a national debt. They also realize that debt repayment has been a major contributing factor to the general economic decline. In Niger, Togo, Benin, and Mali, participants in the national conferences were divided on the question of foreign debt. Some participants called for debt forgiveness, on both ethical and humanitarian grounds. Others questioned outright the legality or legitimacy of foreign debt. However, both groups supported their governments' efforts at debt repayment, out of fear of economic, financial, or military reprisal from international powers.

Whether heeded or not, protests continue in Africa over unilateralism in international relations. Perhaps Western journalists, intellectuals, and politicians do not want to hear from the Vaclav Havels of Africa because they have long labeled them "leftists" or anti-Western. France was even reluctant to support the government of Togo when, in the fall of 1991, the military attempted to annul the results of the national conference by staging a coup. The popularly elected government of Joseph Kokou Koffigoh appealed to Mitterand's government for assistance, but to no avail, although France had once sent military troops to support President Eyadema's dictatorship. During the same period, France, the United States, and Belgium, which, in the guise of anti-communism, more than once had rescued Mobutu Sese Seko from his opponents, failed to protect democratic reformers in Zaire when Mobutu suspended the national conference. Western troops moved in to protect their own nationals and stood by as Mobutu's troops massacred civilians. Following the 1991 post-national conference crisis in Togo and the events in Zaire, many African reformers, nationalists, and leftists have began to wonder whether Western advocacy of democracy includes justice and fundamental political transformations. To the young professionals and students in Mali, Benin, Cote d'Ivoire, the Congo, and elsewhere who protested in front of Western embassies on those occasions, the answer to their question is dangerously frightening.

Glasnost, Perestroika, and the *New* New World Order

Many African intellectuals view with suspicion the effectiveness with which Western powers worked through the UN to attain their Gulf War objectives. Africans and other Third World proponents of a progressive new order argue that any reappraisal of the international system intended to bring about international stability will have to involve a rethinking of the conflicts and dynamics between the North/West and South. For many years, liberals and conservatives in the West have attempted to blame the present failures of African countries solely on the mismanagement of the past years, ignoring the effects of centuries of oppression and exploitation.

The economic crisis in Africa has little to do with a lack of traditions of, or experience with, free exchange of goods and skills. Prior to conquest, complex civilizations had long existed in Africa that included traditions of fair exchanges with other parts of the world, including

Europe. Beginning with the slave trade in the 1500s, up until the early 1960s, the form and nature of economic dynamics between Africa and Europe was primarily determined by Europe's desires. In short, Africa's current position in the world economy is Western-made.

The West continues to share responsibility for Africa's problems. Some of the most corrupt leaders of today's Africa were either installed by the former colonial powers or are kept in power by their good offices. Mobutu Sese Seko replaced Patrice Lumumba thanks to U.S. intervention and manipulation of Zaire's post-independence power struggle. Lumumba was a socially conscious nationalist and a parliamentarian who raised sensitive issues relating to independence. He had to be silenced.

Like the Vaclav Havels of today, Lumumba spoke the language of political self-determination and economic empowerment for the majority, but within a different context: one of international hostility and internal uncertainty. This context lent itself to Cold War activism and destabilization of Africa. Patrice Lumumba's case, though the most visible, was not unique. Ruben Um Nyobe, Felix Moumie, Ouezzin Koulibaly, and many others were politically, and physically, eliminated before independence was granted to their respective countries.

The lack of Western support for popular African demands has led to political alienation, violence, and anti-Western sentiments. Thus, to Islamic fundamentalists in Algeria, Tunisia, Morocco, and Libya, the harsh economic realities, IMF conditions, and Western support for authoritarian, if not corrupt, leaders or regimes signify an anti-Muslim, anti-Third World "conspiracy." This argument is echoed by disaffected and unemployed youth in African cities.

The dissolution of the Soviet Union has effectively ended the rivalry within the UN Security Council, lifted the veil of international antagonism and mistrust, and liberated human and material resources previously held hostage to an ever more expensive arms race. Ideally, the international system will now be restructured to allow all nations to actively participate in decisions that affect them. To many in the Third World, the end of the Cold War offers a unique opportunity for the establishment of international cooperation. However, skeptics in Africa believe, with some justification, that the new thinking and economic restructuring associated with the New World Order are doomed because these measures are not complemented by reform within the international system.

Many Western policymakers have called for a reactivation of the UN in a manner that increases the policing role of the Security Council. These professionals use language that seems inclusive: international cooperation, peace, and stability. In practice, the New World Order they describe is one dominated by the West, in which the Security Council, and the UN in general, lends legitimacy to Western interests and hegemony.

One obvious question heard in Nicaragua, Libya, New Caledonia, the West Bank, and elsewhere in the Third World is whether such a restructuring will include a review of the rules of procedure of the Security Council to strengthen its dispositions concerning conflicts of interest. The majority of conflicts, civil wars, and international tensions in the postwar era have directly or indirectly involved the permanent members of the Security Council. Indeed, the permanent members, more than any other countries, have consistently defied the international system and the International Court of Justice.

Empirical consistency and concern for the future of the globe—and the human species—dictate that we link the restructuring of the international system with issues of global concern, at both the national and international levels. While African and other Third World peoples have suffered more from poverty, repression, and exploitation, conditions in the South may soon affect the world at large. Desertification and the disappearance of the rain forest are a threat to us all. The decrease in per capita income first affects Third World peoples but then also Western banks, industries, and other investors. Refugees, whether displaced by war or famine, are cause for global concern. So are epidemic diseases like AIDS.

Not long ago preoccupied with consumption, Westerners have increasingly had to deal with the issues of conservation, waste management, and the efficient use of resources. These issues have taken precedence where production was once the priority. Considering also the threat to the human race and the planet of the spread of nuclear and chemical weapons, many in the West have had to reassess the meaning of global security. Humanity is now faced by a global environmental challenge on a par with the economic crisis.

The post-Cold War order must not be approached with old ways of thinking which combined evolutionism and a racist mentality with arrogance and imperialism. We need to rethink our approaches to global security, peace, and stability. Professionals and scholars must design new fields of study, analytical methods, and intellectual assumptions, as well as reshape their political agenda. What happened in Eastern Europe, and is happening in Africa, should be seized upon as an opportunity to rethink human solidarity and global interdependence. We must not construe recent events as the last chance for selected countries and their dominant classes to perpetuate world domination. We might still save ourselves from global catastrophe if we apply new thinking to the future course.

Notes

1. Great Britain, Parliament, *Declaration by United Nations*, Treaty Series No. 5, Commons, Cmnd. 6388, 1942, p.1.
2. United Nations, *Charter of the United Nations and Statutes of the International Court of Justice*, D.I.L-24, Articles 24 and 25; and Chapters VI, VII, VIII, and XII.
3. Ibid., specifically, articles 25-32.
4. Richburg, Keith B., "Why is Africa Overwhelmed While East Asia Overcomes?" *The International Herald Tribune*, 14 July 1992, pp. 1 and 6.
5. N'Diaye, Karamoko, "Retrouve nos sous Zorro!," *Aurore Quotidien* (Mali), 11–18 April 1991, p. 5; Malick Kante, "Les comptes bancaires à l'étranger des anciens dignitaires ont été bloqués," *L'Essor Quotidien* (Mali), 26 April 1991, p. 3.

References

Antonius, George, *The Arab Awakening: the Story of the Arab Nationalist Movement,* New York: J.B. Lippincott Company, 1929.

Arechaga, Eduardo J., *Voting and the Handling of Disputes in the Security Council.* New York: Carnegie Endowment for International Peace, 1950.

Asamoah, Obed Y., *The Legal Significance of The Declarations of The General Assembly of The United Nations,* The Hague: Martinus Nijhoff, 1966.

Awolowo, O., *Path to Nigerian Freedom,* London: Faber and Faber, 1947.

Azikiwe, N., *Renascent Africa,* London: Cass, 1937.

Chowdhury, Ramendra Nath, *International Mandates and Trusteeship Systems: A Comparative Study,* Gravenhage: Martinus Nijhoff, 1955.

Erickson, Richard, *International Law and the Revolutionary State,* New York: Oceana Publications, 1972.

Esedebe, Oliansanwuke P., *Pan-Africanism: the Idea and Movement: 1776-1963,* Washington D.C.: Howard University Press, 1982.

Falk, Richard A., *The Status of Law in International Society,* Princeton, NJ: Princeton University Press, 1970.

Geiss, Immanuel, *The Pan African Movement,* New York: Africana Publishing Co., 1974.

Gerig, Benjamin, *The Open Door and the Mandates System,* London: George Allen and Unwin Ltd., 1930.

Great Britain, *Parliament, Declaration by United Nations,* Treaty Series No. 5, Commons, Cmnd. 6388, 1942, p. l.

Green, L.C. and Olive P. Dickason, *The Law of Nations and the New World Order*, Edmonton Alberta: University of Alberta Press, 1989.

Jackson, Henry F., *From the Congo to Soweto: US Foreign Policy Toward Africa Since 1960*, New York: William Morrow and Co., 1982.

Joseph, Richard, "Glasnost for Africa," *The New York Times*, 28 December 1989.

Kahng, Tae Jin, *Law, Politics, and The Security Council*, The Hague: Martinus Nijhoff, 1964.

Kante, Malick, "Les comptes bancaires à l'étranger des anciens dignitaires ont été bloqués," *L'Essor Quotidien* (Mali), 26 April 1991.

Lipson, Charles, *Standing Guard: Protecting Foreign Capital in the Nineteenth and Twentieth Centuries*, Berkeley: University of California Press, 1985.

Mahoney, Richard D., *J.F.K.: Ordeal In Africa*, New York: Oxford University Press, 1983.

N'Diaye, Karamoko, "Retrouve nos sous Zorro!," *Aurore Quotidien* (Mali), 11-18 April 1991.

Okeye, F.C., *International Law and the New African States*, London: Sweet and Maxwell, 1972.

Richburg, Keith B., "Why is Africa Overwhelmed While East Asia Overcomes?," *The International Herald Tribune*, 14 July 1992, pp. 1 and 6.

Rocha, Geisha Maria, *In Search of Namibian Independence: The Limitations of the United Nations*, Boulder, CO: Westview Press, 1984.

Solonim, Solomon, *South-West Africa and the United Nations: An International Mandate in Dispute*, Baltimore: Johns Hopkins University Press, 1973.

Umozurike, Umozurike O., *International Law and Colonialism in Africa*, Enugu, Nigeria: Nwamife Publishers Limited, 1979.

United Nations, *Charter of the United Nations and Statuses of the International Court of Justice*, D.I.L-24, Articles 24 and 25; and Chapters VI, VII, VIII, and XII.

United Nations, General Assembly, *Report of the Council*, A/C.4/L.166, 17 December 1951.

United Nations, General Assembly, *Report of the Trusteeship Council*, A/C.4/226/add.1, 22 December 1952.

United Nations, General Assembly, *Report of the Trusteeship Council*, A/C.4/226/corr.2, 12 January 1953.

United Nations, General Assembly, *Report of the Trusteeship Council*, A/C.4/255, 28 November 1953.

United Nations, Trusteeship Council, *Resolutions. Eleventh Session.* Supplement 1. New York, 3 June-24 July 1952.

United Nations, Trusteeship Council, *Resolutions. Seventh Special Session,* Supplement 1 and 2. New York, 12-20 September 1957.

Africa and the New World Dis-Order

Francis M. Deng

When the end of the Cold War began to manifest itself in the democratization process in the Soviet Union and Eastern Europe, it seemed to imply that a new and promising era was being ushered onto the global scene. On the other hand, some voices in the Third World began to whisper apprehensively that the end of the Cold War might result in the withdrawal of the superpowers' attention from the concerns of the developing countries. While removing harmful ideological confrontations, such an outcome would also risk marginalizing those countries and deny them the support they needed for building their nations.

What was clearly not anticipated was that the bipolar confrontation of the Cold War would be replaced by the disintegration of the Soviet Union; that Yugoslavia, which had stood as a model of unity in diversity, would fall apart; and that ethnic tensions and conflicts would proliferate in many parts of the world.

Economic liberalization and the introduction of market economies into the former socialist countries, initially hailed as reflecting the victory of capitalism over communism or socialism, seems, at least in the initial phases, not to have brought the instant prosperity which the peoples of these nations clearly aspired to and expected. On the contrary, both productivity and equitable distribution, even of essential commodities, have been severely curtailed, resulting in humanitarian disasters.

The Gulf War was another dramatic episode that signaled a transformation in the international system in which the West, and more specifically the United States, emerged as the dominant actor. The United States mobilized the international community, not only to free Kuwait from Iraqi occupation, but also to override Iraqi sovereignty to protect the Kurds and ensure their welfare, albeit temporarily. Statements of President George Bush about the emergence of a New World

Order and the leadership role of the United States in that new, largely undefined, order stimulated speculation and creativity as to what might ensue.

Much of what has since ensued indicates that the new order is by no means uniformly orderly, but it has certainly created an atmosphere for rethinking arrangements that had been taken for granted as almost sacrosanct. One of the most conspicuous areas requiring rethinking is the notion of sovereignty within the international borders as defined by the old order. Two contradictory trends toward enlarged unity and fragmentation seem to be occurring concurrently: progress toward European unity illustrates the first, while the developments in the successor states of the former Soviet Union, Yugoslavia, and Ethiopia dramatize the second. These two models would seem to suggest that in this new order, those who have been oppressed by the concentrated power of the centralized system of the nation-state are asserting the need for self-determination, while those already free are choosing to modify sovereignty and move toward larger cooperative frameworks.

Nowhere is the tension between the opposing trends of unity and autonomy or independence as pressing as it is in Africa, where the colonial borders have been perceived as both artificial and sacrosanct. The signal from the developments at the international level is that old assumptions are now under severe scrutiny, to say the least, and Ethiopia, which appears set to give its ethnic groups the right of self-determination, may well prove to be a test case for the future. The time seems ripe for revisiting the colonial borders which were artificially drawn on the map by European powers some 100 years ago.

The Constraints of the Old Order

During the Cold War, the debate on conflicts around the world, and especially in Africa, centered on whether they were internally rooted or provoked by the ideological rivalry between the superpowers. The question was critical to how those conflicts should be addressed and managed. If the causes were internal, then remedies had to be sought internally. If they were related to the superpowers' rivalry, then not only had the solutions to be sought through them, but their support for their allies was a given. The debate generally dichotomized positions between those who welcomed and even sought external intervention as necessary and those who resisted it as an undesirable complication and aggravation of internal or regional conflicts.

The fear that the end of the Cold War would result in the major powers withdrawing their attention from Third World concerns has been borne out. This has decidedly removed the external factor and placed African problems in the regional and the national contexts. Causes and effects are now increasingly recognized as primarily internal, a development which has both positive and negative implications.

Previously, Africa was hooked to the global structures and processes, first by colonial intervention and then by ideological linkages into a chain of interdependency. The end of the Cold War meant de-linkage in varying degrees, which is making self-reliance increasingly imperative. This applies not only to governance, especially the resolution or management of conflicts, but also to development. However, having been dislodged from the context of indigenous values and institutions as resources for self-enhancement from within, Africans are left hanging between the local and the global systems.

The crisis of this development is manifesting itself in the devastating conflicts which no longer seem to draw world attention as they might have done in the past. The decolonization of Namibia, the process of dismantling apartheid in South Africa, and the peace process in Angola were all undertaken at a time when the Cold War was being replaced by cooperation between the superpowers in the management of ideologically polarizing conflicts around the world. In sharp contrast to the world attention those situations received are the cases of Liberia, Ethiopia, and until recently, Somalia. The worst scenarios are those in Mozambique and Sudan.

The only African issues in which the world still manifests interest are the unfolding developments in South Africa and the humanitarian assistance, often in the form of famine relief for the starving masses, in drought-stricken and war-ravaged countries. And of course the International Monetary Fund and the World Bank adjustment programs keep the continent tied to the dictates of the international financial and economic system. Otherwise, the challenge for Africa is to go beyond the empty slogans and give meaning to true independence through genuine self-reliance.

Africans are reacting to the situation in a pragmatic way that points at two seemingly contradictory, but in fact complementary, lines of action. First, they are recognizing that the world does not care much about them and that they must take their destinies into their own hands. At the same time, the imperatives of global interdependence propel them to resist marginalization. Putting the two together, the operative formula is for the Africans first to put their houses in order and then to get back to the international scene with a renewed sense of legitimacy.

In reality, these moves are not sequential but concurrent. Recent years have witnessed a wave of earnest self-criticism in Africa among the intellectuals and even incumbent political leaders. The promotion of democracy and human rights has become a high priority in the African debate. The Organization of African Unity Charter on Human and Peoples' Rights, the so-called Banjul Charter, was a major accomplishment in this process. The Conference on Security, Stability, Development, and Cooperation in Africa (CSSDCA), the so-called Helsinki process for Africa, initiated by General Olusegun Obasanjo's African Leadership Forum, endorsed by the Kampalla Conference in 1991, and now under consideration by the Organization of African Unity (OAU), is one of the manifestations of this process of self-criticism and the search for practical ways of advancing the cause of security, democracy, human dignity, and development. Envisaged in the process is the creation of an African Council of Elders, comprising mostly former heads of state and government who have retired respectably and can continue to offer leadership beyond power. Among other functions, they are expected to help mediate between parties to domestic and regional conflicts and promote the cause of peace and security in the continent.

The Organization of African Unity has also reorganized its institutional arrangements to be more effective in conflict resolution and the promotion of peace and security, both domestically and regionally. In addition to reactivating the dormant Commission on Mediation, Arbitration, and Conciliation envisaged in the OAU Charter, the secretary-general has recently established a conflict resolution unit in the Secretariat.

Africa's resistance to marginalization at the international level is likely to benefit from the reforms now being undertaken to promote democracy, human rights, and the liberalization of the economies.

The Challenges of the New Order

There is now no doubt that African problems, whether they relate to conflict management or socio-economic development, must be approached from the perspective of the local, regional, and national contexts. This should entail a close analysis of the root causes of conflict, appropriate arrangements and strategies for conflict resolution, protection of human rights, promotion of democracy, and the realization of sustainable development.

Politically, the starting point, as in most matters pertaining to Africa, has to be the colonial nation-state and its unification of the diversities which it paradoxically kept separate and unintegrated. Ethnic groups were broken up and affiliated with others within the artificial borders of the new state system. While the colonial masters were the third-party moderators of ethnic co-existence and interaction, they imposed a superstructure of law and order that maintained relative peace and tranquility.

The independence movement was a collective struggle for self-determination that reinforced the notion of unity within the artificial framework of the newly established nation. Indeed, independence came as a gross national product that did not initially disaggregate who was to get what from the legacy of centralized power and wealth. And indeed, colonial structures and processes of control had divested the local communities and ethnic groups of much of their indigenous autonomy and sustainable livelihood and replaced them with a degree of centralized authority and dependency on the welfare-state system. Once the control of these centralized institutions and sources of survival passed on to the nationals at independence, the struggle for central control became unavoidable, especially as the colonial system had been stratified along ethnic and regional lines. The inevitable outcome was conflict over power, wealth, and developmental opportunities. These conflicts invariably led to gross violations of human rights, denial of civil liberties, disruption of economic and social life, and consequential frustration of development.

Given the Cold War conditions that pervaded the international system, these conflicts were not perceived in the domestic context of competition for power and resources, but rather as extensions of the superpower ideological confrontation by proxy. Rather than help resolve them peacefully, the rival ideological camps only added fuel by providing military and economic assistance to their allies or satellites.

While the end of the Cold War has removed this aggravating external factor, it has also removed the moderating role of the super-powers, both as third parties and mutually neutralizing allies. As Liberia, Ethiopia, Somalia, Mozambique, and Sudan illustrate, the results have been unmitigated brutalities and devastations.

It can credibly be argued that the gist of these internal conflicts is that the ethnic pieces that were welded and kept together by the colonial glue, reinforced by the old world order, are now pulling apart and reasserting their autonomy or independence.

The objective of self-determination, which had triggered the independence movement but had been interrupted by the constraints of sovereignty and the territorial integrity of the colonial borders, now appears to have been resumed with vigor and vengeance. Old identities that were undermined and rendered dormant by the structures, values, and institutions of the nation-state system are reemerging and redefining the standards of participation, distribution, and legitimacy. In fact, it may be even more accurate to say that the process has been going on in a variety of ways within the context of the constraints imposed by the nation-state system.

From the dawn of African independence, such slogans as Senghor's Negritude, Nkrumah's *Consciencism,* Kenyatta's *Uhuru,* Nyerere's *Ujamaa,* Mobutu's *Authenticité,* and Kaunda's Humanism have symbolized African leaders' search for cultural legitimation of their political and economic objectives and strategies. Oftentimes, they were rationalizations for preconceived ideas and practices that were adopted from foreign prototypes and dressed up in local garbs, but they nonetheless expressed a genuine yearning for building on the culture of the people.

With the end of the Cold War, this trend is acquiring a rebirth with a deeper sense of the real world which verbalism or empty slogans can no longer manage. Africans are now called upon to find workable solutions to real problems. They must now face the challenges of their immediate problems in the framework of the New World Order.

It is in this context that the revivalist Islamic trend in North Africa and the Middle East should be understood. The movement, at least in the Sudan, developed as a reaction to both colonialism, which promoted Christianity and Western concepts of secular nationhood, and the collaboration of the traditional Muslim leaders with foreign powers. The latter was always a reinforcement of traditionalism and conservatism in a situation which called for radical transformation, that is modernization. A twin movement in this direction, indeed the first to be born, was communism. Not only did both movements have a great deal in common, but they also were first and foremost reactions to the domestic conditions, utilizing ideological linkages to their international dimensions only as tools of management in an interconnected world.

With the demise of communism, first locally in the Sudan after the abortive coup of 1971 which was used to justify a debilitating blow to the Communist Party, and then internationally with the collapse of the

Soviet Union and Eastern Europe, Muslim fundamentalists remained the only credible alternative to the traditional political forces that were becoming outmoded. The Muslim Brothers, who politically transformed themselves into the Islamic Charter Front and the National Islamic Front, infiltrated the army and won the support of the officers who took over on January 30, 1989, in the name of the Revolution for National Salvation, with Islamic revivalism as their agenda.

In the Sudan, Islam has been closely associated with Arabism as a composite racial, cultural, and religious identity. Seen in the context of pluralism, however, the challenge that faces the Muslim revivalists is how to reconcile their religious legitimacy and basis of power with diversity and conflicting value systems within the nation and the still interdependent world.

Even among the Muslims, Western values and institutions that have thus far dominated the nation-state system have been adopted and internalized by a sizable portion. The separation of religion and the state is an integral aspect of that system. In the southern part of Sudan, national identity has evolved along indigenous African, Christian Western, and secular lines that contrasts with the Arab-Islamic model of the North. Indeed, the two appear to thrive on their mutual antagonism and struggle for survival. Beyond that, there is the challenge of meeting universally accepted standards of human rights which conflict with the relativist approach of religious and cultural groups to whom these universal standards are foreign, both in terms of the institutional means by which they were defined and their substantive content. This is not to mention the imperatives of the world economic order in which all nations and peoples remain incorporated, even though in some cases only marginally so.

These considerations, however, do not invalidate the quest for cultural legitimization and the need for contextualizing nation-building and the process of self-sustaining development from within the cultural context. The search for workable formulas must consider the conflicting demands for autonomy and equitable unity being made by various groups within the nation-state system. The operative principles in this respect must be autonomy, equity, and justice. But the observance of these principles requires a third party as mediator, moderator, peacemaker, and lawgiver. While regional organizations have a role to play, the most obvious institution called upon to play a pivotal role is the United Nations.

It has to be admitted that once the colonial powers accomplished the brutal task of conquest and pacification, they established a system of public order and justice that brought peace to inter-ethnic relations which had been afflicted by chronic violence throughout recorded history. This was certainly the case between the Arab Muslim North and the more African South in Sudan. While colonial intervention understandably provoked nationalistic reactions that ultimately culminated in the independence movement, the postulated role for the United Nations aimed at establishing peace, justice, stability, and prosperity has a more compelling and disarming justification. A political, economic, social, and cultural system that autonomously utilizes local resources and resourcefulness within the framework of regional and global interaction and interdependency can be designed to reconcile the lofty ideals of unity with the imperatives of segmentation and fragmentation. As units of participation and social orientation, the family, the clan, and the tribe can indeed be complementary rather than antagonistic to the nation and the global order.

The United Nations in the New Order

Until the Gulf War, the Western perception of the United Nations was that it was a Third World club and a forum for bashing the West, in particular the United States. The Gulf War and its aftermath turned the organization, in the perception of the Third World, into a Western, specifically a U.S., tool for global control.

The United States, more appropriately the president, has not shied away from the role of leadership which the new perception of the organization places on the West, and in particular, the United States. Despite resentment of the inequalities of a system that has hitherto paid lip-service to the principle of equality among member states, the real test is the extent to which the United States lives up to the ideals of political, economic, and moral leadership, whether it operates individually or through the international institutions.

Although states are usually assumed to be motivated by national interests in their bilateral and multilateral policies and strategies, the role of a world leader certainly carries with it burdens that should transcend national interests. There was considerable controversy in the United States about what President Bush meant by a New World Order, what responsibilities he envisaged for the U.S. leadership in that order, and what financial baggage that leadership might entail. The United States will have to be clearer on what the new order means, whether and how the United States will assume the leadership role, what the guiding principles of that leadership will be, and how it will translate itself in the specific regions of the world where international action is needed to address urgent issues. The former Yugoslavia is an obvious urgent case, but there are many more candidates, and the ultimate objective should be a comprehensively peaceful, just, and orderly world.

Conclusion

If progress is assumed to be an integral part of human development, then the New World Order which is emerging must signify an improvement on the way things have been. The central themes of this improvement must be realizing seemingly contradictory trends, the quest for autonomy and the need for broadening circles of cooperation regionally and internationally. Leadership at the international level must pursue the ideals of freedom, democracy, justice, and prosperity for all nations and peoples throughout the world. World leaders cannot discriminate between their own favored nationals and the marginalized nationals of foreign nations, at least not to the degree of dispossession. Liberating Kuwait must only be defended on universal principles, not for limited national strategic objectives, if the role of the United States as the driving force behind United Nations action is to be viewed as global leadership. The same principle is more glaring in the case of protection for the Kurds in Iraq. This in turn imposes an obligation on the United States and the United Nations to exercise the same responsibility in comparable situations of need for international action.

It goes without saying that the tragic situations in Liberia, Somalia, Sudan, and Mozambique cannot be left to local actors when the magnitude of human suffering and destruction to life and property far exceeds what should be tolerable even by minimum standards of human dignity and global responsibility. Otherwise, what we are witnessing is the emergence of a new world disorder.

Over a century ago, the major European powers met at the Berlin Conference and carved the African continent into pieces of real estate in which they extended colonial domination. Perhaps the time has come for another Berlin conference with a different venue, participants, and guiding principles. "Conference" in this context is intended as a metaphor for re-thinking the colonial borders to give greater meaning to self-determination and the principles of democracy and human dignity.

New World Order: Old Arab World Problems

Nahla Abdo

The Gulf War, viewed from a historical perspective, can be seen as the latest in a string of crises which have confronted the Middle East for the last quarter of this century. During the so-called Cold War between the two superpowers, people in the Middle East were experiencing quite hot and bloody wars: from the 1967 war to the 1982 Israeli invasion of Lebanon, and including the 1973 war and the 1979 Iran-Iraq war. This continuous state of war has drained the economies of the countries involved and ensured their continuous dependency on the superpowers, primarily the United States. Instead of channeling funds for human development projects, industrialization, health, and education, many Arab states such as Syria, Egypt, and Iraq were preoccupied with entrenching their regimes and the military-authoritarian nature of their respective states.

The end of the Cold War, crystallized in the collapse of the Soviet Union and the Eastern Bloc as an independent power, coupled with the defeat, or rather destruction, of Iraq, has given the United States a particular hegemonic status: a new power with very little, if any, official challenge. It is within this context that the so-called New World Order must be understood.

While the Gulf War was just one driving force in the emergence of the so-called New World Order, the war was unprecedented in the history of humanity because it utilized not only the most advanced technologies in weaponry, but also in communication, mass-control media, and dissemination of information, to effect massive destruction in a relatively short time period. Thus in addition to the hundreds of thousands of Iraqi children, women, and men said to have been wiped out during the war, UN and other international agencies continue to estimate child and infant deaths at a rate of 300-400 per day and warn of the environmental catastrophe which has plagued the region (including Iraq, Kuwait, and the poor nations surrounding the Gulf).

In this chapter, I will examine some aspects of change which have affected Arab countries at the global, regional, and local levels. My point of departure will be the event (the Gulf War) and not the ideology (New World Order). The major argument which will be advanced here is that the Gulf War and the New World Order have not invented the new disorder, chaos, regional discrepancies, and the many conflicts and contradictions currently gripping the Arab world. The old order of the Arab world was, in fact, plagued with all sorts of social, economic, ethnic, and gender conflicts prior to the Gulf War. The aftermath of the Gulf War has basically intensified and speeded up Arab disorder by exposing most Arab regimes and state policies. To carry through this argument, I will look at regional conflicts in the Arab world and examine the relationship between Arab states and their citizenries. The last segment of this article will focus on the special position of the Palestinians and the peculiar room prepared for them in the New World Order. Emphasis in this last segment will be placed on the role and position of Arab Palestinian women.

Old Problems in a New Form

One of the major debates which arose during the Gulf War has focused on the nature of the "alliance" between Arab countries, primarily Egypt and Syria, and the United States. While for some such an alliance was viewed as just a temporary tactical maneuver, others have seen it as a dramatic new shift in Arab states' policies. Those who argued that the changes were tactical pointed to the financial incentives which both countries were offered, such as the cancellation of Egypt's foreign debts by the United States, and financial aid and some other promised rewards to Syria for negotiating with Israel about the return of the Golan Heights.

The other camp, which viewed these policies as "new shifts," has focused on the consequences for "Arab unity," arguing that these policies will create or accelerate divisions within the Arab world. One area where a rift was seen as imminent was between the Maghreb—notably Tunisia, Algeria, Morocco, and Libya, and the Masreq—especially Syria, Egypt, and Jordan.[1] These debates, I propose, are superficial in that they fail to address local and regional conflicts and discrepancies already existing in and between the Arab countries. These debates, conducted in the spirit of Arab nationalism, fail to account for the internal class, gender, religious, and ethnic conflicts plaguing most Arab countries. They also ignore the unequal relationship of exchange between large poor countries, such as Egypt, Syria, and Sudan, and the tiny oil-exporting monarchies of the Gulf.

Arab nationalism has long been placed on the back burner in most Arab countries. In fact, various Arab scholars have observed that the defeat of the Arab armies in 1967 by Israel constituted a major blow to the Arab unity project. The end of Nasser's era and the rise of the Sadat regime, which has brought about the *infitah* (or the open door policy), marked the beginning of a new political economy in the Arab world. The coming of Sadat to power, his open alliance with the world capitalist system and the United States in particular, and his signing of the Camp David Accords with Israel eliminated the last glimmer of hope held by Arab nationalists.

Moreover, Egypt's political alliance with the U.S. camp has not guaranteed it economic self-sufficiency, let alone economic independence. Instead, Egypt has been dragged into an IMF and World Bank style of development, incurring heavy foreign debts and distorted development. By the early 1980s, Egypt had turned into the major labor-exporting country in the Arab world. An estimated labor force of over two million Egyptian workers is currently employed in the non-skilled and semi-skilled sectors of the Gulf. One of the calculations of the Mubarak regime during the Gulf War was that if his government did not receive immediate financial rewards it would at least be guaranteed some role in the reconstruction of Kuwait. His calculations, as Haseeb and Rouchdy have pointed out, were misplaced. The overwhelming majority of reconstruction-related projects were controlled by the United States itself, with some smaller projects grabbed by Britain and France, which managed to contact the Kuwaiti government early on.[2]

While the overwhelming problems of Egypt are directly related to the political economy of its state, it is definitely not alone. Structural and regional problems exist in and among all Arab countries. Lebanon, Somalia, Libya, the western Sahara, and Mauritania have all been experiencing active civil wars or border conflicts. Whether these conflicts were manifested in the suppression of the Sunnis by the Alawite regime of Syria, the suppression of the Shia' by Saddam Hussein, or, more importantly, the suppression and massacres against the Kurds by the latter, all these conflicts have had debilitating effects on Arab regional stability.

Viewed from this perspective, one can hardly find a common ground for regional cooperation, let alone unity, among Arab countries. There remains one single issue which for many years has been adopted by almost all Arab states as a common theme, namely the declared aim of liberating Palestine and the Palestinians. While this issue was at the top of the Arab agenda until the Gulf War, history shows that the Palestinian issue was no more than a propaganda card, used by Arab states in an attempt to deflect popular attention from increasing social, economic, and political hardships. In fact, the 1987 *intifada* has dispelled any remaining illusion about the position of the Arab regimes on the Palestinian issue; in some sense it withdrew their bargaining card.

The primary result of the Gulf War in the Arab world has been to accelerate already existing conflicts, intensify old, yet partly masked, discrepancies, and fuel local and regional contradictions which the state of impasse in the Arab nationalist movement has failed to address. The Gulf War has sanctioned direct contacts between various Arab regimes and the state of Israel, contacts which otherwise would have been made secretly and in private. For example, the recent "Israeli-Egyptian summit" was held in Cairo at the invitation of Mubarak, and a series of meetings between Syrian officials and Israeli Labour Party officials were facilitated by King Hassan of Morocco just prior to the Israeli elections. The recent Syrian-Israeli deal in which the former has agreed to import water pipes manufactured in Israel carries a special weight in regional considerations. Syria, which for the longest time has been claiming to be the champion of Arab nationalism and of the Palestinian people, is not only contradicting its own claims but also exposing the shaky regional treaty signed in 1973, known as the Arab economic boycott of Israel.[3]

State and Society in the Arab World: Old Tensions with New Fuel

Regional conflicts and self-centered interests which have marred all Arab regimes during the past 20 years have largely been responsible for the increasing gap and tensions between states and societies in the Arab world. Tensions that were expressed through mass demonstrations during the Gulf War were not just a response to the war, as some may have thought. Except for the states of Syria and Egypt, which had policed their nations and suppressed popular demonstrations, almost everywhere in the Arab countries masses took to the streets. Arab popular sentiments, revealed during the Gulf War in Algeria, Tunisia, Morocco, Jordan, Lebanon, and elsewhere, expressed more than anything else people's frustration and resentment at Arab regimes in general, and their own states' policies in particular.

The three major Arab countries in the Maghreb—Morocco, Tunisia, and Algeria—have been crippled for the past decade by worsening economic conditions. To varying degrees all three countries were facing rising unemployment, widespread poverty, "bread uprising," youth demonstrations, women's protests, and most notably a revival of Muslim fundamentalism, with Algeria being most affected. Algerian social structure has been crippled by the failure of the National Liberation Front's (FLN) one-party rule to implement its economic projects, which led to high rates of unemployment and worsening living conditions among the rural poor, making space for the Islamic Salvation Front (ISF) to emerge as a strong political alternative with considerable mass support. Further tensions were also rising at the gender level, partly due to the attempts of the ISF to turn the country back into a traditional patriarchy with strict religious codes. All these tensions were played out actively in the streets of Algeria prior to the Gulf War. The frequent antiwar demonstrations throughout January 1991, whether organized by Left and opposition groups, the ISF, or women's organizations, were all expressing the deep social, gender, economic, and political conflicts embedded in the Algerian system.

A similar reading can also be made of the popular demonstrations held in Morocco and Tunisia. During the Gulf War much of the concern of Arab states, and of the Maghreb in particular, has not been about Iraq and its destruction as much as about the security of the regimes from the people themselves. In Morocco, for example, despite the "balancing" or rather vacillating position of King Hassan, he could not control the popular resentment and a demonstration by over 300,000 people in the streets of Rabat. Commenting on Morocco during the war, David Seddon observed:

> In Morocco, where the Islamic movements had been effectively repressed for the time being, the main concern was the enormous potential for social unrest associated with the unpopular economic reforms of the government and the associated deterioration in living conditions among the mass of the people, which was dramatically revealed when a general strike called by the trade unions in December degenerated into large-scale demonstrations and violent clashes with the security forces in several major cities, giving rise to over 200 deaths and hundreds of arrests.[4]

Furthermore, as the Algerian women's mass demonstration of January 24, 1991, showed, the enemy of the Arab people was not only "Bush" but "the emirs" as well. The "emirs" in this demonstration symbolized Arab popular resentment of the policies and lavish lifestyles which the Gulf sheiks and emirs have been practicing while millions of Arabs have been perishing from malnutrition, starvation, and ethnic conflicts. Grassroots sentiments against the emirs and sheiks were in fact brought home through the experiences of millions of Arab expatriates (both laborers and professionals) who for the past 20 years have lived and worked in the Gulf states. Commenting on the lavish lifestyle of the sheiks and emirs, Sayigh has the following to say: "...enough time has passed since the oil-boom of 1973-74 for stories of sexual excesses (whether true or not), spending sprees in Western capitals, and the gambling away of millions of dollars at casinos (even gambling by satellite) to have filtered down to the most illiterate and impoverished in the farthest corners of the Arab world."[5]

Class, gender, and ethnic problems have long characterized the social systems in all Arab countries. These problems were heavily entrenched in Arab regimes whose economic dependence on the world capitalist system has kept them in a perpetual state of debt, while simultaneously strengthening their authoritarian rule. For their regimes to be maintained, Arab rulers realized that the status quo must be preserved and their state machinery must be prioritized over any human development concern, a position welcomed by the U.S. and other Western powers, and especially by big capitalist agencies such as the IMF and the World Bank. It is not surprising, therefore, that most states' budgets get spent on excessive military buildup with very little funding channeled to educational, health, employment, and other programs.

Misallocation or mismanagement of state funds, whether the decisions are made consciously or not, has also characterized oil-producing Arab countries. The United Nations Development Program's *Human Development Report 1990* states that oil-producing countries have "failed to translate their recent wealth into human development." The same report talks about the poor performance of Middle East and North African oil producers, including Oman, the United Arab Emirates, Saudi Arabia, Libya, and Algeria, and suggests that the life expectancy in these countries is "often no better than the average for the Third World, while the literacy rate is frequently well below the average. The rate of female literacy, in particular is said to be low."[6]

The poor, women, and other ethnic and social groups have been the primary victims of the Arab authoritarian states and of the regional disparities between rich and poor countries within the Arab world. It is these same groups who have been most affected by the Gulf War and who will continue to be marginalized in the new Arab world "order."

What Does the Gulf War and its Aftermath Hold for the Palestinians?

While one cannot prioritize suffering or victimization, one particular Arab national group, namely, the Palestinians, presents a unique case and requires special attention. In this section, we will deal with the direct and indirect impact of the Gulf War on the Palestinians. The availability of data on the impact on, and role of, Palestinian women will also enable us to provide more gender analysis.

In order to appreciate the real magnitude of the economic impact of the Gulf War on the Palestinians, a brief account of Palestinian economic history under Israeli occupation is necessary. During 25 years of Israeli military occupation, massive land expropriation has taken place.[7] While not all these lands have been successfully settled by Israeli Jews, the impact of this expropriation on the Occupied Territories has been devastating. Masses of proletarians have been created; unable to survive in the territories, they have been forced to sell their labor power in Israel. The Palestinian migrant labor force employed in Israel is estimated at over 150,000 workers. The working and living conditions of these workers, according to many reports, including the recent report by the Israeli human rights activist Israel Shahak, are worse than those experienced under South African apartheid.[8]

The Occupied Territories of the West Bank and Gaza Strip have been turned into a pool of cheap labor power for the Israeli labor market. This process has been enhanced partly by Israel's water policies, which aimed at diverting the waters from West Bank and Gaza agriculture to newly built Jewish settlements in expropriated land, and partly by Israel's various military regulations, which have restricted Palestinian agriculturists and hampered agricultural production. By the late 1980s and early 1990s, the Occupied Territories have been turned into an almost fully dependent economy with all the features of underdeveloped dependency: insignificant industrialization, maintenance of labor-intensive agriculture, and insignificant technological development. It is within this context of an underdeveloped dependent society experiencing military rule that one must view the economic impact of the Gulf War on the Occupied Territories.

In the aftermath of the Gulf War, hundreds of thousands of Palestinians found themselves not only jobless, but also forcibly expelled from the Gulf states, particularly from Kuwait.[9] This new Palestinian exodus is a major catastrophe for the people, second only to their expulsion from Palestine after 1948. For many Palestinian families, Kuwait has been a place of residence and work for over 30 years. Palestinians see themselves as major contributors to the development of the economy and infrastructure of some Gulf states, especially Kuwait.

While other Arab expatriates, such as Jordanians and some Egyptians, were expelled from the Gulf, only Palestinians had no state or country of their own to go back to; Palestinians with homes and families in the Occupied Territories were prevented by Israel from returning. The impact of mass Palestinian expulsion from the Gulf has been comprehensive because of the chain effects it had on other Palestinian families, whose very survival has for many years depended on remittances sent by expatriate family members in the Gulf.

The annual losses of the Palestinians in the form of income and remittances have been estimated between $1,309.5 million and $10 billion.[10] The elimination of remittances as a source of income for many Palestinians has been compounded by drastic cuts and the withdrawal of funds from various health, labor, and educational institutions. In addition, the Gulf War and its aftermath have drastically reduced exports from the Occupied Territories to the Gulf states. Particularly affected have been citrus fruits and olive oil. This sector had been instrumental in providing income for many Palestinian agricultural laborers.

The ramifications of these heavy economic losses go beyond their mere impact on individual Palestinians. Palestinian employment has been experiencing further hardships with the immigration between 1991 and 1992 of over 400,000 Soviet Jews to Israel. Unable to find jobs in their professions—most Soviet immigrants came as professionals—Soviet Jews were ready to accept any menial, unskilled, or semi-skilled job available. The employment of Soviet settlers thus came in large part at the expense of Palestinian migrant labor.

The onus of all these hardships has fallen largely on the shoulders of women and children. Prior to the Gulf War, a number of women's groups and scholars already had warned against the emergence of new and disturbing social phenomena: increased child labor and escalation in school drop-outs, especially among female students, and early and often forced marriage of young women, with the reappearance in some cases of polygamy.[11] Worsening economic conditions as the result of the Gulf War, the inability or lack of interest on the part of Arab states in solving the Palestinian problem, and the unlimited support Israel has been receiving from the United States—including the approval late in 1992 of $10 billion in loan guarantees for Israel's settler project in the Occupied Territories—will probably intensify these social problems. The real danger here lies in the long-term consequences these social problems might produce.

Unlike expatriate families in other Arab countries, Palestinian women in the West Bank and Gaza do not easily get to see or unite with their male breadwinners. The phenomenon known as "the feminization of the Arab family" is widespread in the Occupied Territories. Partly due to economic hardships but also for political reasons—currently more than 13,000 Arab men and young males are held in Israeli prison camps—many families, especially in the refugee camps, are solely supported by women. Whereas, for example, in rural Egypt, women can till the land or work as hired agricultural laborers, such a possibility is not available for camp refugee women.

During the Gulf War a number of democratic and open-minded Palestinians resented what they viewed as U.S. "double standard" policies. Underlying their argument is the belief that the United States has adhered to international law in its war to "liberate Kuwait," and that consistency in U.S. foreign policy would require it to follow suit in liberating the Palestinians. Yet, as Bishara has rightly observed, the United States neither followed international law, nor did it care about Kuwait's liberation. Its primary interests have been economic and geopolitical, both of which require a degree of stability in the region.[12]

North American media coverage of the Gulf War was full of ironies, racism, demonization, and dehumanization of Arabs. Yet, most ironic, I believe, has been the media preoccupation with the Palestinians and their responses to the war. The media, while ignoring mass demonstrations in many Arab countries, singled out the Palestinians as the only antiwar and pro-Saddam forces. The irony here is that at no time was the media interested in the well- or rather ill-being of the Palestinians. At no time has it condemned the brutal military regime of Israel, and at no time has it recognized the Palestinians' long struggle for human dignity and political rights. More importantly, while the media was focusing on Palestinian refugees' protests in Jordan, it ignored the fact that at the same time more than two million Palestinians in the West Bank and Gaza were living under emergency regulations, with a blanket curfew imposed on them for the whole duration of the war.

In fact, outside of the Gulf region, the only people who were living under constant fear during the war were the Palestinians of the Occupied Territories. They feared massive expulsion and massacres like those of 1948; they feared a massive retaliation by Israel when no foreign media were allowed in; they also feared chemical weapons when gas masks were not available for them.[13] Neither Palestinian fears nor their hopes were or are of interest to the United States. On the contrary, the Palestinians have been targeted and singled out because for a long time the Palestinian problem, created by Israel and the Western powers, has been a major stumbling block for full U.S. hegemony in the region.

The New World Order and Palestinian Independence

The *intifada,* which for the past five years has been able to stand up against Israel, one of the most formidable military powers in the region, is now undergoing some major changes, facing special hardships at both the local-societal and the international level.

Grave economic difficulties, combined with Israel's continuing expansion of settlements and the lack of serious international efforts at finding a just solution to the Palestinian question, are taking their toll on the masses, many of whom are sensing a state of *ihbat* (frustration and hopelessness). Undoubtedly, those most affected by these circumstances are refugees, rural and urban poor, and women. In fieldwork I carried out in the summer of 1990 among female grassroots organizations in the West Bank and the Gaza Strip, the mood of women activists in these organizations was one of hope and optimism, despite the many hardships Palestinians were facing. Women's mass participation in the *intifada* had given them a sense of empowerment and conviction of their ability to effect change in the social, gender, and economic structures of their society. Equally important was women's belief in their ability to combat the rising Islamist movement Hamas.[14]

However, the impasse they now face has altered the mood among many. From a sense of empowerment expressed in terms like "no going back," a large number of activists are currently expressing a sense of *raddah* or going nowhere. The *raddah* among Palestinians is attributed to the development of new factors, social and cultural as well as political and economic. For most Palestinians, the popularity of the *intifada* and the strong national unity they achieved in the initial stages gave them the impression that an immediate political solution was in sight. This feeling was further enhanced by the PLO declaration of the independent Palestinian state and its recognition of the Israeli state. Yet, when the declaration of political independence failed to result in any real solution, a state of *ihbat* began to take its toll among the population.

In the meantime, Israel intensified its campaign of occupation, clamping down on the Palestinians both economically and politically in an attempt to weaken the *intifada* and weaken, if not dismantle, the Unified Leadership. These conditions were evolving, as we have seen above, in an unfavorable international context which saw the demise of political independence for most Arab Middle Eastern countries after the Gulf War. Amidst all these frustrating conditions, fundamentalist Muslim groups began to emerge as an alternative leadership, encouraged at the beginning by the Israeli military. Some of these groups, especially

Hamas, began to launch an aggressive campaign of fundamentalist revival, if not reinvention. As expected, the most vulnerable group for religious fundamentalist activities has been women.

In the Occupied Territories and especially in Gaza, a startling "return" or, more properly, reinvention of Muslim fundamentalist culture, expressed in the veil, religious dress codes, and the "domesticization" of women, began to take hold. Most often women find themselves coerced into adopting the new dress codes and, more importantly, forced out of the public sphere.

Notwithstanding this, it has become clear that Palestinian women have emerged as a major social force to be reckoned with. Their long struggle has accorded them significant recognition both locally and internationally. A major achievement for the women of the *intifada,* one which is not likely to fade out, is the role they have played in politicizing the Israeli women's movement as well as in generating not only sympathy but also solidarity and support among various feminist groups internationally. The formation of a number of Jewish organizations such as Women in Black and Women Against Occupation in Israel, Europe, and various North American cities attests to this.

It is important to realize, however, that, like other social groups and women's organizations in the Middle East and probably globally, the Palestinian women's struggle is dialectically linked to the general environment within which it is placed, and as such will always be undergoing changes and transformations, depending on changes in that environment. What makes their struggle different, however, is that they are part of a national liberation movement and not struggling within the confines of a state as yet. A more credible evaluation of Palestinian women's social status and role will be possible when and if the national liberation movement wins international recognition as a state.

It is this very issue, namely, the future of the Palestinian struggle, which is currently placed at the top of the agenda for the so-called New World Order. While I do not want to speculate on the outcome of the ongoing "peace talks," a couple of observations are in order.

The *intifada* has exposed Israel's real and ugly face of military occupation and unmasked Israel's apartheid and racist system. While these realities have not altered the Likud policies, they appear to have embarrassed the enlightened Zionists of the Labor Party and more so the U.S. government, which wants Israel to appear as the only democracy in the Middle East. Hence, this destabilizing force must be somehow solved or ended. With the September 1991 Madrid Conference, a process of transformation has begun: the diplomatization of the Palestinian political struggle, or, more properly, the hijacking of the Palestinian struggle.

At this historic juncture, which is characterized by a unipolar system (U.S. hegemony), the balance of power is not likely to favor Palestinian independence. Judging from what has already taken place during the various "talks" or discussions, there is little hope that a just and comprehensive solution to the Palestinian diaspora will be placed on the international, or rather the U.S., agenda. For example, in the two most important conferences held until now, Palestinians were either entirely absent or their very basic rights were ignored. Thus, in the conferences on refugees held in Ottawa in May 1992, the most important right of Palestinian refugees, namely, the right to return, proclaimed by the UN Security Council resolution 194, has been entirely absent from the negotiations, while earlier on, in the conference on water in Moscow, the Palestinian, Jordanian, and Lebanese delegations, the primary victims of Israel's water policies, were altogether absent.

While for many, the Palestinians are considered the heart of the Middle East conflict, one should not be very surprised if they end up with less than minimum rights. The old formula of self-government and confederation with Jordan, suggested by Israel more than ten years ago, approved by the United States, and at the time rejected by the Palestinians, appears to be back on the U.S. "Peace Talks" agenda. Finally, the New Arab World Order allows enough room for all kinds of speculations, one of which could be that the so-called normalization of Arab-Israeli relations will be pushed ahead, even if that happens at the expense of Palestinian independence as well as at the expense of the Lebanese and Syrians under Israeli occupation. The place of the Palestinians in the New World Order remains to be seen.

Notes

1. For more on these debates see Dina Haseeb and Malak S. Rouchdy, "Egypt's Speculations in the Gulf Crisis: The Government's Policies and the Opposition Movement," in *The Gulf War and the New World Order,* Bresheeth, Haim, and Nira Yuval-Davis, eds., London: Zed Books, 1991, pp. 70-79; David Seddon, "Politics and the Gulf Crisis: Government and Popular Responses in the Maghreb," in ibid., pp. 104-116.
2. Haseeb and Rouchdy, p. 76.
3. For details on this specific Israeli-Syrian deal, see the Arab newspaper, *Kul al-Arab,* published in Nazareth, Israel, 7 March 1992, p. 2. The same newspaper

reports various meetings between King Hassan of Morocco, Shimon Perez of Israel, and various Syrian officials.

4. Seddon, pp. 106-107.

5. Sayigh, Yezid, "The Arab Grassroots Response to the Gulf Crisis," in *The Gulf War and The New World Order,* pp. 143-44.

6. Quoted in Moghadam, Val. "The Neopatriarchal State in the Middle East: Development, Authoritarianism and Crisis" in *The Gulf War and the New World Order,* p. 203.

7. In 1986, Meron Benvenisti estimated land expropriation at 52% in the West Bank and 49% in Gaza Strip, (Benvenisti, Meron and Shlomo Khayat, *The West Bank and Gaza Atlas,* Jerusalem, 1989). In 1991, according to Al-Haq, 60% of the land in the West Bank and over 55% in Gaza have been expropriated. Cited from *News from Within,* 2 October 1991, p.3.

8. Shahak, Israel, "Israeli Apartheid and the Intifada," *Race and Class,* Vol. 30, No. 1, (1988), pp. 1-12.

9. Of the estimated 700,000 Palestinians who have been expelled from the Gulf states, about 30%, or 230,000, were workers. Included in this number are the overwhelming majority of Palestinians living in Kuwait, estimated at 350,000-400,000, who were driven out immediately after the War. (Ibrahim, Nabil, "Impact of the Gulf Crisis on the West Bank and Gaza Strip," a report prepared by the United Nations Development Program, Business Development Centre, Jerusalem, January, 1991, pp. 1-54.)

10. *al-Quds,* 16 November and 6 December 1990.

11. For a better understanding of the social problems in the Occupied Territories, see "The Intifada and Some Women's Social Issues," a conference organized by the Bisan Centre of Development Research, Jerusalem, December 1990. A short version of the proceedings of the conference was published by Bisan Centre.

12. Bishara, Azmi. "Palestine in the New World Order," *MERIP Reports,* No. 175, Vol. 22, No. 2, (1992), pp. 2-8.

13. A graphic illustration of the psychological impact of the Gulf war on the Palestinians has been provided by Kathy Glavanis in her "Changing Perceptions and Constant Realities: Palestinian and Israeli Experiences of the Gulf War" in *The Gulf War and the New World Order,* pp. 117-135.

14. Abdo, Nahla. "Women of the Intifada; gender, class and national liberation," *Race and Class,* Vol. 32, No. 4, (1991), pp. 19-34.

Malama 'Aina

Take Care of the Land

Haunani-Kay Trask

Aloha mai. Aloha kakou.

I am Haunani-Kay Trask, a descendant of the Pi'ilani line of Maui and the Kahakumakaliua line of Kaua'i. I greet you as an indigenous woman, as an American-subjugated Native, as part of a non-self-governing people—Hawaiians—and as a Polynesian member of the pan-Pacific movement for self-determination that has been growing in our part of the world for the last 30 years.

We in the Pacific have been pawns in the power games of the "master" races since colonialism first brought Euro-Americans into our vast ocean home. After Western contact destroyed millions of us through introduced diseases, conversion to Christianity occurred in the chaos of physical and spiritual dismemberment. Economic and political incorporation into foreign countries (Britain, France, the United States) followed upon mass death. Since the second World War, we Pacific Islander survivors have been witness to nuclear nightmare.

Now, our ancestral homelands—Hawai'i and the Pacific—are planned convergence points of the New World Order. In our geographic area, the coalition of "wealthy political entities" that Brecher analyzes has resulted in extreme U.S. militarization of our islands and increasing nuclearization of the Pacific Basin; exploitation of ocean resources (including toxic dumping) by Japan, Taiwan, Korea, the United States, and others; commodification of island cultures by mass-based corporate tourism; economic penetration and land takeovers by Japanese and other Asian money; and forced emigration of indigenous islanders from their nuclearized homelands that can only be termed "diaspora."

"Unregulated transnational corporate activity," as Brecher names it, has resulted in tremendous environmental and cultural destruction as well as the steady death of our people due to inundation by a mad industrial nationalism.

But as John Brown Childs points out, "industrial" is the key adjective. As indigenous peoples, *our* nationalism is born not of predatory consumption, nor of murderous intolerance, but of a genealogical connection to our place, Hawai'i and—by Polynesian geographical reckoning—the Pacific.

In our genealogy, Papahanaumoku—Earth mother—mated with Wakea—sky father—from whence came our islands, or *moku.* Out of our beloved islands came the *taro,* our immediate progenitor, and from the *taro,* our chiefs and people.

Our relationship to the cosmos is thus familial. As in all of Polynesia, so in Hawai'i: elder sibling must feed and care for younger sibling who returns honor and love. The wisdom of our creation is reciprocal obligation. If we husband our lands and waters, they will feed and care for us. In our language, the name for this relationship is *malama 'aina*: care for the land which will care for all family members in turn.

This indigenous knowledge is not unique to Hawaiians, but is shared by most indigenous peoples throughout the world. The voices of Native peoples, much popularized in these frightening times, speak a different language than old-world nationalism. Our claims to uniqueness, to cultural integrity, should not be misidentified as "tribalism." We are stewards of the Earth, our mother, and we offer an ancient, umbilical wisdom about how to protect and ensure her life.

This lesson of our cultures has never been more crucial to global survival. To put the case in Western terms: biodiversity is guaranteed through human diversity. No one knows how better to care for Hawai'i, our island home, than those of us who have lived here for thousands of years. On the other side of the world from us, no people understand the desert better than those who inhabit her. And so on, throughout the magnificently varied places of the Earth. Forest people know the forests; mountain people know the mountains; plains people know the plains. This is an elemental wisdom that has nearly disappeared because of industrialization, greed, and hatred of that which is wild and sensuous.

If this is our heritage, then the counter to the New World Order is not more uniformity or more conformity, but more autonomy, more localized control of resources and the cultures they can maintain. *Human diversity ensures biodiversity.*

Unremittingly, the history of the modern period is the history of increasing conformity, paid for in genocide and ecocide. The more we are made to be the same, the more the environment we inhabit becomes the same: "backward" peoples forced into a "modern" (read "industrial") context can no longer care for their environment. As the people are transformed, or more likely, exterminated, their environment is progressively degraded, parts of it destroyed forever. Physical despoliation is reflected in cultural degradation. A dead land is preceded by a dying people. As an example, indigenous languages replaced by "universal" (read "colonial") languages result in the creation of "dead languages." But what is "dead" or "lost" is not the language but the people who once spoke it and transmitted their mother tongue to succeeding generations. Lost, too, is the relationship between words and their physical referents. Here, in Hawai'i, English is the major language, but it cannot begin to feel the physical beauty of our islands in the unparalleled detail of the Hawaiian language. Nor can English reveal how we knew animals to be our family; how we harnessed the ocean's rhythms, creating massive fishponds; how we came to know the migrations of deep-ocean fish and golden plovers from the Arctic; nor how we sailed from hemisphere to hemisphere with nothing but the stars to guide us. English is foreign to Hawai'i; it reveals nothing of this place where we were born, where our ancestors created knowledge now "lost" to the past.

The secrets of the land die with the people of the land. This is the bitter lesson of the modern age. Forcing human groups to be alike results in destruction: of languages, of environments, of nations.

The land cannot live without the People of the land who, in turn, care for their heritage, their mother. This is an essential wisdom of indigenous cultures and explains why, when Native peoples are destroyed, destruction of the Earth proceeds immediately. In Hawai'i, the uprooting and great dying of my people was quickly followed by massive and irreparable changes to the land. Under U.S. control, Hawai'i has been transformed into a tinsel version of the fragile beauty it once was. As a 19th-century plantation economy gave way to a modern tourist/military economy, our lands and waters have been increasingly poisoned, developed, or destroyed altogether. Militarism and tourism—twin engines of *haole* (white) U.S. culture in Hawai'i—have increased their rapacious consumption of our physical and cultural heritage as we enter the 21st century.

Now, we Hawaiians have no control over the massive tourist industry which imports more than six million foreigners into our tiny islands every year. Multinational corporations sell our beauty; the world's rich buy it in two- and four-week packages. These foreigners, mostly *haole* and Japanese, think of our homeland as theirs, that is, as a place they have a claim to visit, pollute, and destroy by virtue of their wealth. Our role, as indigenous people, is to serve and wait upon these visitors, to illuminate and fulfill their dreams. Throughout the Pacific Basin, First World tourists play out this racist fantasy of an "island vacation," ruining our waters and lands, degrading our living cultures. When they leave, tourists have learned nothing of our people or our place. They have not listened to the land or heard her singing.

And still Western stupidity knows no bounds: our islands are also nuclear hotspots. While tourists flock to our homelands, the U.S. military continues to maintain bases and airfields and storage sites and dumping grounds and tracking stations. The white war machine, including nuclear submarines and missiles, is well-oiled and ready for deployment on a moment's notice. Hawai'i, like most of the Pacific, is a nuclearized paradise.

Of course, the rush to sameness is resisted by indigenous peoples everywhere. Indeed, indigenous peoples are among the most resilient in the face of the existing world order.

And yet, Native peoples' resilience depends on certain physical conditions: our homelands must be protected from destructive developments, like deforestation, industrial projects, and mass-based tourism; immigration and in-migration into Native areas must be regulated or restricted *by indigenous peoples for our benefit;* and indigenous human rights, like those enunciated in the current draft of the Universal Declaration on the Rights of Indigenous Peoples now being considered at the United Nations, must be guaranteed—for example, rights to self-determination on an aboriginal land base; rights to our languages, to our religions, to our economies, to integrity as distinct peoples, to the security of our families, especially our children, and perhaps most urgent, the right to be protected from physical and cultural genocide. Above all, modern nation-states, especially the super-industrial powers like Japan, the United States, and European countries, must honor and protect these rights because they are the nations most responsible for chronic violations.

But can we, as Native peoples, resist the planned New World Order by ourselves?

Probably not. The state of the world gives us little hope. Native resistance can be and has been crushed. As indigenous nations die out, our peoples reach a point of irreparable harm. We cannot sustain our numbers, our cultures, our stewardship of the Earth. Even while they plan our demise, First World countries and those aspiring to that status memorialize our passing. We are not heroes, or models, to an unsung world.

The choices are clear. As indigenous peoples, we fight for Papahanaumoku, even as she—and we—are dying.

But where do people in the industrial countries draw *their* battle lines? On the side of mother Earth? On the side of consumption? On the side of First World nationalism?

If human beings, Native and non-Native alike, are to create an alternative to the planned New World Order, then those who live in the First World must change their *culture,* not only their leaders.

Who, then, bears primary responsibility? Who carries the burden of obligation? Who will protect mother Earth?

A Very Bad Way to Enter the Next Century

Petra Kelly

Europe after the Cold War

We were all unprepared for the idea that the Iron Curtain would suddenly dissolve, that there would be rampant revolutions in Eastern Europe, that communism would be falling apart at the seams. It was the time for utopia. Two years ago, I wrote "we have this big hope." The world can change. We can have disarmament and conversion and a peace dividend. We won't have resource wars. And then came the Gulf War and Panama. And Eastern Europe became a kind of Latin American backyard for Western Europe.

At first we received the East Germans with champagne, we were crying, we were dancing in the streets. After three months it was all finished. The chance we had, the vision of how to make a confederation rather than unification, of how to treat East Germany in a more dignified way, of how to help them become an ecological society—we're not doing this. East Germany has become a kind of dump for West Germany. We're sending our poisonous things to them, we're sending our bad industries to them, we're building nuclear power plants for them.

In the alternative movement in Western Europe in the last 20 years we achieved a certain amount more of democracy, of citizens becoming their own experts, an understanding about alternative technologies. All of this is back at square one. Everything we learned in Western Europe, our friends in Eastern Europe are now facing. And they say to us, "We haven't got a chance. How are we supposed to resist your banks, your companies, your know-how, your government? We just got out of 40 years of dictatorship, and now you're telling us it's wrong again."

Petra Kelly originally offered to write a contribution for this book but, pressed for time, proposed an interview instead. This piece is edited from a two-hour interview conducted by John Brown Childs on June 13, 1992—one of the last given by Kelly before her death. Despite her grim appraisal of the state of the world, she sounded full of fight, and said "I'm going to be running, I hope" in the 1994 parliamentary elections.

In East Germany, groups that I know to be very good and very radical say to us, "Don't talk to us about experiments any more. We just had one for 40 years that went wrong. So now let us simply try to get a little bit of the pie." They're afraid it could go wrong again. And of course it's gone all wrong.

I don't see Eastern Europe having the chance of its revolution again. The chance was there, the round tables met. They had the most incredible constitutions worked out. We had one of the bravest and most feminist and ecological constitutions worked out for a new Eastern Germany. Kohl made sure to tell the world, "We don't like this kind of radical Germany. We don't want it."

We had big hopes that once East Germany was liberated, there would be no military there. Now German troops are stationed there and NATO troops are going to go there. They moved into headquarters that were first occupied by Hitler and then occupied by Honnecker's army; now the German Bundt is living in them.

There are strong feminist women who have come into politics in Eastern Europe, but the elections after the revolutions put fewer women to the parliaments than before. When the elections came, the men took the seats. In Czechoslovakia, Havel has tried to nominate many women to key ambassador-level jobs, but in parliament they lost out, and in East Germany just as much. There are eight alternative people from East Germany, but most of the strong women are missing.

We had a strong Green Party in Czechoslovakia. In Poland the ecological clubs are very strong. In Russia I met many excellent groups in Leningrad and Moscow—small, but very hard-working. In Bulgaria there was Ekoglasnost; in Romania there were some small but brave groups. But the Greens were almost decimated in the elections. In Czechoslovakia the ecological groups were expected to get up to 10%, and I think they were down to about 1 or 2%. Even the Civic Forum, the group that supported Havel, has in the recent elections dropped down below 5%. You just want to scream, because it was the most powerful force in Czechoslovakia, it was like Solidarnosc in Poland at one point. And in Poland, there has been a strong reactionary Catholic influence. Lech Walesa, now that he's president, is no longer the radical Lech Walesa he used to be.

There are small Green groups still present and working hard. In Hungary, for example, they have been effective working against the building of the Danube electrical plant, but they have made little difference in the elections. In Slovenia, there are about ten members of the Green Party who are ministers. They are doing good things like trying to stop a reactor project, but they are of course totally unnoticed because of the war. The Green Party there gained many votes on the platform of nonviolence, of having no military intervention whatsoever, and doing nonviolent training, but it's gotten completely lost. In the Baltic republics there have been Green movements and the governments took a strong nonviolent position, saying they didn't want to have military forces—they'd like to have a civilian defense.

There is a Green alliance in Eastern Europe that meets every few weeks with the Greens of Western Europe in the European Parliament. But when you speak to them you don't have a feeling of hope that they will get into Parliament. They've been decimated by the broad Christian democratic, social democratic, liberal tendencies of the big parties.

The Rise of Nationalism

In Yugoslavia we knew many environmental and human rights groups coming from all different parts of the country. When the civil war broke out, they split. They hated each other, although they had worked together in the underground for 20 years. This is one of the saddest things I can imagine. Yugoslav human rights advocates told me in tears that all the friends with whom they fought year after year in the underground have fallen apart into these separatist, nationalistic tendencies, saying, "I'm a Croat," "I'm a Serb." "I can't speak to you any more. I'm sorry; it's finished."

In Czechoslovakia, before this all broke out, I had the feeling that they were rather united, that they really wanted to uphold a humanistic system and try to live together, but the groups are losing their loyalties to each other and saying, "I can't speak to him any more because he likes to have a separate state and I don't." The same in Romania. Suddenly your dialect, where you come from, your historical problems, historical hatreds, your historical relationship to each other becomes the most important issue. Even in Germany, activists from Yugoslavia or Czechoslovakia who live here end up saying, "I can't stand him any more, the barber or the person I take my coffee with, because he's a Croat." And they had been together as friends up until the time of the war.

This is something that nobody was prepared for, nobody understood it. I'm waiting for the Basques in Spain to start; I'm waiting for the Irish to begin. It would seem very natural for them to start it as well. While the European union is supposed to be being built up, and we're

supposed to get this common currency, all of Europe is falling apart. It's
the most ironic situation.

We had an organization called the Unrepresented Nations and
Peoples Organization, UNPO. It includes peoples and nations who have
no seat in the United Nations, so there were Eskimos and Hawaiians
and Tibetans. Some talked about becoming sovereign or becoming an
independent country. You can understand that. But in the process of
saying they would like to become that, they began separating themselves from everything around them. And suddenly you realize they're
not talking about one world. It's first of all this idea of their own song
and their flag and their identity and their language, and you can
understand it so well, it seems to be very positive. But then it takes on
a rightwing expression because jobs are missing, because economically
they can't survive, and it goes into a very ugly nationalistic tendency.

Racism and Neofascism

In Germany you can read every magazine—*Stern* or *Krek* or
Bundt—and you will see "Asylum seekers get better housing." Next
week it will say, "Asylum seeker rapes woman." Next week "Asylum
seekers don't eat German food." It's building up the typical, normal,
average hatred of a normal, average German.

I can go into a beauty shop and the person who cuts my hair,
who's a very liberal person, starts telling me "I don't want any foreigners
working in my beauty shop any more. I don't trust them. They lie." I go
into a cafe and there will be a foreigner sitting next to us, and the next
thing I hear, somebody is saying, "Get up, you old man, get back into
the forest where you came from." This is suddenly normal in Germany.

Our Tibetan and Chinese friends in Germany, especially in Eastern
Germany, cannot be in the streets after 6:00 at night. I never go into a
subway any more at night. I can't take seeing that people are literally
thrown out of the window in subways. Alone you can't really help
anyone because there's no German who will get up and help you to
protect somebody.

There are groups with fascist connections throughout Europe and
with the American Nazi Party and those connected to David Duke. In
Germany they are burning crosses. It's explosive in France; it's very bad
in Sweden, in Denmark against the Kurds, in Great Britain.

You get a tendency now to make Europe into a fortress. European
laws are being changed dramatically to keep out foreigners. The interior
ministers would like to have a European police force, a European

Interpol, to make sure the European Community wards off all these people that are hungry and need to be clothed. People that I know to be liberal, not in any way rightwing, have turned completely rightwing because they see foreigners as taking away your home, taking away your jobs, none of which is correct.

There is a strong alliance between the press, the church, and rightwing politicians in Germany. Every week people get told on television that 50 or 60% of foreigners misuse the right of asylum, that they're all economic refugees, that they all take drugs and kill people. Of course, no German takes drugs or kills anybody.

Our courts in Germany are clearly showing sympathy for young people who attack foreigners. There will be a young man, a German neo-Nazi, driving a truck and hitting a Senegalese person, then dumping some kind of poisonous gas on top of him, and then driving over his arm. And the judge will say, "This is not very good what you did, but you were drunk. Because you were drunk, I have to be lenient." And he ends up getting a very mild sentence. If any peace activist had ever even touched an arm of a policeman, let alone driven a car toward him, he'd be in prison for the next three years.

All the tendencies toward xenophobia are coming back again. I don't think Germany has really ever worked them through. I believe we're not ready for a multicultural society. This ridiculous fear of strange things, of foreign things, makes Germans say, "Germany for the Germans" again, and "Germans are far better; we're still better than the rest of the people. We are something special."

I didn't notice this before reunification. It has been forced by the large number of Germans, almost 85 million, coming together, and the idea that we have this influence over Eastern Europe. We're bullying people around again. And the first victim this time has not been the Jew, it's the foreigner. It's another form of anti-Semitism; it's now the foreigner who's bad, who's done everything, who's ruining your whole country.

It's amazing how many people supported Mr. Schoenhuber of the Republicans in Baden Rutenberg in the last election. You ask people in the streets, "Why did you vote for this demagogue?" And they simply say, "Because I want to have quiet and peace, and I don't want any foreigners living in my villa."

Human Rights

Human rights to me is the most essential element in foreign policy. Whether it be the way Indians in the United States are treated, or how the people seeking asylum are treated in Germany, or whether it be Tibetans or the Chinese. In Germany, just as in the United States, human rights are instrumentalized. You use human rights to your own advantage when you can criticize an enemy, but once any of your friends are committing violations, like the Turks against the Kurds, then you shut up. In the Cold War attitude, the enemy of my enemy was always my friend. China was the enemy of Russia, so China was good. This kind of thinking brought about double-standard human rights policies.

The Green Party is the only group that I know of in Europe—especially in Germany—who never succumbed to this instrumentalization. We always said when human rights are trodden anywhere and we can do anything we'll get ourselves involved. The impression we got from many governments was that the Greens should shut up and not do this. We demonstrated in Turkey, in Moscow. I was arrested in East Germany for our demonstration on the Alexanderplatz in '83. We went to the South African embassy and occupied it for 48 hours, tied ourselves to the chairs and didn't leave.

These were small but powerful actions which had a multiplicatory effect. But the momentum was only possible as long as we were strong in the Parliament, when we had all the machinery, all the fax machines, all the financial help. And now that the Greens are no longer in the national Parliament, this has broken down. It shows that the effort of just a few committed people can make a big difference in human rights.

You have to be very public, you have to be rather courageous in the actions you do, and you also have to target the companies that are dealing with regimes that trod on human rights. For example, for many years I followed in Parliament the case of German weapons being sent to Iraq to Saddam Hussein. The Greens had a list of companies who had done this. We tried to boycott them. But there has been no public outcry; there has been no consumer boycott.

For eight years I was kind of the lobby for people in China and I tried very hard to get parliamentary legislation to stop German credits from going to China. In fact, right after the terrible massacre at Tiananmen Square I got two Green resolutions unanimously accepted by the whole Parliament to stop development aid, all high-level visits, and all credits to China. And in fact I held it until I had to leave Parliament. After I left Parliament the friends who helped me stuck to it, but the government got very strong and revised it. It was very painful, because I had kept at this for eight years.

It showed me that unless you have very strong public action, nonviolent action in front of the embassies, a lot of Amnesty International activity, a lot of grassroots activity, you cannot pressure even your own government. But because I did have a lot of backing from the democracy movement in China, and a lot of help from the Tibetans, I was able to apply pressure very well in Parliament. We were able to do both: be out in the street and apply pressure in Parliament.

We tried to boycott German companies who were sending cattle prods to China, which are used against Tibetans. We tried to boycott Mercedes Benz, which was exporting telephone systems to South Africa. The small committed groups would help, but the majority of the people had a feeling that you couldn't move anything with this.

We tried to get a toy boycott going against Chinese toys. We couldn't get it going because if you did an act in front of the Chinese Embassy, if you got arrested—which happened to me rather many times—you would get very high fines. And the other colleagues who were not in Parliament just couldn't pay the fines any more. So they stayed away.

There's a lot of pressure against human rights activists in Germany. As soon as you upset any of the major economic allies, you are upsetting the whole apple cart. So it's a very long, difficult road, but to me human rights is the most important part of politics; for me it's the cornerstone. It's the testing ground.

Connecting the Local and the Global

When I compare the Third World activists, like people in the Chipko movement or the people in Malaysia in the Third World Network, I always feel they are far more radical and far more in solidarity with the global scene. When I look at European groups, they're very Eurocentric. And when I look at U.S. groups—I spoke at the National Organization for Women convention in San Francisco two years ago—my impression was that their's is just like the German attitude that we have to liberate ourselves first. Those in the Third World confront violence and structural violence much more directly than we do, so they are more radical in their whole analysis. I think we have to learn from them. But we tend to look at them and say, "Well, we've done it all in the '60s and the '70s." I feel very embarrassed in meetings where the

Western women or men act condescending. We end up like the rich aunt or uncle saying "We'll tell you how to do it."

I have a Tibetan foster daughter living in the community of the Dalai Lama in Dharma Sala; I've often gone to North India to visit her. Traveling through India, I met many incredible grassroots groups, for example women who did nonviolent action in front of missile sites that were being built with German money involved. They were completely informed about who was building them, why they were building them, and they were doing terrific nonviolent action. And none of us knew about this.

There seems to be a feeling that, "Well, what we don't know doesn't seem to be important," and very little solidarity toward these people. There's solidarity morally, yes, but not financially. We had a network where German Green women helped women in Thailand open up an office so that prostitutes could get legal and medical help and, if they liked, retraining for another job. As soon as the Greens had to give money, the problems began. "We need this money more at home." In the beginning, in the late '70s when we began the Greens, there was much more openness toward that, much more solidarity. Now we've become kind of self-important, arrogant about our own goals, and very restrictive about the money, forgetting that we have to share our resources with those groups in the Third World.

We talk about how governments should do this, but we're not doing it ourselves. The more powerful the German Greens became at home, the more we took domestic issues to be the most important ones. To prevent some street being built is more important than to prevent the rain forests from being cut down. Politics then becomes very much narrowed down to the small goal that a minister is about to take on. I feel that the more important and powerful we become, the more we have to connect the local to the global issues.

For eight years I helped bring printing presses and photocopiers illegally to Prague. We got stopped many times and I got in trouble over it, but it was a very helpful thing. Just after President Havel got elected, Jane Fonda, who I never knew before, called me and asked if I could help arrange a trip for her to visit him. She said, "What can I bring?" We asked Havel. He said, literally, "I need a fax, a phone, and a photocopier." And she actually took two suitcases full of computers, fax machines, and answering machines. We went to the Civic Forum and the people did not even have photocopiers. They were writing letters over and over again by hand. And I remember saying to myself, "This is so ridiculous. This is a revolution that's just happened and they haven't even got a fax machine." So you can imagine what an office looks like in India.

I think this infrastructure is one of the most minimal things that we can do. If we tell governments to give their technology, we must also share our grassroots equipment. In India and other countries it's very difficult to spread the word, to print things, to photocopy texts, to get material about how to stop a nuclear power plant, to distribute action manuals. We don't realize how difficult it would be for us if we didn't have any of these means.

The Earth Summit

The Earth Summit has failed terribly. There's been no move toward democratization of the World Bank and the IMF. There has been no reduction of the debts the South owes the Northern banks, which was one of the key demands of the environmental movement in the South. Protecting indigenous people living in rain forests across the world was not taken up.

Transnational companies like those that made the Bhopal disaster were sitting secretly at the table in Rio, but they were not there to be controlled or to get information about the damage they have done. Up to 80% of all environmental damage has been done by transnational companies. They're completely uncontrolled, even after Rio. They can go home and laugh at this whole summit because they have not been put to the test.

There's been no discussion about what kind of system has allowed this. Capitalism has won after the Eastern European revolution, but after you look at Rio, you realize you can't go on with such a capitalistic system either. This system is probably going to drive the whole world to its death.

Bush came out saying we need even more growth. And we keep saying it's the wrong kind of growth he's talking about. The world won't allow our standard of living to be given to every Chinese, to every Indian. That means we have to reduce our lifestyle. The rich countries have not been able to say one self-critical thing. They point their fingers at the South and say, "You are now going to pollute because you're going to grow. You're going to have more people, more cars, more energy." It's the North that has been responsible for two-thirds of all environmental destruction. But there has been no discussion about reducing affluence and saying simply that we can't go on doing what we've been doing. This is what has not happened in Rio.

For the first time there has been a really big difference between the European Community's position and the United States' position. That's rather unusual because usually the European Community gives in when the United States is opposing anything. When Bush said he wouldn't sign the Species Protection Convention because it would hurt the U.S. biotechnological industry, there were big cries of shock in the German newspapers, even conservative papers. They felt that, at the minimum, the conventions for the tropical forests, for CO_2 emissions, and for the protection of species should be binding and should be signed by all industrial nations including the United States.

Another idea had been to make a kind of an alternative Earth council. Collect experts, jurists, and scientists in every area—tropics, CO_2 emissions, or atmospheric pollution—and set up Earth councils that review governmental policies in every part of the world, forming a kind of a body of the elders, of elder statesmen or stateswomen, to act as a public conscience. Of course a binding court system would be even more effective.

The idea of an environmental court crept up at the preparatory meetings for the Earth Summit. This is an idea that has been proposed by Manikka Gandhi, who at one point was minister for forestries and nature in India. She advocated regional, national, and international environmental courts which could try cases like Chernobyl or Bhopal or the chemicals Swiss companies put into the Rhine. There has never been a tribunal where they could be tried, where all of the facts could be given to the public, on the model of the International Court of Justice. But, of course, that is not taken seriously any more either. I remember when the United States said about Nicaragua, "We don't care what the Court decides. We'll go ahead and do it anyway."

The Future of Alternative Movements

When I look at the alternative movement I can say, "Well yes, there is still a small hope that one day eventually we'll somehow get into the institutions, we'll break through and get into Parliament, maybe break through and get into government." But overall, it's far too small. Four years ago the German Greens were at 8 or 9%; now we're back down to 4%. The Green Party in Great Britain has dropped down to only 5%; they were at 20% in 1987, I believe. In France the Greens split into two groups because Mitterand build up a second Green group to destroy the first one. I see it breaking down in Spain, in Holland. There are now two groups in Belgium.

It was supposed to be our decade. At the moment, it seems we have lost the battle. We are all hanging in, but we don't seem to have much influence any more. The democratization we felt would swoop from Eastern Europe back over to us again, the kind of glasnost that we said we needed at home as well—it hasn't happened.

Look at what is happening to Siberia. There's Japanese, German, U.S., and Korean companies exploiting every bit of it, burning down the last Siberian forest. I think we'll have none left in 20 years. Siberia is being taken apart piece by piece by Western companies. And the people there have no say-so, they have no codetermination, they have no idea what is happening. All they know is that the companies destroy everything and they have nothing from it—just poverty.

To me this is the symbol. This last untouched region of the world is now completely scorched and destroyed. And we the alternative movement were unable even to understand how quickly it happened. To read suddenly there's a Korean company with 2,000 workers cutting down the forest. There's a German company, there's a U.S. company, and a Canadian consortium. They're all destroying it in front of our eyes and we can't even get ourselves together, let alone stop anything.

When we get letters from Russian friends who say, "Please come and help us," we just sit there and say, "How on Earth are we supposed to help now? What are we supposed to do?" And they tell us "You're democracies, stop your companies from doing this." It's a kind of testing ground. We can't stop German companies. If you take a look at their legal situation, you realize you can't stop them in Parliament. They operate outside of your legal means. There's no legal means to control them.

We don't have one world. Ms. Bruntland was correct when she wrote in her report, "We may be one Earth, but we're not one world." That's really a very bad way to enter the next century. It's probably the worst possible way.

Part III

Globalization-from-Below:
Alternatives

For an Alliance of Hope

Muto Ichiyo

The Hope and Spirit of Our Time

The slogan at the beginning of the 20th century was progress. The cry at the end of the 20th century is survival. The call for the next century is hope. It is impelled by that hope in the future, and with a keen sense of urgency, that we begin our Gathering of the People's Plan for the 21st Century in Minamata.

It is significant that we meet in Minamata, a place in the world which symbolizes to all of us development at its most murderous. As it did to the people of Bhopal and Chernobyl, a giant organization with advanced science, technology, and production methodology brought to our hosts at Minamata fear, sickness, and death, and brought to their beautiful bay deadly damage that may not be repaired for decades or centuries. These three disasters—Minamata, Bhopal, and Chernobyl—can be taken as benchmarks of our time. At Minamata, the industry of a capitalist country poisoned its own citizens. At Bhopal, a huge Northern multinational corporation poisoned people of a country of the South. At Chernobyl, a socialist government spilled radiation out over its land and people, and beyond its borders to the whole world. There is no need here to repeat the long and mounting list of eco-catastrophes. These three tell the story: there is no place to hide.

We know that the 20th century, the Age of Development, brought us many things which we value. But we also must be coolly realistic. The 20th century has brought us more, and more murderous, wars than any time in history. The technology of killing has advanced beyond the wildest imagination of any previous era. The state, which was supposed

---

This was the keynote speech at the first People's Plan 21 gathering in Minamata, Japan in 1989, which brought together people's organizations from all over the Asian-Pacific region. (Minamata was the site of widespread mercury poisoning in the 1950s, caused by the Chisso Company.) Muto Ichiyo was National Coordinator for PP21. A second PP21 gathering was held in Thailand in December, 1992. A PP21 group was also established in Central America in 1992.

147

to be our great protector, has turned out to be the greatest killer, killing not only foreigners in wars, but also killing its own citizens in unprecedented numbers. Economic development, which was supposed to raise the world out of poverty, has so far only transformed undeveloped poverty into developed poverty, traditional poverty into modernized poverty designed to function smoothly in the world economic system. The 20th century has added two grim new words to our vocabulary: genocide and ecocide. The practices that gave birth to these words have all grown out of advanced science and technology. And they have occurred in the name of what we have called "progress" and "development." We must ask, is there not something profoundly wrong with our understanding of historical progress, with our picture of what to fight for, with our image of where to place our hopes?

Mr. Hamamoto taught us a beautiful word in the Minamata dialect, *Janakashaba*. Literally it means "a world that does not stand like this." It is an exciting word, telling us there can be a quantum leap, a break, from what we are, what we have, what we are resigned to accept as our fate. This is precisely what is being acted out before our eyes today by millions of people in Asia and the Pacific region. They do not accept what has been foisted on them as their fate, they are ready to take the leap, and they are taking it. We witness wave after wave of peoples' movements emerging, spreading, cutting across state boundaries, complementing each other, and sharing an increased sense of contemporariness fostered by new networks of communication. The major struggles of the Korean, Philippine, and Burmese people have shown explosive power. Recently they have been joined on a tremendous scale by the new democratization movement of the Chinese people. In these big countries and in the smaller ones, in every prefecture, town, and village, the people are on the move. And they are aware of each other as never before, watching each other, communicating, joining in unprecedented ways. All of this is new. It is the main force defining our situation and the main reason for this conference. *Janakashaba* is the spirit of the people in our time. This is why we do not hesitate, despite everything this century has brought us, to declare that the 21st century will be the century of hope.

State of Our Region

These new movements are growing up within the context of a peculiar contradiction that is appearing in the role of the state. Our region is being organized by transnational capital, which is bringing together far-flung and heterogeneous areas and peoples into a single, vertical division of labor. The state, as the agency which mediates the entry of transnational capital within the national boundaries, is serving as a vigorous promoter of the emerging pattern. At the same time, trans-nationalization of the economy undermines the basis of the state, placing its claim to sovereignty and its pose as protector into question, and weakening its legitimacy. The state seeks to protect itself through inten-sification of repression and violence, as we are seeing today in a series of "developing" countries including China, or, as in the case of Japan, through an intensification of the attempt to implant statist ideology into the minds of the people.

In this same process, the engine of development has overheated in Japan and is running wildly out of control, producing a saturation economy. Japanese work an average of 2,200 hours a year, mostly in heavily managed situations in which they are virtually powerless. They are bombarded with advertising that urges them to compensate for frustration by consuming. At the same time, virtually every human activity and every bodily function has a whole shelf of consumer goods or commercial services associated with it. The manner in which one combs one's hair, wipes one's nose, or scratches a mosquito bite are all the subjects of intensive market research and intense product and service competition. The commodification of every aspect of human life in-cludes the commodification of sex, which has produced a huge sex industry in which hundreds of thousands of women, many imported from other Asian countries, are made to serve in order to satisfy the Japanese male taste for alienated sex. The world's most powerful econ-omy does not empower its citizens, but rather seeks to make them powerless and fragmented. And it has also reproduced within its bound-aries a "North" and a "South." The "South" includes millions of poorly paid women part-timers, subcontract workers, day laborers, and increas-ingly, migrant workers from South and Southeast Asia, as well as farmers who are being rapidly marginalized.

Here too the system has begun to undermine itself. The economy has pushed itself to such absurd lengths that more and more people are simply fed up with it, and are beginning to search for a different way of living.

New Approaches

In this turbulently changing situation, we need new maps. We need a new picture, a new paradigm, of the society in which we can live together in dignity. But we need not go far to find this new paradigm.

We can partly see it already, emerging out of the peoples' movements themselves. This is no romanticism: we are referring here to specific new concepts emerging from certain of these movements.

First let us look at the Asia-Pacific people's movement itself, as it has emerged in the last couple of decades. Everywhere we see the patient, dedicated efforts to promote empowerment—of community people, ethnic groups, women, labor groups, urban slum dwellers, people organizing themselves against "development" imposed from above, or asserting their independence and autonomy. The major national explosions of popular will are in most cases prepared in these small-scale accumulated efforts of empowerment and "conscientization." It is here that the notion of the people as sovereign is being nurtured in concrete form. In the face of this new movement of the people, many grassroots thinkers, religious and intellectual, have drawn on the liberating elements in their teachings to shape them into new forms through which the people can express their anger and hope. The various peoples' theologies and practical philosophies developed in recent years, as well as indigenous values found in folktales and traditional popular arts, are given new light to rebuild people's identity.

This grassroots movement for empowerment points to a new form of democracy, a democracy which we have never seen before, and whose outlines are not yet clear to us. But we can say for certain that it is something more than "democracy" as a form of state. It is a kind of "democracy on the spot," a community-based democracy through which the people build power over the things that matter in their lives.

Then there are the indigenous peoples' movements. The revitalization of their struggles of survival and self-determination has enabled us to re-read the history of modern civilization originating in the West. At the same time, the Aino people in Japan have revealed to us the whole history of Japan's invasion of their lands. Also, their struggles and values show us a different way of living in harmony with nature, of which we also are part.

Women's movements and feminist ideas have also contributed to new ways of viewing history and understanding the present. They have shown, for instance, that the dominant notions of politics, economics, organization, and culture have been profoundly characterized by the structural domination of women by men. They have shown that social sciences dedicated to revolutionary change by and large have ignored the all-important process of reproduction of human beings and have thus misconceptualized work and labor and the importance of human life itself. They have shown that male-dominated values have done violence not only to women but also to nature. And they have offered a profound and exciting new alternative—that a society reordered on the basis of harmonious and equal relations between men and women would naturally tend to move in healthier, less destructive ways.

Ecological movements since the 1970s have addressed the issue of establishing a harmonious relationship between human beings and the environment. They have shown us that unlimited economic and technological growth cannot be sustained on this planet. They also project, and partially practice, a social relationship with minimum domination, which corresponds to their human-being-within-nature model.

There is a striking concurrence of views among those new movements of different origins in that the social, historical, and ecological approaches are integrated in a single context. It is important to note now that though some of these movements started in the West, the issues they address are becoming life-or-death issues for the most marginalized populations in the Third World, where the very basis of subsistence is being destroyed at the hands of transnational corporations and their agents.

Common Themes

In order to aid our search for an alternative model of future society, we designated five areas as a common agenda for all the conferences of People's Plan 21. They are: 1) Humankind and Nature—From destruction to harmony, 2) Liberation from Oppression—Creating new society and culture, 3) Overcoming Rule by the Strong—Changing the state and changing international relations, 4) Taking Back the Economy—From a relationship between things to a relationship between human beings, and 5) For a Common Future—Ethics and spirituality for people's solidarity. The subtitles indicate what we wish to counterpose to the existing realities in each area. Let us briefly introduce the items (except the last, which covers all the rest and so is discussed in the concluding part).

Humankind and Nature—From destruction to harmony
By now, nobody denies that nature on this planet is in danger. Even big powers now talk about conservation; even the Japanese government has offered a lot of money for preservation of the world environment. But such abstract conservationist cries sound hollow when nothing is said about who is causing the destruction of nature and for what.

Bringing our civilization into harmony with nature is difficult, yet urgent. It brings us straight to the question of an alternative model of development. It is no longer a matter of how effectively to continue to exploit nature, but how to change drastically our relationship with nature.

Here we have among us people rich in wisdom on just this question. Indigenous people from Hokkaido, Canada, Sarawak, Australia, Aotearoa, and elsewhere, considering nature their partner and source of life, have been protesting for years against its exploitation and plunder. Here, the bottom line may be that no exploitation of nature should be allowed without the affected people's consent, and that what the indigenous people say on these matters is given the greatest weight.

Also, the way science and technology have been developed should be called into question. The techno-utopian solution is even now proposed by governments and business, but that is absurd: it is precisely the arrogance of technology that has wounded the world. We should begin by renouncing patently harmful technologies and their application, nuclear weapons and nuclear power among them. Soil-killing use of agricultural chemicals also must be stopped. Large-scale technology which aims at the so-called "conquest of nature" also tends to disempower the workers and farmers who use it. What are the technologies and modes of work which both empower the worker and reestablish harmony between humans and nature?

There should also be a clear recognition that we, human beings, are part of nature. Doesn't violence against nature, regarding it as a mere object of exploitation, entail and justify a similar treatment of human beings and human bodies?

Last, are harmonious relations with nature possible within a capitalist system which is unable to survive without endless accumulation?

Liberation from Oppression—Creating a new society and culture

The task is to dismantle, nationally and transnationally, the vertical integration that predominates and to replace it with a horizontal integration of individuals and groups.

By vertical integration we mean the socioeconomic class structure and other forms of hierarchical formations where individuals or groups are judged and treated by criteria chosen by those at the top and to the advantage of those at the top. It also means the division of the human community into the rich and powerful North and the poor and suppressed South. Pyramidal formations have entrenched themselves all over the world in government bureaucracies, corporate organizations, and military systems. Society as a whole has this kind of division, by status, profession, gender, caste, alleged physical and mental capacity, birthplace, religion, and other criteria for discrimination.

Aside from the state, the most powerful vertical formation is the corporation, particularly transnational corporations which exploit the fact that the people remain divided. How can we deal with them? Here, our response should also be cross-border.

To overcome this discriminatory system, we should demolish the social, institutional, and economic systems that generate or benefit from discrimination. For that to be done, we need to create new egalitarian values. Underlying these egalitarian values are what can be termed "simple personhood" or "peopleness," which we refer to later. In this way we all work to reorganize the vertical integration into a horizontal cooperation of individuals and peoples' groups. It is important here that horizontal cooperation encourages diversity as a source of wealth for society, while vertical integration imposes uniformity.

Overcoming Rule by the Strong—Changing the state and changing international relations

Here we deal with the state and inter-state relations. Our main concern is how we can overcome the state, which no doubt still remains the strongest entity in the world today. We need a dual approach: never losing sight of our long-term goal, we should also fight to make the state and its policies more accountable to the people and to transform regional international relations in favor of peace and justice. We shall come back to this duality later.

A new fluidity in the global international situation seems to have created a space in our region for the people to intervene. The regional political situation is turbulent, and diverse factors and actors are at work: declining U.S. power, perestroika and resultant foreign policy changes, the rise of Japan as the world's most dynamic economic power and Japan's military buildup as part of U.S. strategy, provision of huge Japanese Overseas Development Assistance (ODA) funds; rampant intervention by the United States with Japanese help in the Philippines, New Zealand's nuclear-free policy, China after Tienanmen, confrontation on the Korea unification issue, and moves toward an Indochina solution, to name only some.

How can we jointly intervene in this regional situation to weaken the rule by the strong? What are our action programs? What should our priorities be?

In Japan, the state is emerging as a strong force managing the rest of Asia and the Pacific for the interests of transnational capital. Internally Japan is a state with a system of discrimination and domination, a state based on corporate supremacy, discrimination against "aliens," minorities, women, and the weak, and the negation of the people's independence. The state falsely claims that Japan is a mono-ethnic country and negates even the presence of Ainu as an ethnic minority. There are also 700,000 Korean people living permanently in Japan, who were taken to Japan against their will, or whose parents or grandparents had been, to be put to hard labor or who had to move to Japan as a result of Japan's colonization of their country. Instead of being compensated, they are subject to blatant discrimination in all aspects of life. Okinawa, with its distinct historical identity, is treated practically as Japan's internal colony. In fact, the postwar Japanese state has never admitted the crimes the country committed against other Asian peoples, or toward the minorities within its territory, since the Meiji period. All these injustices should be confronted and overcome.

We in Japan need to strive to go beyond Japanese statehood, ultimately overcome this state from within, and establish ourselves as people who can live together with our neighbors, in a confederation of the peoples of the archipelago.

Taking Back the Economy—From a relationship between things to a relationship between human beings

How can we remake this world economy which, for its survival, keeps billions of people starving or undernourished, landless, poor, and overworked in the South, and makes waste and saturation consumption a necessity in the North?

However difficult this task may be, it is obvious that we cannot go on this way much longer. An economy that can operate only through infinite growth measured by GNP will soon enough bump into the wall of the limited capacity of this planet. Nor is it sustainable in an historical period where the people's power is on the rise, for the majority in the South will not tolerate the continued disparity. We who live in Japan should refuse to contribute toward further increasing GNP and further increasing production. We should slow down our activities and reduce the productivity and efficiency of the most "advanced" sector of our industry. If we are told that such action would invite disaster, then we must say that it is the system that has to be replaced.

It is important that we begin with basics—what we need for a decent living and how those things should be produced, distributed, and consumed. Value added ('GNP') should cease to be the measure for economic activities. Instead, satisfaction of human needs in a human way should be our yardstick.

Economic activities should be reintegrated with the life of the people—people in the community. Production and consumption should be organized as material aspects of communities. On this basis, communities need to be horizontally linked so as to exchange their surpluses. This is not an image of subsistence economy, nor is it a call to go back to pre-modern society. It is an image of a new affluence made possible by accumulation at the grassroots level, by people themselves. Here, people-to-people relations regulate the economy, and not vice versa. This is what we mean by "taking back the economy."

It is here that we must examine the role of innovative economic systems which counter mainstream systems. A variety of such movements are now developing: cooperatives linking organic farmers to urban consumers, workers' production collectives, people-to-people trade, buffalo banks, and credit associations. How far and in what way can these people's economic systems be a basis for our future economic systems?

Another major problem is how the relationship between agriculture and industry, between the city and countryside, should be transformed. The concentration of power and wealth has caused a concentration of population in huge urban centers like Tokyo, Seoul, Bangkok, and Shanghai. Can our envisioned decentralization of power and wealth lead to more or less smooth dispersion of the pathologically aggrandized metropolis?

Transborder Participatory Democracy

Now we have sketched what kind of alternative model of development we have in mind. But isn't it a utopia?

As we have said, our alternative model of development is not a utopia. It is rooted in reality—in the reality of the world today, in the reality of the people, and—most importantly—in the reality of the people's movement. Even so, we must not naively conclude that because of the growing power of the people we can expect someday to wake up in a changed world. We cannot reach this new world without a serious search. We need to identify in the people's struggles of today those facets which reflect the new realities of the world, and in particular those facets which point to a liberated future. And we need to find ways to consolidate these elements and relate them to the 21st century to which we aspire. In other words, we need bridges.

As one such bridge, we propose a new concept of political right and political action, which we provisionally term "transborder participatory democracy." We present this as the specific people's alternative, the counter-system to stand against the particular formation that oppressive power has taken in our time: the state-supported globalization of capital.

Transborder participatory democracy is the name both of a goal and of a process. As a goal it means worldwide democracy practiced by the people of the world. It is a picture of a world order clearly distinct from the conventional idea of world government or world federation, which presupposes states as the constituent units. Yet, as our goal, it still remains a remote vision of the future.

As a political process, transborder participatory democracy has two aspects. First, it is a practical method for criticizing, confronting, intervening in, and changing the power formation of globalized capital. In this sense, it is a form of action that corresponds both to present socioeconomic reality and to the logic and necessity of the people's movements. Second, in the process of transborder political action, the people's groups and organizations gradually form themselves into transborder coalitions, eventually leading to the formation of a transborder "people," by which the division of the world into North and South can be overcome.

The dominant tendency in the Asia-Pacific region today is regional integration by state-backed globalization of capital. In this system, most of the major decisions which affect the lives of millions of people are made outside their countries, without their knowledge, much less their consent. Even those decisions made inside the country are made outside the communities of those affected, in the power centers in cities. Most of the decisions are made in the core countries, by their governments, by transnational corporations, or by collective agencies such as IMF, the World Bank, big power summits, or international business bodies.

For a time there were high hopes that it was the state which could rectify the growing international inequalities. In the 1950s the Bandung Spirit prevailed, and the people expected the coalition of the newly emergent independent states to work on their behalf, promoting import-substituting programs. For some years in the 1970s, the UN Conference on Trade and Development (UNCTAD), bearing the banner of the New International Economic Order, seemed to be effectively pressing for redistribution of the wealth of the world in favor of the majority. Both failed. Illusions about the state as the tribune of the people have faded as almost all the Third World states—including China—have made a definite shift to the position of promoter of the logic of multinational capital and mediator of capital globalization within their own territories.

The situation calls for the declaration of a new right: the right of the people to intervene in, to modify, to regulate, and ultimately to control any decisions that affect them. This should be established as a universal right which recognizes no borders. It means that the people's action is no longer confined within the bounds of a state, nor to acting only through the state political structure. Transborder participatory democracy is a new principle, by which not the state but the people themselves can emerge as the chief actors in determining the course of world politics and economics. "The people" here means, first of all, the people directly affected by external decisions. But transborder participatory democracy goes beyond this. It operates to form a transnationally coalesced people who emerge as the principal actors.

Take, for instance, a decision by a giant publishing company in Tokyo to inaugurate a new, glossy, useless magazine printed in millions of copies to gain advantage in the competition among publishing houses. This will further increase Japan's pulp demand. It will lead to accelerated plunder of tropical forests in Sarawak and mangrove trees in Papua New Guinea, in turn further destroying the basis of the lives of the people there. We say that the people who live there have just the same right to intervene in this decision as they would if it were being made in their own village. It does not matter where, or by what agency, the decision is being made. What matters is that the people's lives are being affected by that decision. We declare that there exists no artificial right—neither the right of private property nor the right of state sovereignty, nor for that matter the treaty-based rights of international agencies—that can take precedence over the natural democratic right of people to speak and act directly against decisions that are destroying them, no matter where or by whom those decisions are being made.

Direct intervention by people from the rain forest countries is not only a means of self-protection. It would also have an important effect on Japan. There are people here already who have their own reasons for questioning the outlandish waste of paper for junk magazines with their people-fooling messages. There are people who work for those magazines, who feel the dull despair of knowing they are devoting their lives to producing a bad product over which they have no control. If these people can learn directly what disastrous consequences the publishing industry has on far-off people, they have an opportunity to see what this "publishing industry" is in a new perspective, and to join with the affected people in protesting and intervening.

Transborder participatory democracy leads toward transborder coalitions of people, and aims ultimately for the formation of a transborder "people." In particular we can expect to see this process having an effect on the people of the northern or core countries. In Japan, for example, people engaged in this process will move away from their identity as "Japanese," in the sense of identifying with the so-called Japanese national interest—which is often synonymous with corporate interests. For years, movement people in Japan have been saying that we produce, consume, and waste too much; some argued that in principle we should fight to lower the standard of living, but that such a strategy would be political suicide. This argument is abstract and is an expression of guilty conscience. And it misses the point, which is not a general, abstract lowering of the standard of living, but finding the specific ways in which the country can be changed to allow us to coexist with our neighbors. And as our neighbors begin demanding their legitimate right to participate in those decisions made in Tokyo which affect them, those ways will begin to become clear to us. If accompanied by a paradigm change, can't this be a way to begin first to narrow and finally to eliminate the gap between the South and North?

Transborder participatory democracy does not mean participation in the exclusive decisionmaking process of monopolies. It is not like the company union's "participation" in management decisions. On the contrary, it aims to abolish that exclusivity of decisionmaking.

Take the Japanese automobile industry, for instance. Today it is producing 12 million cars a year. By any standard, this is too many. But no one outside the closed rooms of the corporate directors has any say in this. Now we say that affected people both inside and outside Japan—the regular employees of the manufacturers, subcontract workers, subsidiary assembly workers overseas, users, city dwellers, and all who are concerned about excessive motorization—can and should assert themselves in determining what should be made, how many, for what purpose, how they should be sold, and with what kind of advertisements. Imagine what "Toyota" or "Nissan" would be in such a situation. They could no longer operate only for profit. The purpose of production would have to change. They would be forced in the direction of becoming publicly responsible and accountable. We can see how this would lead toward structural transformation of the profit-oriented nature of production.

I repeat, this is not the model of a utopia. What we describe here grows out of tendencies that already exist in the world. For some time now it has been widely accepted that in the matter of human rights there is no such thing as "intervention in internal affairs." At Berlin in 1988, the IMF-World Bank conference—where governments had gathered to negotiate on the Third World debt—was met by a huge mobilization of people from all over the world, trying to intervene against the imposition of a rich-power solution. Again, several years ago when the Japanese government announced its plan to dump nuclear wastes into the Pacific Ocean, the Pacific Island peoples sent powerful delegations to Japan and, in collaboration with Japanese movements, effectively stopped the dumping. Transborder participatory democracy begins in this way as a movement. The experience of acting together situates people in a new universal context, in which each individual action acquires new meaning and direction.

Dialogue between Short-term and Long-term Perspectives

Here short-term and long-term perspectives must not be confused. In many Asian and Pacific countries it is the immediate task of the people to establish their democratic, national states. The great struggle of the Korean people for national unification, as their path toward liberation from the big-power intervention which keeps them divided, is a case in point. The people's struggle in the Philippines aimed at establishing a national democratic government accountable to the people is another. In many of the Pacific Islands, where foreign powers are keeping people subjugated for colonial or strategic reasons, independence through the establishment of peoples' own states is essential. And at a time when most of the Third World states have degenerated into agencies for joining the big core capital interests with the interests of the local rulers, it is important to continue to try to "internalize" the state, to make it into a barrier against the dominant powers. In this sense a new alliance of people-oriented states, if such could be resurrected again, would broaden the people's opportunities.

Changing and improving state policies is also important for people in the core countries. In Japan, major policy changes are needed in the field of commitment to U.S. military strategy, in overseas development assistance, and in the entire stance of the country toward the Asia-Pacific region as well as in the area of domestic accountability. The postwar Japanese state has never clearly disavowed what Imperial Japan has done against the neighboring Asian countries since the Meiji Era; it is essential for the Japanese people to fight for a set of clear principles, based on a thorough review of the past history of national arrogance, which the Japanese state must follow.

Crucial as these struggles are, they should not be separated from the long-term perspective. Given the fearsome degree to which the region is being integrated, we cannot expect national solutions to stand by themselves as we could several decades ago. The times call for transborder solutions, and the only means for such solutions is the transborder participation of the people themselves. There should be a constant interaction, a dialogue, between the long- and short-term perspectives. The moments of history overlap in our time. Against colonialism, the people struggle to establish their national states. Against the development-dictatorship state, the people struggle to establish democratic accountability. Against state-supported global capital, the people begin to marginalize the state, and carry the fight directly to the centers of capital wherever they are. This is not a formulation that divides the people's movements into more- and less-advanced. Transborder participatory democracy means that we join all of these struggles together. If we can begin the dialogue between our dreams and realities here, we are already on our way to the shaping of the people's future.

Peopleness and Inter-People Autonomy

The key to transborder democracy is the people. But what is "the people?" Cynics whisper, "Are you not romanticizing the people? Are you not setting them up as a god?" Let us clarify.

We can begin by defining the people as we always do in this kind of discussion: they are the oppressed, the exploited, the manipulated masses. This is so, yet such "people in general" do not exist. The people are divided into a multitude of groups with their respective identities: gender, ethnic, religious, geographical, cultural, class, nation-state. These groups overlap, and individuals belong to more than one. But today, these groups are being forced to live together under conditions imposed upon them. State-supported global capital is organizing all these groups into a system of international and hierarchical division of labor. This new order is lauded as the world of interdependence. Interdependence, yes. But it is an interdependence forced upon the people and permeated by hostility and division. The dominant system perpetuates itself by organizing internal division, and setting one people's group against another. National chauvinism, religious fundamentalism, contrived communalism, cultural exclusivism, sexism, and the whole varied panoply of racial and ethnic prejudices all serve the ruling elites well in their efforts to establish a great organization incapable of its own unity.

The struggle of the people begins on this terrain, in this divisive structure. It does not begin as the full-blown struggle of the people the world over. It begins rooted in each group's identity, and asserts the group's dignity as well as its immediate interests. Or movements may begin as single-issue movements.

Thus each struggle nourishes its seed of liberation. But for the seeds to germinate, they must interact with other struggles and movements.

Suppose a Japanese workers' movement regards fellow workers from other Asian countries who are underpaid because of their illegal status as merely a threat, and shows no concern about their conditions; then their movement is no people's movement. It is operating within the borders of the compartmentalized structure which perpetuates mutual hostilities. However "militant" its action may have been, it has allowed its seed of liberation to be poisoned and eventually die.

All movements start in this compartmentalized terrain; the point is to fight our way beyond it, to destroy the whole divisive structure and replace it with a spontaneous alliance of the people's own choice and making. In this process the movement can free itself from captivity. Experience shows that interaction with other movements transforms the movement, helping overcome its narrowness and oppressive practices inside it, if there are such.

In this process, what Xabier Gorostiaga once called "the logic of the majority" should of course be the guideline. "The majority" here means the global majority, that is, the most oppressed. They have the prerogative. In the hierarchy of the 20th-century world, each stratum of the people has its own interest not only to assert against those immediately above it, but also to protect against those immediately below. Whenever the lower is forced to concede to the higher, that strengthens the existing order. It is the part of the higher to be prepared to concede to the lower. And our new ethic for the 21st century must include a way of seeing such renunciation as entailing a gain, and not a loss, in dignity.

Is this alliance, which we call the Alliance of Hope, possible? Let us call that which makes it possible "peopleness."

Peopleness manifests itself most dramatically when people risk their lives in struggle. When the people take to the streets, fight the police, expose themselves to danger, and help each other, the people's spirit becomes visible. We have seen this in Rangoon, Seoul, Kwangju, Manila, Beijing, Bangkok, and even Tokyo. Men and women, young and old, many meeting for the first time and by chance in the tear gas fog, find each other comrades. If one falls, others help, braving gunfire. There is natural equality and compassion. People transcend their immediate self-interests. A strong human bond is forged that leads people to make extraordinary sacrifices.

But this extreme expression of "peopleness" should not be separated from its roots in daily life. Here we are alike in what really matters. Each of us was born a helpless infant, each has a life to live, each faces death. Some of us have privileges, but no one is so privileged as to be exempt from these basics of human existence, or from the constant exposure to the risks of living. We all eat, excrete, sleep, and love; many of us bear and rear children; we hate, celebrate, enjoy, toil, ponder life, fall in and out of confusion, weep, get sick, express ourselves in our own cultural ways, grow old if we are lucky, and prepare to die in dignity and repose. These simple aspects of human existence are common to all of us, and should give us a basis for relating to each other in compassion and equality. Yet so often this common peopleness is hidden from us by centuries-long relations of domination. Or, in this century, it is plastered with the fetishism of money, ambition for promotion, avarice for commodities, and craving for power. If plastered too thick, this simple personhood, peopleness, is lost, and with it the capacity to relate to others. Japanese society today is one where this capacity has been lost to a pathological degree. But if the cult of "things" is a burden, then the rediscovery of peopleness is a path to liberation.

Peopleness is not an idealist construct. It is what is actually at work in the existing solidarity movements among seemingly very different groups of people. It is what is behind the real sympathy and compassion for other people's struggles. It is what is behind the sacrifices being made for the people's cause everywhere. Denying the working of peopleness would be to deny the reality of these movements—or to render them incomprehensible. Peopleness represents our radical equality and our equal radicality.

Only by recourse to peopleness can we expect to overcome internecine conflicts between people's groups and imagine the formation of the people worldwide as the subject of transborder participatory democracy. This is a dynamic process of action and counteraction—not like the signing of an agreement in a ceremonious atmosphere.

When peoples' groups begin to regulate their mutual relationships spontaneously and for themselves, thus destroying the system of forced mutual relationships, then we shall have inter-people autonomy cutting across the state barriers and replacing the interstate system. Inter-people autonomy will represent the people of the world collaborating with each other while developing all their rich diversities.

Inter-people autonomy thus is an affair of billions of people, and it is still a vague picture of the 21st century. But one thing that is certain is that the alliance of hope of billions should be preceded by an alliance of hope of tens of thousands or hundreds of thousands: an alliance based on inter-movement autonomy, an arena and network where people's movements from different concerns and backgrounds meet, recognize each other's peopleness, and enter into a dynamic process of interaction. Let us engage in this task.

Reforming North Economy, South Development, and World Economic Order

Martin Khor Kok Peng

The nongovernmental organizations (NGOs) represented in the Third World Network have been spending most of their energies at the national and international levels fighting to conserve forests and other natural resources and fighting against the effects of toxic chemicals and wastes. We have been very actively communicating with agencies such as the World Bank, the Food and Agriculture Organization (FAO), and the European Economic Community, giving detailed critiques of the environmental and social effects of programs and specific projects they have been funding. We have also been active within our own Third World countries helping local communities protect their forest and land resources, and advocating policies with our own governments that would reduce resource depletions and would improve standards for food, environment, and occupational safety.

From the perspective of groups working at the community level, we realize that unless ecological issues are linked simultaneously with social issues of equity and economic issues of having sufficient income and financial resources, we will not solve the environmental problems at local, national, or international levels. For solutions at the local level, we also have to link up to national and international policies and structures. This is why many grassroots groups in the Third World are now allocating some of our resources to international networking, as we realize that local solutions require a conducive international environment.

Environment and Economic Crises Linked

The global environment crisis is accompanied today by increasingly severe economic and social crises in most parts of the Third World. The per capita incomes in most African and Latin American (and some

163

Asian) countries fell during the 1980s, in some regions declining to the levels of 20 or 30 years ago. Poverty has increased, and health problems (like cholera epidemics in Latin America and Africa) have returned.

These two phenomena—the global environment crisis and the socioeconomic decline in the South—are interconnected and have resulted together from an inequitable world order, unsustainable systems of production and consumption in the North, and inappropriate development models in the South.

Among profit-centered economic institutions, the operating principle of competition has made economic growth a necessity. This principle operates within social systems that have a very unequal distribution of resources and incomes, thus resulting in uneven distribution of the benefits of growth and development. Much of the world's output and income are channeled to a small elite (mostly in the North but also in the South), while a large part of humanity (mostly in the South, but also a growing minority in the North) has insufficient means to satisfy its needs.

In addition to this uneven distribution, the high rate of growth has led to the rapid depletion and contamination of resources, pollution, proliferation of toxics, and climate change threats. This, then, is the social-ecological crisis of our times: the accelerating exhaustion and pollution of Earth's resources through inappropriate technology and production processes producing ever increasing volumes of goods and services, the majority of which are channeled to filling the luxury wants of an elite, while too few are going toward fulfilling the basic human needs of the poorer majority. And resources to meet the justifiable demands of future generations will be even scarcer.

From this perspective, the environmental and economic crises are the result of the same fundamental sources: the inappropriate and wasteful economic model of the North, the unequal distribution of resources and income at global and national levels, and the inappropriate development models in the South. The global link between the North's model and the South's model is obvious: the South's development model is only a subset or a subsidiary of the dominant Northern economic model.

The North's model was transferred to the South during colonialism (when the pattern of exchange between Southern raw materials and Northern capital and consumer products was established), and accelerated in the post-colonial period through multilateral institutions that advised on macroeconomic policy and facilitated the continuation of the North-South production and trade pattern.

The post-colonial development model promoted by the World Bank and adopted by most Third World countries called on the developing countries to expand their exports of commodities. This has led to higher volumes of production, oversupply, lower prices, and continuous fall in the terms of trade, with a disastrous growth in poverty. In environmental terms this has meant the acceleration in the depletion of natural resources such as oil, forests, minerals; the import of inappropriate Northern technologies that replaced the more ecologically sound systems of agriculture, fishery, animal husbandry, etc., that existed in the South; and the transfer to the South of polluting industries, unwanted and unsafe products, and toxic wastes. It can be seen that the environmental crisis is really a side-effect of international economic relations. It is the same economic and development model that created social problems like poverty, social inequities, and unbalanced development, as well as depletion and contamination of resources.

Given the pattern of world distribution of economic and technological power, the North, with 20% of world population, uses up 80% of world resources and has a per capita income on average 15 times higher than that of the South.

The major part of the problem of depletion and contamination of resources is thus located in the North. One could simplistically say that four-fifths of the problem lies in the Northern economic model and a fifth in the Southern development model.

At the UN Conference on Environment and Development (UNCED) there was a lot of focus on the South's flawed development model and the need to change to "sustainable development." Very little has been concretely discussed about the Northern economic model, which is after all the dominant model on which the South's development model is based. Very little has been planned about changing the North's economic model.

We often hear it said that it is true that the production and consumption patterns have to change, but that it is politically impossible to actually do it because no politician who advocates lifestyle change or diverting from economic growth would survive election. If this kind of "pragmatism" is to reign in the North, how then can we expect the much poorer South to be able to change its economies?

If a Northern politician is afraid to advise his or her public to have fewer cars per family, and to use less gas per car, can a Southern government be expected to tell the people to tighten their belts further to make way for two structural adjustments: the structural adjustment forced on them by external debt and the new structural adjustment dictated by ecological imperatives?

Burden Sharing

If we agree that we must reduce the depletion of resources and also spend more to lower the ecological costs of pollution, waste, and climate change, then it is inevitable that the volume of output has to go down. For instance, to save forests we have to reduce logging and cut down on wasteful use of wood. There is, then, the crucial question of sharing the burden of economically adjusting to an ecologically sound pattern of production and consumption. This was surely the heart of the issue at UNCED: international burden sharing, and burden sharing within nations.

At the international level, there are at least two ways by which adjustment could come about. The first is if the powerful countries were to say: "I'm strong, you are weak. I want your resources that are getting more scarce; give them to me; too bad if you don't agree." In this solution, there will be "triage," the strong throwing off the weak in order better to survive. The poor will be made to die off without help, sovereignty over resources will be eroded, and there will be a return in parts of the world to direct colonial rule.

The second way is for the governments of the world to agree on cooperation for the mutual survival of their peoples. The North would thus say: "We have a mutual problem. We belong together as part of humanity. The overriding principle is that we all survive together. I am strong but perhaps I was wrong. In the colonial past and now in this present system, we've taken away from Nature, and yet many of you are still as poor, if not poorer. And many of us frankly don't need so much to enjoy life. Maybe we could adjust this unequal relation and have a real partnership to save Nature and thus ourselves together."

The North's responsibility in this new partnership is or should be obvious. The era of colonialism saw military conquest, extraction of natural resources, and enormous flow of economic resources from the South. In the post-colonial period, the same phenomena have continued. Moreover, North-controlled multilateral institutions provided wrong advice or imposed inappropriate policies (such as increased commodity production or structural adjustment) which have resulted in social and ecological problems.

Sometimes, too, decisions made by a few major Northern countries (with no participatory rights from the South) resulted in enormous losses for the South: for example, the realignment of exchange rates and interest rate increases caused many Southern countries' external debt stock and external debt servicing flows to jump. Finally, of course, it is predominantly the overconsumption of resources and the pollution emissions in the North that have caused the global environment crisis.

This does not mean that the South is absolved from all blame. As NGOs in the South, we spend a lot of our time pointing out the weaknesses and problems associated with the establishment and the elite. In many parts of the South, there is a combination of corruption, political patronage, financial mismanagement, and of course the adoption of inappropriate technologies and environmentally unsound policies.

We do, however, realize that even in these national-level problems, there are Northern-controlled institutions that play a role. For instance, while some political leaders are corrupt, it is the transnational corporations (TNCs) that offer the kickbacks; one should not blame the "lady of the night" without simultaneously putting the spotlight on the client. And, as pointed out earlier, much of the misallocation of resources in the South can also be traced to the wrong macroeconomic advice or conditionalities given by multilateral financial agencies and bilateral aid agencies.

We thus have to recognize that there are strong historical and intellectual grounds establishing the principle that the North should take measures to reverse the South-North transfer of resources and to provide not charity but a revival of moves to improve the South's terms of trade, to put life back into commodity pacts, to relieve the financial burdens weighing down the South, and to provide genuine aid for ecologically sustainable programs.

The North-South impasse is the major impediment to forward movement. We observe that Southern governments are reluctant to negotiate seriously on the technical areas such as biodiversity, forests, and climate, because the fundamental framework (namely, the social principles of sharing the burden of adjustment) has not yet been discussed or established.

National and International Democracy

As national NGOs, we in the South have spent a lot of our energy in broadening the democratic spaces in our own national societies, in removing the barriers to people's participation, in helping social movements regain their right to land and other resources, and in promoting their right to good health and adequate nutrition, to safety, housing, and a sustainable environment. All these things, as we know, are needed for both social justice and a sound environment and development policy.

At the same time, we now realize that the fight for democracy also has to be extended to the international arena where the lack of democracy is so obvious. International democracy is needed just as much as national democracy. Therefore, the UNCED process should also be an opportunity for us to expand the democratic spaces in the international institutions that shape world policy and, through that, the national policy of our countries.

The world economic order is obviously unbalanced, a fact so well-worn with analysis-without-remedial-action that few people are bold enough to even whisper the once popular catch phrase "the new international economic order" that the UN General Assembly adopted in a declaration in 1974. There cannot be concrete moves toward this new order unless the international economic institutions are democratized. And until there are moves toward a more balanced world economic order, there is little hope for any genuine partnership on the environment.

There must thus be a review of the performance of the major economic factors, including the transnational corporations, the international banks, the World Bank, the International Monetary Fund (IMF), and the General Agreement on Tariffs and Trade (GATT). These institutions, which make the decisions that affect so much of our lives, including the environment and development aspects, should be made much more accountable to the public. The decisionmaking processes in these institutions must be opened up for public participation and scrutiny.

Not only Southern governments but also local communities in our countries must have the opportunity to participate in the design of programs and the monitoring of effects. The public has the right because the public suffers the consequences if something goes wrong, whether it be the Bhopal residents dying from chemical poisoning, or the more than 100,000 farmers dying from pesticide poisoning annually, or the hundreds of millions of people suffering the social and economic effects of structural adjustment policies imposed by the World Bank and IMF.

Institutional Arrangements

If the North has to reduce wasteful production and scale down wasteful consumption, what kinds of institutional arrangements can be established within and between Northern countries to make these changes possible? Within each Northern country, how can the necessary adjustments be made to output levels and lifestyles, when we are told this kind of change is "politically impossible"? (If it is practically impossible to implement the changes that are needed to make it possible for us and Earth to survive, then surely we are doomed).

What institutional arrangements are needed in society to make the majority of people accept change? For instance, if the adjustment burden is equitably shared so that (for example) the incomes of the bottom 20% of households are increased to above poverty line, incomes of the top 10% are reduced (through tax or other mechanisms) by a large percentage, and incomes of the lower deciles are reduced but by progressively lower degrees, then it may be possible to get the majority to accept a scheme to change production and consumption patterns. Changing the volume and composition of output may be possible within a socially accepted framework, for the mutual survival of all. Thus, environmental concerns, economic changes, and social equity have to proceed hand in hand.

Institutional arrangements have also to be made among the countries of the North so that the respective countries would not feel that changes they make unilaterally for a sounder environment would give unfair commercial advantage to other countries. What role can be played by the Organization for Economic Cooperation and Development or by other Northern forums to plan for coordinated adjustment in the North as a whole and in individual North countries?

In the case of the South, what international institutional changes are required to promote the kind of economic environment that facilitates the transition to sustainable national development? What arrangements can be made to review and, if needed, revise the policies of technical agencies such as the FAO, the UN Development Program, and also private agencies to ensure that their programs conform to just and sustainable development? As for the Bretton Woods institutions, how can the World Bank, the IMF, and GATT be democratized, with fairer opportunities for Southern governments and NGOs/social movements to participate in decisionmaking, planning, evaluation, and revision of policies and programs? How can their processes be made more transparent and publicly accountable?

Since, in our analysis, these agencies have been responsible for a lot of the things that have gone wrong with the environment and development in the South, no more resources or power should be invested in these institutions unless and until they are democratized and have proven that they have the technical competence to deal with development and the environment. Otherwise, the logger would be provided with a more powerful chainsaw, and we are sure that is not what we mean by good institutional arrangements.

There is also the need to establish a new or more comprehensive international trading institution under UN and democratic principles, whose objective would be the promotion of a more balanced North-South trade relationship, where the need for trade is tempered by the need of the South for stronger domestic economies simultaneously with a stronger position in world trade and economy. The role of the UN Conference on Trade and Development (UNCTAD) in giving a more favorable balance to the South should be promoted in this regard, but also should undergo prior assessment in the light of sustainable development imperatives. For instance, it is already outdated to promote the expansion of supply of (or even demand for) Third World raw materials, for this depletes natural resources.

The key issue in commodities (that combines environmental and economic concerns) is how to reduce the volume of production and exports (to conserve resources) while raising prices to reflect their social and ecological values, thus enabling the Third World exporting countries to retain their export earnings. The shortfall in volume can be made up for by price increases; thus, there would be North-South (or producer-consumer) cooperation in the sharing of the economic burden of adjusting to ecological principles. A reformed UNCTAD with more environmental expertise and more political teeth could play a role in combining economics and ecology in new trading arrangements.

We hope we have made the point that environmental and economic issues have to be resolved simultaneously, in a well-balanced manner, within the context of North-South relations, and with the operating principles of ecological sustainability and social equity. If there is a fairer North-South balance at the international level, it would make it far easier or possible for NGOs in the South to facilitate genuine people's participation in endeavors toward socially just and environmentally sound forms of development. At the same time, we are always reminded by the objective facts that the North has to change within itself, and that the battle for that adjustment in the North will also be as difficult as it is necessary.

The Transformations Must Be Deep and Global

Luiz Inacio Lula da Silva

We are now nearly five-and-a-third-billion people on this Earth. Three people are born every second; three-hundred-thousand a day; a hundred-million a year; and in the present decade there will be more than a billion new human beings. About 90% of this population increase will take place in the poor countries of the southern half of the planet.

If we set these population trends alongside the present concentration of income in the world, the data are truly frightening. We see that the industrialized countries of the North enjoy a per capita income of nearly $15,000 a year, and consume an average of 25 times more per person than the "developing" countries of the South.

Now that the popularity of Cold War militarism is at an end, we have entered a period characterized by great transformations and much political instability. The progress of new technologies, changes in the patterns of production and in the systems for its administration, the tendency toward the globalization of strategic sectors of the economy—all of these are producing a new context for the international structure of production, one which has as its basic characteristic the increasing widening of the gap between South and North.

The economy of the future is an economy of knowledge and know-how. The poor countries of the South are losing the comparative advantages of cheap labor and traditional raw materials. At the same time the configuration of the great economic blocs and their mega-markets are imposing new scales of production and very high levels of productivity with which the fragile economies of the South cannot compete. The concentration of income, wealth, and power is increasing at a rate seldom seen in history.

This extremely adverse context for the poor economies of the South is made even worse by the offensive of the neoliberal strategy

This chapter is based on two speeches given in New York and Sao Paulo in 1992. Translations by David G. Sweet and Joe Weiss.

being pushed by the great centers of international power and by the principal multilateral agencies such as the IMF and World Bank. Concern with the development of poor countries and with international cooperation to that end has simply disappeared from the agenda of international politics. On the neoliberal horizon, development is viewed as a question internal to each country. Privatization and free trade are proclaimed and clearly defined as magical means to achieve a return to economic growth.

The disturbing signs of recession are growing in the developed countries, and the economic crisis deepens in the peripheral economies, especially in Latin America. My country, Brazil, has been living between stagnation and recession for 12 years.

Some of the countries on this continent, which are applying tough "economic adjustment" programs, have had some success in the control of inflation, but none shows any improvement in its social situation. We see growing unemployment, poverty, and misery throughout Latin America. Our precarious systems of education, health, and welfare are coming undone. Epidemics such as cholera are returning, bringing death to thousands of the poorest. Millions of youth and children are in deep despair, abandoned to the streets, prostitution, or violent crime.

For these reasons I want to warn that the key threatened species in our countries—and especially in Brazil—is the human being.

This silent genocide has its economic causes, which are also the bases for our countries' environmental degradation. One of these causes is the foreign debt, which we have paid many times over and which is growing each day. Another is the deterioration of our foreign trade, as the rich countries impose the end to our protective tariffs while they openly practice protectionism. Another is the bargain-selling of our industry, condemned to strangulation in the face of the neoliberal offensive and outdated technology, which every day separates us more from the developed world.

But there are political reasons too. Some governments try to reduce the planet's environmental issues to preserving the forest, especially the Amazon. As Brazilians, with indisputable sovereignty over most of the Amazon, we are pleased by the growing interest of developed countries in saving the Amazon forest. We are open to international cooperation on the environment and vehemently reject the false nationalist rhetoric of Latin American elites and governments which raise the phantom of external intervention as a pretext to continue the criminally predatory policy which has produced such gigantic devastation. But we have to demand that rich countries be equally concerned with air pollution, the destruction of the ozone layer, and other forms of pollution that continue in their territories.

Sustainable development is not simply a struggle against misery and for the preservation of strategic natural resources. The construction of a sustainable development which is committed to enhancing the quality of life for future generations must begin with the premise that the pattern of growth and consumption that has characterized the Northern countries cannot be generalized to the whole planet. The limits of the ecological equilibrium of the Earth are evident and insuperable; but the consciousness of economists, politicians, and duly constituted authorities appears to be very far from encompassing the historic urgency of the environmental problem. Problems accumulate on all fronts, and the establishment of alternative policies continues to be postponed.

For example, a water crisis is clearly predictable. It is enough to note that 98% of the water on the planet is salty, and that, of the remaining 2%, only a tiny fraction is available for human use. This explains why 3.4 billion of the 5.3 billion people on the Earth have the use of an average of only 50 liters of water per day—one 117th part of the average consumption of a North American. In some poor countries of the South, more than half of the illnesses suffered are water-borne. We need not even talk of cholera; it is enough to note that 60% of hospital admissions in Brazil result from infections acquired from water.

Air pollution has been much discussed, and the increasing impact of the greenhouse effect and the thinning of the ozone layer are well known. The difficult problem is negotiation aimed at reducing the sources of pollution such as carbon dioxide emissions and the burning of fossil fuels. The governments of the countries of the South are reluctant to accept the strategic role that the tropical forests play in the maintenance of ecological equilibrium. In the North there is no serious discussion of the changes that are needed in the prevailing patterns of production and consumption. It is easier to transfer to the South the responsibility for recycling the air, which is more and more burdened by consumerism.

Soil pollution is another emerging problem. Great expanses of land are being salinized, alkalized, or turned into desert. Since 1950 we have lost about 60,000 square kilometers per year of the cultivatable surface of the Earth. The devastation of the tropical forests, at the rate of 20 million hectares a year, will destroy some 40% of the presently existing forest cover of the Third World by the end of this century. No less than 100 species of animals disappear each day. Without even considering the nuclear threat and the challenge of diminishing energy sources, we have the problem of garbage and toxic wastes, industrial byproducts within an enormous complex of problems related to the consumption of nonrenewable resources. There is no way to face this accumulation of environmental problems if we do not achieve a genuine rethinking of the patterns of development and consumption, and an improved international distribution of wealth.

The pattern of consumption and growth of the industrialized countries of the North is never questioned. But a careful analysis of the situation serves to confirm that we are facing the challenge of building an alternative kind of development. Nothing is accomplished by transferring to the South the dirty industries, the production which consumes a large amount of energy, or by masking the problems of the North. The transformations must be deep and global.

In Brazil during the '80s we built with thousands of workers a new social movement. We renewed the unions and established a party which gave a voice to those who had always been marginalized. This party is concerned with the environment because we are a party of workers. Rural and urban workers are the main victims of environmental degradation: in the factories, the polluted neighborhoods, the fields infested with chemicals.

The Worker's Party is environmental because it is socialist and democratic. As socialists and democrats, we teach new ways to organize production, new working relations, incompatible with the polluting and authoritarian output-based criteria of capitalism and bureaucratic socialism. We want to build a new society, founded on the values of liberty and social justice. A preserved environment is one of the benefits we want to will to future generations.

That is why so many environmentalists participated in founding and building the Worker's Party. Because they understood that the ecological struggle is—more than anything else—the workers' struggle. It cannot succeed as long as the land is concentrated in the hands of the few, factories are still living infernos, and living conditions in the cities remain poor.

Some of us began in the union struggle. Others, defending the environment. Others, fighting for improved housing, health, schooling, or transportation. Others, fighting for women's rights. And others, out of intellectual, ethical, or religious convictions. We all walk the path that leads to a free and just society capable of preserving nature and building new political and moral values. Many have landed on this path. By their example they have lit the way we still have to travel.

Facing the New International Context of Development

Gay W. Seidman

For most of us, the end of the Cold War evokes the demise of the dual-superpower order: the world is no longer divided into two spheres of influence. But as Jeremy Brecher points out in his introductory chapter, there is another dimension to global dynamics in the 1990s: increased mobility of capital and new patterns of international investment have eroded nation-states' control over economic growth, reshaping economic linkages in ways we are only just beginning to understand.

This restructuring seems to have reduced governments' options. Even in historically industrialized areas, social services and corporate taxes have been cut in the effort to retain investments. For countries in what has been called the Third World, capitalist development has been characterized by severe inequalities, and global economic trends have long been out of the control of individual nation-states; possibilities for promoting welfare as well as growth are now even more restricted. In the 1990s, as the Mexican writer Carlos Vilas puts it, "The international conditions that enabled some Third World countries to choose a socialist strategy no longer exist, but those that forced them to do it are stronger than ever."[1] What possibilities exist for challenging the constraints of the New World Order, in which existing models of socialism have been thoroughly discredited, and monetarist policies appear hegemonic? What development strategies might be pursued by activists seeking to redistribute the benefits of economic growth?

Changing Categories

In the 1990s, all nation-states, whatever their historical positions, have lost some degree of control over multinational investment policies; increasingly, even historically powerful nations find themselves competing with other nations, hoping to attract investments and jobs by offering

companies a more attractive deal. But for countries in what has historically been considered the Third World, this process has been even more
significant.

Through this century, the economies of most countries in Asia,
Africa, and Latin America experienced a relatively similar pattern of
incorporation into the world economy: dependent on producing and
exporting primary products, they generally imported manufactured
products from the more industrialized areas of Western Europe and
North America. But since World War II, a handful of these countries
began to develop significant industrial sectors, reflecting both international capital's shift into direct manufacturing investments and
developmentalist states' efforts to attract foreign investment and foreign
loans into dynamic industrial sectors.[2] While most Third World countries
remained dependent on exporting agricultural and mineral products, a
small handful, including Taiwan, South Korea, Brazil, and South Africa,
seemed to have overcome the obstacles to industrial growth posited by
modernization and dependency theorists alike.[3]

By the late 1970s, the emergence of "newly industrialized countries" (NICs)—countries which had been relatively unindustrialized at
the end of World War II, but which by the 1980s produced their own
manufactured goods and even exported manufactured products back to
already industrialized countries—marked a shift in global possibilities.
Even in countries still oriented toward primary commodities exports,
uneven processes of development sometimes created regional industrial
growth poles around major cities. New industrial growth seemed to have
altered geographic relations, both between countries and within them.

This spread of industrial production to new parts of the world also
tended to alter patterns of social organization. Academics writing about
how global restructuring affected workers have generally emphasized
the degree of workers' victimization implicit in capital's search for cheap
labor. Multinational capital's increased flexibility seemed to weaken
organized labor; in an effort to attract investments, developmentalist
states have often repressed workers' organizations. Indeed, some observers suggest that low wages are inherent to global restructuring. Since
global industrial production is oriented toward global consumers, the
Fordist link between producers and consumers may no longer hold:
perhaps employers need not pay workers enough to create a domestic
market for their mass-produced goods, because they can now find
markets by exporting products to middle- and upper-class consumers
anywhere in the world.[4]

New Sources of Opposition?

Certainly, less-skilled workers in new industrial plants around the world have rarely been permitted much control over labor processes or working conditions, or even an organized voice through which to demand higher wages or better living standards. But in a few cases, the reorganization of economic production has sometimes allowed workers to insist that they, too, receive some of the benefits of greater productivity. Recognizing that the use of mass-production technologies—especially of technologies which require skilled and semi-skilled workers—could create new possibilities for shop-floor organization, workers in some NICs began to demand a greater share of corporate profits. In Brazil, in South Africa, and in South Korea, militant workers' movements emerged in the heavy industries which expanded rapidly during the 1970s. Although they arose in very different contexts—facing different kinds of authoritarian states and different institutional frameworks for labor unions, and drawing on very different cultures—these new unions, supported by working-class communities, used industrial action to persuade unwilling employers to negotiate, and to persuade authoritarian states to allow more autonomous worker organization.

In Brazil, for example, the military regime which came to power in 1964 had severely restricted political organization and used corporatist legislation to control unions. In the late 1970s, militant strikes erupted in the automobile industry. Drawing on working-class community support, relatively skilled metalworkers won concessions on the shopfloor and launched a labor movement which spread rapidly through Brazilian society. Within a few years, a new labor federation, the Unified Workers' Central (CUT), included less-skilled workers in textiles, construction, and transport, and even landless farmworkers. More importantly, the labor movement laid the basis for a new class-based politics, insisting that the demands of workers and their families be considered during the transition to civilian rule. In 1989, the Worker's Party candidate, a charismatic metalworker universally known as Lula,[5] came close to winning Brazil's first free presidential elections in 20 years.

In South Africa, where the black majority has been denied political and labor rights for most of this century, the unionism which emerged in the 1970s became a cornerstone of the broad anti-apartheid movement. Workers in newly expanded heavy industries used shop-floor strikes, supported by consumer boycotts and community stay-aways, to push employers to negotiate with workers, as well as the state to reform labor legislation. By the mid-1980s, the Congress of South African Trade

Unions (COSATU) represented nearly a third of the organizable black workforce, including less-skilled workers in mining, textiles, domestic service, and the like. The new unions worked with community organizations to mobilize the uprising that spread across South Africa in the second half of the 1980s. As South Africa moves toward democracy in the 1990s, few observers doubt that COSATU will continue to play a major role in shaping the transition, and in articulating workers' demands for a greater share in the country's wealth.[6]

South Korea also experienced rapid industrial growth in the 1970s and 1980s, and its authoritarian government directed new investment into heavy industries and, later, into export-oriented production. For most of this period, South Korea had a more egalitarian income distribution than either Brazil or South Africa, and workers' real wages rose during rapid industrialization. The South Korean state strictly controlled political groups and labor organization, but Korean workers probably still had more hope of improved living conditions than the "cheap labor" vision of Third World industrialization would suggest. But in the 1980s, when the Korean state began to promote export-oriented industries, real wages began to stagnate, and relatively skilled workers began to use shop-floor strikes to demand higher pay and better working conditions. As in Brazil and South Africa, militant strikes were supported by working-class communities and student groups; membership in these new unions grew rapidly, and their campaigns for better wages were successful enough that South Korean employers could no longer count on unlimited supplies of cheap labor for their factories.[7]

Each of these labor movements exhibited different features, reflecting the different institutional and cultural contexts in which it emerged, yet there is one crucial similarity: in each case, workers responded to new organizational possibilities, using their position in new production processes to mobilize pressure on employers and authoritarian regimes. Rather than concentrating only on improving the conditions of skilled workers, each labor movement included in their political agenda issues from outside the factory gates, issues reflecting the concerns of their wider communities. Instead of focusing only on workplace reform, all three movements also challenged state control over workers' communities, articulating the demands of a broad working-class constituency.

In each case, these labor movements expressed a vision of democratization that included, beyond the right to vote, some kind of redistribution of resources and wealth. They challenged state policies which had historically benefited the dominant classes, using their social base in the industrial working class to back up that challenge.

In other parts of the Third World, workers may not be able to win as many concessions, but popular movements based in poor urban communities often express similar demands. Especially in countries which have experienced authoritarian rule, popular movements tend to include not only political rights and civil liberties, but also socioeconomic rights as goals of the transition to democracy. For them "democratization" implies more than simply giving people the right to vote every few years; it includes an understanding that citizens are entitled to demand a living wage, a reasonable standard of living, and basic social services like education, health, and housing. By the 1990s, many democratization processes were highly contested as popular movements sought to impose visions of change which would redefine development goals to include improved welfare as well as more traditionally defined economic growth.

Narrowed Options

The dynamics of global restructuring raise several questions about the strategies available in the 1990s. Even if a government sympathetic to popular demands took power, how much could it do? In the past, militant labor activists often believed they knew how to proceed once they gained control of the state: programs of nationalization and state ownership, which seemed especially attractive in countries where colonial powers and foreign capital provoked anti-imperialist sentiments, were supposed to ensure that property and national resources would be used for the benefit of all, rather than a tiny elite. But with the collapse of Eastern European states, a general pessimism about statist solutions was reinforced. Moreover, most Third World movements recognized that socialist experiments have proved extremely risky. In the 1980s, the record of bloody destabilization in Nicaragua and Mozambique illustrated the dangers inherent in challenging existing property relations: nationalization had proved no panacea, and the dominant powers of the new international order seemed unwilling to tolerate attempts to use the state to redistribute wealth or services. Monetarist ideologies, which insist that growth requires unlimited freedom for capital, seemed to have become internationally hegemonic.

By the 1990s, few labor activists were sanguine about pursuing the economic policies traditionally advocated by socialists—and they were even less optimistic about whether governments in less-industrialized countries, with little capital or technology of their own on which to draw, could use nationalization to pursue redistributive policies.[8] Capital's global flexibility seemed to make economic growth dependent on attracting private investment to a particular geographic area, and any move which private investors feared would reduce profits seemed likely to reduce a country's chances for future growth.

The need to reassure investors immediately raised questions about many of the more obvious equity-oriented measures which popular governments could once have chosen: land reform or higher corporate tax rates might threaten capital's willingness to locate in a particular area. Armed with the rhetoric of the free market and the ability to move around the globe, capitalists seem increasingly intolerant of any regulation. Business leaders may not always seek identical state policies, but they tend to agree on maintaining high returns to capital—which generally means they also agree that workers and their families should not demand too much from either employers or the state. If nation-states seem too sympathetic to popular demands for redistribution, will they frighten away private investors?

At the same time, donor agencies, no longer concerned with the political allegiances which often shaped aid policies during the Cold War, tend to see improving the climate for private investment as a basic condition for giving development loans or assistance. Thus, policies that might alienate private capital seem likely also to alienate aid agencies, and in the 1990s, international donors and lenders have made it clear that only governments which support and protect private investment can expect help. Multilateral lending agencies like the International Monetary Fund tend to predicate major loans on economic structural adjustment—programs which usually involved privatization and currency devaluation, and emphasized export of primary commodities. Instead of promoting the growth of domestic industries or a domestic market, development aid thus seems likely to recreate patterns of dependence on the world market and on private investors. Although most international development experts talk about the need to improve living conditions or to increase human resources in order to attract private investment, development aid in the 1990s seems unlikely to reshape the basic outlines of the New World Order.

Yet without alternative sources of funds and technology, few countries can afford to reject international packages. For heavily indebted countries like Brazil, the fear that redistributive policies might threaten future loan negotiations could play a real part in political choices: the Worker's Party's threat to renounce interest payments, which could consume half the country's foreign exchange earnings, almost certainly worried middle-class voters fearful of economic isolation. They turned instead to a conservative candidate who promised to continue Brazil's interest payments—although he also promised economic recession. Even in South Africa, where the transition out of strict racial apartheid lends great moral legitimacy to redistributive policies, union-affiliated economists have expressed doubt about the likelihood of radical change in patterns of ownership. Like Brazilians, most residents of the world's poorer countries recognize that unless they manage to attract international capital and technology, their economies will be unable to offer possibilities for a higher living standard.[9]

Restructured Capitalism?

In the early 1990s, popular movements in both Brazil and South Africa attempted to address the question of what policies a popular movement might use to improve living conditions for the majority of the population if they could not control investments directly through state ownership. Economists affiliated with many popular movements have begun to seek ways to improve distribution without slowing growth— recognizing, in the words of one South African economist, that even when governments favorable to labor take power, in the 1990s it looks as if "capitalism will survive its own transition, so that socialism is not on [the] agenda for the next round." The crucial struggle now, he suggests, lies in the effort to

> intervene and shape a capitalist order which is both more humane and more dynamic than has been true of...capitalism in the past, a capitalist order which could be more favorable for socialist prospects in the longer run, by enabling the working classes to become considerably better off, economically and politically, than they have been.[10]

In the past, developmentalist states in the successful NICs have allowed, even supported, private capital accumulation, but they have also used tax incentives, subsidies, and so on to push private companies toward specific kinds of investments. Economists linked to popular movements ask whether future democratic developmentalist states might not be able to use similar policies to attain not only growth but also redistribution. Within a framework of private investment and the existing international context, could some states manage to negotiate a better deal?

Some economists suggest that government programs which provide services to working-class areas, such as electrification and housing schemes, would simultaneously provide jobs and increase domestic market size. Rather than promoting investments in new export-oriented agriculture or manufacture, governments responsive to popular movements might well be able to promote private investment in social services which would first employ workers, and then increase consumption and markets. Instead of spending state revenues on expensive public works programs—outside the reach of most governments in the 1990s—governments could try to persuade private investors they could do well by doing good. But while this approach could improve conditions for those who gained jobs or services, its limitations are obvious. Development strategies which rely on private investors need cooperative capitalists, willing to let long-term concerns about the economy override short-term profitability issues. Will the kind of long-term profits available in domestic market expansion prove more attractive to private investors than the profits they could earn by exporting goods made with cheap labor to a global market? How many employers would be willing to pay higher wages—a crucial step in creating domestic markets? Those who believe the only feasible development strategy for the late 20th century lies in negotiating with private investors have yet to propose an easy strategy for ensuring reasonable returns to labor as well as capital.

Alternative Possibilities?

Designing a redistributive development strategy based on private investors is going to be difficult; indeed, it was an awareness of these difficulties that prompted early socialists to propose nationalization in the first place. But an alternative approach to political economy is beginning to emerge simultaneously within several broad social movements, stressing bottom-up mobilization rather than top-down investment incentives. Recognizing that states must negotiate with private investors, popular movements like the Brazilian Worker's Party increasingly stress the need to develop a counterbalancing weight within the political arena.

By developing organizations in what is sometimes called "civil society," independent of the state, popular movement activists hope to create a source of pressure on democratic states to develop social programs, and to respond to demands formulated in local grassroots organizations and expressed through political mobilization. Trade unions, community groups, women's organizations, associations of peasants—all these could become forums through which demands for redistribution could be placed in the public arena for discussion and debate. More and more activists argue that these associations could use political participation—or, if necessary, more disruptive methods such as strikes and demonstrations—to insist that states respond to the needs of poor and middle-class citizens, as well as the needs of capital.

But this approach, too, carries risks. First, if grassroots movements representing poor and working-class members are free to organize and mobilize, property owners will be able to organize, too—often with many more resources to back them. Will the existence of grassroots movements really diminish the influence business associations already exert over policymakers?

Second, even if it were possible to privilege groups formed by poorer citizens, how can activists ensure that these groups will be internally democratic? That they will avoid the pitfall of mobilizing ethnic, rather than more universal, identities? That they will resist manipulation by populist politicians, or by groups with hidden agendas? That their strategies and goals will reflect the needs of a broad range of citizens, rather than a handful of members of dominant groups whose resources enable them to present private interests as public issues? Even if it proves possible to ensure that groups in civil society remain democratic and universalistic, how willing will developmentalist states be to tolerate the rather unpredictable, sometimes messy, processes of such open democracy? Especially in countries that have recently experienced authoritarian rule, vigorous mobilization may provoke dominant classes or militaries to take over the state and close down politics once again.

And if these dangers can be avoided, a responsive democratic state trying to promote growth, equity, and participation simultaneously would still face other challenges. If social movements grow in importance, how will states arbitrate conflicting claims? While tension between different constituencies of political parties can be creative, it can also prove problematic—especially when demands arise from the concrete conditions of widely varied local areas, and when grassroots participants lack the broader perspective required for developing national schemes. Deepening democracy involves increasing participation, but it may also require developing a broader vision that encompasses a range of conflicting goals.

Advocates of this approach to democratic socialism will have to consider the question of what kinds of internal political processes will allow a broad-based popular movement to create and sustain the kinds of coalitions required to make significant reforms in political processes and in national policies. Strategies which aim to incorporate socioeconomic rights in the meaning of democracy rely heavily on grassroots mobilization, but these movements—even articulated with and through a strong political party—may find it difficult to grapple with the complex realities confronting dependent capitalist economies, and the dangers posed by capital flight or even military takeovers.

The Brazilian Worker's Party probably offers the 1990s' most successful example of a party bringing together a militant labor movement and social movements organized around the conditions of daily life. Its activists combine popular mobilization with political participation, replacing a tradition of clientalist populism with what appears to be real debate. Yet even the Worker's Party has been unable to move beyond an oppositional stance, or to offer concrete proposals for what it might do on attaining parliamentary power. Two of its leaders recently offered a list of issues that the party has only inadequately addressed:

> A national project is not something that can be produced through the intellectual effort of a few technocrats or politicos, however capable they may be, nor in the exclusive ambit of a political party. It requires the active involvement of civil society and social movements, a fertile interchange between diverse political and social subjects.…However, a party of the left disposed to confront this challenge will have to deal with some vital questions. These include the redefinition of the economic function of the state and the public sector, reformulation of the electoral system and of criteria for parliamentary representation, reform of the legislature and judiciary, democratization of the means of communication, administrative reform, an end to military control, a struggle against violence and the defense of human rights, the establishment of democratic norms for the control of the state by society, etc. Also essential is a group of economic and political reforms which foresee a development strategy oriented toward the promotion of citizenship. Among these we would underline a development policy for industry, science and technology, a policy for wages and income distribution, policies for relating to foreign capital and the world economy, and for dealing with the foreign debt, agrarian reform, agriculture and nutrition, taxes, etc.[11]

The list of policies still undefined is somewhat overwhelming: any party based in social movements will have to create channels through which party members and groups can represent their demands, but which also allow state policymakers to take account of technical questions.

But perhaps the most difficult question facing those who hope to reform capitalism is the extent to which countries dependent on multinational capital and technology can risk the disruptions that will almost automatically accompany a process that encourages grassroots mobilizations. Investors are generally wary of mobilized labor movements; in the past, they have also proved wary of movements demanding environmental regulation or increased social services. Implicitly, a strategy that seeks to deepen democracy assumes, as Bendix suggested three decades ago, that industrial society offers new possibilities for "the process of fundamental democratization by which 'those classes which formerly only played a passive part in political life' have been stirred into action."[12] In an increasingly competitive international market, confronted by rapidly changing technologies and by ever more internationalized capital, states in any economy dependent on private capital and international commodity markets may find that recurrent demands for inclusion and redistribution create a risky investment climate, threatening economic growth and the support of middle- and upper-class citizens for democratic rule.[13] Even if political parties closely allied with popular movements come to power, how much participation will they be able to tolerate, if participation threatens investment and economic growth?

Internationalism

This last challenge is perhaps the most serious confronting social movements, and few activists in what is still called the Third World have yet grappled with it—perhaps because, despite the grassroots strength of some oppositional movements, none has yet come to power in the new international context of the 1990s. The best answer to the limitations on popular demands may lie outside the nation-state: If the problem facing developing countries is the internationalization of capital, perhaps no development strategy will work unless it, too, incorporates an element of internationalism, taking advantage of the new technologies of communication and information that give capital such flexibility.

At the governmental level, international trade agreements may prove the only way for dependent economies to avoid constantly deteriorating prices for primary product exports, either by setting new terms of trade, or by creating regional economic blocs to create semi-protected markets for fledgling industries. But in recent years, nongovernmental links between social movements have proven even more effective at increasing bargaining power with multinational corporations, as popular demands are repeated and reinforced by coordinated or parallel campaigns in different parts of the world. Workers have sometimes been able to use industrial action in support of workers elsewhere. Usually, this support takes the form of unions sending aid to workers on strike elsewhere, but in the 1980s, U.S. and Swedish workers went on strike themselves to pressure their multinational corporate employers to recognize unions in their Third World subsidiaries. Workers have sometimes boycotted goods from repressive labor regimes; stevedores in several U.S. ports refused to unload South African goods during the 1980s as part of an international anti-apartheid campaign. Such campaigns might be extended. Cross-border campaigns among workers in subsidiaries of the same corporation, or workers in the same industry or sector, for example, might reduce capital's ability to insist on low wages. Similarly, international consumer boycotts might persuade employers to bring working conditions in line with international standards.

But workplace-based internationalism is only one kind. Environmental activists have shown they can coordinate international campaigns on specific issues, using popular pressure to challenge corporate policies; volunteer organizations like Greenpeace, for example, bring together people with common environmental concerns from around the world in well-coordinated campaigns. International consumer boycotts such as the 1980s boycott of Nestlé have been able to prompt new corporate practices—in this case, new advertising restrictions on baby food formulas. Responding to appeals from black South Africans, an international grassroots anti-apartheid movement in the 1980s forced governments in the United States and Europe to impose economic sanctions on South Africa, undoubtedly speeding up the transition to democracy there. If popular mobilization were coordinated internationally, democratic states might find they gained more negotiating room; multinational corporations would find their options limited if they faced similar demands everywhere.

Calls for strengthened international solidarity are older than this century, of course, and neither labor movements nor socialist parties have proved able to achieve it: the same national boundaries that seem so unimportant to transnational capital still play a role in defining political and personal identities. Just as unions tend to defend their members first, political parties represent constituencies within electoral systems, and tend to defend the interests of their nation's citizens above those of others. Yet in the 1990s, adequate representation for national constituencies may require international coordination. Lula, the Brazilian Worker's Party leader, says: "There is no individual way out of the crisis we're facing at the international level." When Third World countries try to renegotiate a better commercial deal with international capital by themselves, "it's like placing a lightweight up against Mike Tyson—no matter how good he is, the odds are stacked against him and he ends up getting knocked out."[14] Perhaps—and this remains only a vague possibility—social movements in different locations can develop a broader vision, which will allow them to cooperate across national boundaries, supporting popular movements and larger global campaigns; without such a vision, states in late-industrializing nations may find their policy options limited by the goals of international capital—goals that do not, in general, include raising the living standards of workers and their families.

Restructuring the Alternatives

Even with coherent plans for growth through redistribution, with mobilized social movements, with democratically constituted popular governments, and with international coordination, what are the chances in an era of global restructuring that any government can manage both growth and even moderate redistribution? How optimistic can we be that historically poor areas of the world can negotiate successfully for a better deal?

There are important differences between newly industrialized countries and more classically underdeveloped economies. Countries like Brazil, South Africa, or South Korea already have relatively developed industrial infrastructures, relatively well-educated workforces, and domestic market potential. It is at least conceivable that even in the current world context, states like these can manage to negotiate new development alternatives. In some cases, surely, investors can be persuaded to accept higher wages, better social services, and even more participatory institutions, in return for access to skilled workers, new markets, and infrastructures—if they confront well-organized working-class movements, backed by states committed to permitting these movements to express themselves, and reinforced by international coordination. Under such conditions, broad social movements might just be able to rewrite the rules—at least enough to spread the benefits of growth beyond a tiny elite, and to make some progress in improving the conditions of daily life for the majority of the world's population.

Notes

1. Vilas, Carlos, in *The Future of Socialism: Perspectives from the Left,* Tabb, William K., ed., New York: Monthly Review Press, 1990, p. 217.
2. Between 1950 and 1970, world industrial production increased at an unprecedented rate of 5.6 percent annually, while world trade increased at an annual 7.3 percent. Gereffi, Gary, "Paths of Industrialization: An Overview," in *Manufacturing Miracles: Paths of Industrialization in Latin America and East Asia,* Gereffi, and D. Wyman, eds., Princeton: Princeton University Press, 1990, p. 21.

3. For modernization theorists, industrialization was generally believed to be blocked by internal obstacles, such as a lack of infrastructure, human resources, or investment capital. Dependency theorists, on the other hand, tended to stress external obstacles, inherent in the way international pressures and markets shaped the economies of former colonies to emphasize the export of primary commodities.

4. See, for example, Lipietz, Alain, *Mirages and Miracles: The Crises of Global Fordism,* trans. David Marcey, London: Verso Press, 1987.

5. Two recent English-language books discuss the rise of the Worker's Party: Sader, Emir, and Ken Silverstein, *Without Fear of Being Happy: Lula, The Worker's Party and Brazil,* London: Verso Press, 1991; and Keck, Margaret, *The Worker's Party and Democratization in Brazil,* New Haven: Yale University Press, 1992.

6. For an excellent history of COSATU through 1990, see Baskin, Jeremy, *Striking Back! A History of COSATU,* Johannesburg: Ravan Press, 1991.

7. Frederic Deyo compares the history and labor legislation of several East Asian NICs, including South Korea, in *Beneath the Miracle: Labor Subordination in the New Asian Industrialism,* Berkeley: University of California Press, 1989. See also Brandt, Vincent, "South Korean Society," in *Korea Briefing: 1990,* Chong-Sik Lee, ed., Boulder: Westview Press/The Asia Society, 1991, pp. 75-96; and Tun-jen Cheng, "Political Regimes and Development Strategies: South Korea and Taiwan,"in *Manufacturing Miracles,* pp. 139-178.

8. South Africa perhaps provided the clearest example of the way dependence on primary commodities could narrow options. South African labor activists once believed the country's gold mines would pay for redistributive measures; nationalization seemed to offer a real source of funds for new social services and redistribution. But by the 1990s, gold prices seemed permanently depressed, apparently because the international financial world, no longer relying on a gold standard to back currencies, finally stopped viewing gold in terms of speculation. By 1991, over 75% of South Africa's gold was used for jewelry, and gold seemed destined to become merely another primary commodity. As a result, South Africa, like most countries which rely on exporting primary commodities to an uncertain world market, is facing fluctuating international demand and unstable prices; even the militant mineworkers' union feared that nationalization would ultimately hurt workers by reducing international investments, and perhaps even by provoking international economic sanctions on a post-apartheid South Africa.

9. Peru's Sendero Luminoso (Shining Path) claimed it would willingly forego those international economic links, arguing that most people in poor countries would never be able to afford the VCRs and computers that increasingly marked the lifestyles of the global middle class, and suggesting that an isolated economy would be better able to ensure equity and growth. However, by the 1990s, most

social movements—especially those representing urban industrial workers—were far less willing to renounce all possibility of gaining access to the technological advances of the late 20th century.

10. Gelb, Stephen, "Capitalism: There is no alternative...for now," *Work in Progress,* 76, (1991), p. 43. See also Gelb, ed., *South Africa's Economic Crisis,* Cape Town: David Philip, 1990.

11. Genoino, Jose, and Jose Eduardo Utzig, "Alternativa positiva," *Teoria e debate* 14, (May 1991), p. 5.

12. Bendix, Reinhard, "Tradition and Modernity Reconsidered," in *Nation-Building and Citizenship,* second edition, Berkeley: University of California Press, 1977, p. 402, citing Karl Mannheim, 1941.

13. Thus, for example, Samuel Valenzuela has argued that the best prospects for a long-lasting democracy lie in "mobilization followed by restraint," in which militant strikes challenge authoritarian rule, but are controlled by labor leaders during the transition to democracy to avoid a return to repression. "Labor movements in transitions to democracy: A framework for analysis," *Comparative Politics,* Vol. 21, No. 4, (1989), pp. 445-472.

14. Interview with Lula, appendix to Sader and Silverstein, p. 162. For more on Lula and the Worker's Party, see his chapter, "The Transformations Must Be Deep and Global," in this book.

Acknowledgments

The author is grateful to Allen Hunter and Jeremy Brecher for comments on earlier drafts of this chapter.

One Man No Chop

Hassan A. Sunmonu

Any traveler in West and East Africa will not fail to notice the writings on the fleet of local transport plying the urban and rural roads. They are the "Matatus" in Kenya, "Molue" in Lagos (Nigeria), and "Tro-Tro" in Accra, Ghana. The captions that I still remember read:

"One man no chop," meaning "It is bad to be selfish."

"Remember Six Feet," meaning "Remember death," that whatever you are, death is the end of everything.

"No condition is permanent." In other words, what is permanent is change.

When one reflects on the selfishness, greed, and insensitivity of the current promoters of a New World Order, one feels sorry for them because of their narrow-mindedness. For them "might is right." They promote double standards, the manipulation of the United Nations and its agencies to further the interests of U.S. multinationals and to terrorize poor Third World countries into complete submission.

The New World Order that we require is based on: equity, social and economic justice for all peoples and countries of the world, rich or poor; freedom, democracy, respect for human rights; peoples' self-determination; empowerment of the people and the accountability to the people of those in authority. Any New World Order that lacks these three essentials is not worthy of being so called.

In most African societies, the principle of the traditional culture is that the welfare of the whole community is paramount and supersedes the selfish interests of the individual. The whole community becomes brothers and sisters. This gives rise to the "extended family," whereby cousins and even distant relatives are part of the close-knit family, whose members help each other in every way.

In the same way, the objective of a New World Order should be to bring peace, democracy, balanced development, and happiness to all peoples and countries of the world. How can there be peace without justice? Can there be democracy without social and economic justice? Can there be balanced development without the judicious use of both human and environmental resources? Can there be happiness in the world when 80% of world resources are appropriated by 20% of humankind?

It is when all of us, individually and collectively, find honest answers to these questions that the objective of a New World Order can be achieved. Take the question of peace and justice. Can anybody solve the Arab-Israeli conflict with justice only for the Israelis and not for the Palestinians? The same United Nations Security Council that imposed an air and arms embargo on Libya for its refusal to surrender two of its citizens, alleged to have been responsible for the Pan-Am air disaster in Lockerbie, Scotland, refused even to discuss Cuba's call for investigation into the "alleged" United States role in the bombing of a Cuban airliner over Bermuda in 1976! The same UN Security Council that waged war and imposed sanctions on Iraq for refusing to obey UN Security Council resolutions following Iraq's invasion of Kuwait on August 2, 1990, turns a blind eye to Israel's refusal to comply with UN Security Council resolutions.

The worst thing any individual, country, or organization can lose is moral authority. Great efforts need to be made by all of us—the citizens of the world—not to allow the big powers to manipulate the United Nations Security Council into taking unjust decisions or resorting to double standards, so that it may not lose its moral authority. The world has not yet found an alternative to the United Nations.

Currently the world is talking about democracy. But nobody is talking about its component of social and economic justice. Why? Because the democracy the rightwing is trying to fashion, particularly for the former socialist countries of East and Central Europe and for Africa, is "government of the rich, by the rich, on behalf of the people." For African countries in particular, "democracy and multipartism" have been made additional conditionalities for aid and technical assistance. And in place of social and economic justice, they are forced to accept Reaganomics and Thatcherism, i.e., "economic liberalization" dictated by "market forces."

Africa has defined her own democratic agenda through the Organization of African Unity's "African Charter for Popular Participation in Development and Transformation." It is based on popular participation, empowerment of the people, accountability, social and economic justice, respect for human rights, and peoples' self-determination. In fact, Africa needs no lessons in democracy from anybody.

The International Monetary Fund and the World Bank force neoliberalism on poor African and other Third World countries. For over five years, the Organization of African Trade Union Unity (OATUU) was the "lone voice in the wilderness" against the inhuman conditionalities imposed by these two institutions through their orthodox Structural Adjustment Programs (SAPs) in Africa. It is gratifying to note that the leaders of the World Bank have been forced by incontrovertible evidence to admit the failure of their SAPs. They admitted that these programs had not adequately addressed the question of poverty. That is putting it mildly; the evidence on the ground is that the middle class has been wiped out in most of the 34 African countries applying the orthodox IMF/World Bank SAPs! To add salt to the wound, the IMF and World Bank refused to support the African Alternative Framework to Structural Adjustment Programmes (AAF-SAP) for Socio-Economic Recovery and Transformation, which had been specifically designed by the United Nations Economic Commission for Africa and adopted by the Organization of African Unity (OAU) and the UN General Assembly.

As far as African workers and the OATUU are concerned, any economic structure or program that does not have the objective of satisfying the basic needs of the African peoples is unacceptable and will be rejected. These basic needs include: food, housing, education, health, water, electricity, roads, transport, communications (radio, telephone, television, etc.), and employment. It is only AAF-SAP that provides the basis for the achievement of these ten basic needs, not the voodoo economics of Reaganomics or Thatcherism nor the orthodox SAPs of the IMF and World Bank.

The undemocratic, one-sided negotiations in the Uruguay Round of GATT are heavily weighted in favor of the multinationals and the developed countries, and against the trade and development interests of the Third World. It has been estimated that if the Uruguay Round of GATT comes into operation, Africa will be losing $3 billion annually.[1] Where then is the economic justice for the Third World in the Uruguay Round of GATT? Those responsible for this grave economic injustice should remember the African proverb that says, "The flea is killing itself, while it unwisely thinks it is killing the dog; doesn't the flea know that the day the dog dies, that is also the day of its own death?" A word is enough for the wise.

Another important area that has to be addressed in the New World Order is the judicious use of human and material resources in order to achieve an ecologically sound and balanced environment for the present and future generations. Much needs to be invested in human resource development; population management, especially in Africa and other parts of the Third World; environmental pollution, treatment of human, industrial, and toxic wastes; the ozone layer and world-wide reforestation. The emphasis on a cleaner and sustainable environment worldwide will lead to the creation of tens of millions of new jobs.

Workers and trade unions throughout the world should be much more committed to solving environmental problems. A good, clean, and sustainable environment offers the potential for a better life with better climate, food security, employment, and overall development.

The Road to the New World Order

In all countries of the world, a tiny minority rules and decides the fate of the overwhelming majority of the population. In most countries of the world, the people are disempowered. The first task of the world community is to ensure the empowerment of the people so that power and sovereignty rest with them.

To be empowered, the people have to be educated. In countries where more than 50% of the people are illiterate, especially in most African and some other Third World countries, literacy programs have to be embarked upon with national and international assistance. That is why we in the OATUU see the cut in subsidies to social services like health and education by the orthodox SAPs as a way of disempowering the people. Those SAPs have a definite, antipeople ideological objective. International nongovernmental organizations (INGOs) should work together on massive literacy programs to ensure empowerment of the people worldwide.

The world community should seize the initiative from the ideologues of neoliberalism and market forces and expose the massive exploitation, oppression, and fraud against the silent, poor majority in the North and South from whom the ideologues are profiting. The battle cry should be, "Satisfaction of the basic needs of the peoples before corporate greed."

The international community should mobilize against all wars, whether civil, national, or international. Great pressure should be brought on all countries to stop the production of tanks, missiles, and nuclear armaments. War industries should be converted to industries for the production of the basic needs of the people. Military personnel should be drastically reduced or re-deployed to environmental protection.

Role of Trade Unions

I have listed three essential elements that affect people all over the world, around which they can be mobilized for action. What should be the role of trade unions in this mobilization effort?

Before trade unions can effectively play their role in mobilization, they themselves have to ensure popular participation and empowerment of the workers among their ranks (trade union democracy) from the industrial union level to the national, continental, and international levels. After all, charity begins at home! They should organize massive workers' education around the objectives of a New World Order: the basic needs strategy, peace and disarmament, sustainable environment, popular participation and peoples' empowerment, accountability, and social and economic justice. They should then mobilize their members for action.

The next step is to forge links with other mass organizations and social forces at national, regional, and international levels. These include women, youths, students, religious, academic, farmers, professional, voluntary development organizations, etc. Two OATUU affiliates, the Union Nationale des Travailleurs du Mali (in Mali) and the Zambian Congress of Trade Unions, successfully overthrew the Moussa Traore military dictatorship in Mali and the Kenneth Kaunda one-party dictatorship in Zambia, using the above strategy. Also, another OATUU affiliate in Benin, the UNSTB, had earlier led the process that brought a peaceful democratic change in that country.

It is regrettable that, in spite of the end of the Cold War, there are still some prominent trade unionists who are bent on pursuing the Cold War within the international trade union movement to its logical conclusions. This is not only counterproductive, but it is also inimical to the unity of the international trade union movement. There should be unity in diversity, and nobody has the right to impose his or her ideology or religion on anybody or any group of persons. It is also undemocratic and against trade union internationalism for any trade union organization to undermine or destabilize another trade union on the altar of ideological purity.

The solidarity and assistance of trade unions and other INGOs will be needed to strengthen many weak trade unions in the South. This much-needed assistance should be given in such a way as to enable them to become independent and self-sustaining, so that they can in turn help less fortunate trade unions and INGOs elsewhere. Assistance that perpetuates dependence is not the type needed in the struggle for the New World Order we want.

Workers all over the world—North and South—are suffering from unemployment, exploitation, and insecurity at the hands of conservative governments and their multinational backers. These are the forces that workers and trade unions should fight to ensure fairness, equity, social and economic justice, peace, sustainable development, freedom, and democracy worldwide. This gigantic task calls for workers and trade unions all over the world to unite.

Notes

1. Onimode, Bade, citing research by O. Knudsen, in a report to the 15th Annual Meeting of ACP/EEC Representatives of Economics and Social Interest Groups, Brussels, Belgium, 2-4 December 1991, p. 9.

Labor Standards and Double Standards in the New World Order

Denis MacShane

Former U.S. Vice President Daniel Quayle came to Geneva, Switzerland on a European swing early in 1992 and addressed the United Nations Commission on Human Rights. He sternly lectured the assembled ministers and international functionaries on the uselessness of their work. The message coming through from Quayle was clear. Now that the Cold War was over, there was less and less room in U.S. diplomacy for human rights as an international issue.

Quayle lectured his audience, people of high sophistication and higher cynicism, on the failings of the UN Commission on Human Rights. It had tried to make employment, or healthcare, or literacy, into a human right. These were interesting questions, said the Vice President, but they belonged elsewhere in the UN's warehouse of committees, commissions, and agencies. What was worse, declared Mr. Quayle, was the presence in the human rights commission of representatives of Cuba, Iraq, and Iran. The accused were sitting in the jury. The worst abusers of human rights were up on the bench sitting in judgment!

Quayle had a point. As Iain Guest has shown in his excellent study, *Behind the Disappearances: Argentina's Dirty War Against Human Rights and the United Nations,* of the UN's efforts to implement its own human rights conventions, the diplomatic rules of the UN do place representatives of the most absurd countries in charge of the most unlikely projects. You do not have to have the shallow American provincialism of a Pat Buchanan to engage in criticism of the feebleness of UN operations in defence of its proclaimed universalist values. In the 1970s, the UN chose an Iraqi to head an inquiry into people who had been "disappeared" by the Argentine military after the 1976 coup. Unfortunately, the Iraqi fell foul of Saddam Hussein, and six months after his appointment to the post, he too, alas, disappeared—in Baghdad.

But as Vice President Quayle read out his speech proclaiming a singular American view of human rights, his listeners waited to see if he would mention the big one. (It was probably at this same time that then-Governor Clinton took 24 hours out of his presidential campaign to fly back to Arkansas to personally oversee the execution of a mentally retarded black man. In Europe such behavior is now seen as barbarous, and for two or three decades no national, let alone minor regional, political leader in Europe has had to soil his or her hands or mind with judicial killings. In the United States, it is, of course, an essential part of manliness to demonstrate one's ability to lead the free world. After all, if you dodged the draft in Vietnam, the least you can do is strap a man of low IQ to a wooden chair and fry him longer than a Big Mac.)

The single most brutal exemplar of human rights abuse in recent years was the massacre in Tiananmen Square. Experts argue over the exact number of dead or the precise location of the massacres, but none deny the cold-blooded nature of the suppression and the continuing arrests, imprisonments, and harassment of pro-democracy Chinese since 1989. Moreover, the symbol chosen by the young Chinese in those weeks of hope in May and June 1989 had been the Statue of Liberty, an American image, offered by France to commemorate in 1889 the centenary of the declaration of the rights of man (sic), and still pregnant with appeal and hope for millions of people deprived of political freedom and economic opportunity worldwide.

Yet Vice President Quayle managed an entire speech without the word "China." Shortly afterwards, Washington announced it was lifting the paltry trade embargo it had imposed on China after the Tiananmen Square massacre. The human rights defenders from Iraq, Iran, or Cuba smiled gently as they sat back in their comfortable leather chairs in the luxurious committee rooms of the Palais des Nations in Geneva. Whatever else was on the agenda of President Bush's New World Order, it certainly was not a universal application, free of double standards, of human rights.

Business as usual? Well, not quite, because the end of European communism has opened a new era in world history in which, as always in the past, we are on the foothills peering up into the clouds wondering what lies ahead. Guides like Mr. Fukuyama, who claim to be on the summit from where it can be safely announced that there is no history ahead to be discovered, are seen to be today's version of "the wisest fool in Christendom." What has happened is that illusions of a First World (northern, U.S.-led), a Second World (communist, Russian-led) and a Third World (nonaligned, Group of 77-led) have, thankfully, been washed away. There was and is only one world. In it, since 1945, the United States has been dominant, but that dominance is now over as a result of the rise of Western Europe and of Asian capitalism. And even U.S. dominance was not quite what it seemed—hard to accept as that may be for those in the American intelligentsia, whether Kissingerite or Chomskyist, for whom their country is, for good or evil, at the center of all world development. Soviet communism, we now realize, though many Europeans were making the point since the mid-1970s, was an empty wasp's nest waiting to be blown away by a passing puff of wind, unable even effectively to sting in Afghanistan or preserve its own imperial unity, let alone a *cordon sanitaire* on its western borders. But as old illusions disappear, it is not a new post-ideological, post-nation-state world that emerges.

As someone of Polish-Irish descent, I will venture only the prediction that the long-awaited demise of the nation-state may yet have to wait awhile. On the contrary, it is the formation of the nation-state that is the single biggest global political surge that can be seen under way in the post-communist, post-unipolar world.

As I write, I have pinned to the wall in front of me two regional maps, one of Europe (Note how language has changed. A quarter of a century ago, Europe was pretty much the world as far as my studies in history at school or in university were concerned. Now it is simply bracketed as a region!) and one of the Asia-Pacific region. It would take too much time to list the rise of new nation-state entities on both maps since 1990 alone. The map of Europe printed in 1991 shows neither Slovenia, Croatia, nor Macedonia. Naturally, the Basque country is subsumed within Spain, Corsica within France, and the six counties of Northern Ireland are shown as part of the United Kingdom. The map of Asia published by *National Geographic* in 1989 goes as far west as Moscow but shows none of the now independent Asian republics once in the Soviet Union. Tibet, Timor, and New Caledonia are all shown under foreign occupation, part of China, Indonesia, and France, respectively. It is neither isolationist, nor nationalist, nor anti-internationalist to note that national passions, and the desire to join the club of nation-states with an independent seat at the UN General Assembly, are waxing not waning. The power of the nation-state directly to control its internal developments and external interventions is declining sharply as a result of the globalization of economic, communication, political, and cultural relations. But the nation remains a far greater focus of attachment and locus of contestation than perhaps is realized by those who seek to wish away national government as more of a problem-posing obstacle to democratic advance than a potential solution offering support to progress and human development.

Thus the obligation to work toward the election of progressive democratic governments in nation-states remains a priority. Just because 30 or 40%, or, in the case of developing countries, 60 or 70% of nation-state authority no longer obtains—as evidenced by Bush's kowtowing to the Japanese to obtain some relief for badly managed U.S. industries—that is no reason to give up seeking control of regional and national government. The miseries and corruptions of all Left parties in government encourage the response of "A plague on all their houses," or the traditional conservative whine of "Politics is a dirty business." Well, so it is, but a constant appeal to a networking, friction-free, millenaristic post-political global community carries opposite dangers of clean hands but little enduring presence or power. Ayn Randism of the Left, effortless moral superiority in which any defeat is the result of evil action, may be good for crowd-pleasing on the seminar circuit of progressives, but leaves the executive committees of the bourgeoisie firmly in control. It is essential to reach out for new forms of governance corresponding to current global social needs and, especially, to break the government-equals-military-force connection that has dominated political philosophy since Hobbes. Representative democracy is now almost replaced by opinion-poll-, combined with lobby-, democracy. Athenian debates are nullified by the direct participation of citizens through push-button choices on the telephone after watching television. As we unleash venom on elected representatives, we should be careful about what will come in their place.

I write as a labor activist, working for nearly half my adult life in the field of international trade unionism. I long for, work toward, and, within the possibilities of what I can do, encourage transnational action by workers. Yet I am more and more conscious that for many progressives the embrace of internationalism may, at times, be a mechanism for avoiding the difficult work of securing advances within their domestic or nation-state context. British and U.S. unions, for example, have rightly criticized the exploitation of Asian workers by electronics multinationals such as Wang, Motorola, or Texas Instruments. They have sought to intervene with their governments, or proposed labor rights-linked trade embargoes, or called down anathema from international bodies such as the International Labor Organization (ILO). Yet the most concrete help these northern unions could give to their oppressed brothers and sisters in Asia would be to ensure the unionization of the electronic multinationals in their home countries. A fully unionized company may behave brutally to workers overseas, but at least is exposed to some pressure on its home turf if it does so. In the 1970s and early 1980s, for example, the United Auto Workers union (UAW) was able to offer some protection to South African union organizers in General Motors and Ford by intervening with the parent companies in Detroit.

So the first act of global solidarity is to organize local solidarity by way of deeds, not words. If U.S. unions altered modes of organization, profile, and external linkages so as to overcome the pathological hostility they confront from the administration, the media, and corporations, and were able to represent 50 or 80% of the workforce instead of the 15% of the U.S. workforce currently in unions, then their ability to intervene internationally would be worth a million times what so far they are able to do.

Global solidarity, like charity, begins at home. In the world of labor, certainly, there is now far more to work with. The doldrums in which northern trade unions have found themselves (though this needs some qualifying, as European unions have achieved remarkable reductions in working time since 1980) are not reflected elsewhere in the world. From Poland to South Africa, from Brazil to South Korea, workers in the past decade have organized independent labor unions which have transformed the political economy of their countries.

Contrary to the utter silliness of claims that a new Holy Alliance between Pope and President was responsible for toppling communism, the plain fact is that it was a worker-centered form of organization, with worker-centered demands, that posed in Poland from August 1980 to December 1981 the major historic challenge to communist rule. Despite his rhetoric, President Reagan and his coterie were delighted with the suppression of Solidarnosc that reinforced his evil empire crusade. It was Swedish, Italian, French, and British socialists who took the lead in supporting the underground Solidarity organization. (I know, as I helped organize sending printing equipment and spent an uncomfortable· few days in the hands of the Polish secret police when I was arrested on an underground mission to Warsaw in 1982). Reagan never lifted a finger to support the democratic opposition anywhere in the world, while the British government under Thatcher actually cut the number of visas issued to Poles after the suppression of Solidarity in 1982. As with the theory, dear to both the U.S. Right and Left, that Western Europe became an anticommunist stronghold after 1945 because of U.S., notably CIA, interventions, the *Time* propaganda of the United States defeating communism via trade unionism is not historically valid. After 1945, it was democratic socialists in Europe, operating within a Marxist framework, who opposed and defeated Stalinism, just as in the 1980s it was the democratic Left which provided most support for Polish Solidarity.

Similarly, in South Africa, white defenders of apartheid capitalism proclaimed that the red hand of Moscow was behind every new strike or labor organization victory in the country in the 1980s. In fact, the rapid industrialization of the country called into being the extraordinary black trade union movement, which took apartheid capitalism by the throat again and again. Faced with imminent throttling, the rulers decided to release Mandela and begin negotiations.

The same wind swept through South Korea in 1987, when six weeks of giant sit-down strikes forced out the ruling dictatorship and replaced it with a still-authoritarian but less directly oppressive political government. In Brazil in 1989, Lula, head of the worker-controlled CUT federation, only a decade old and spawner of the Workers' Party (PT), came within inches of being elected president. In Zambia in 1991, it was the president of the labor federation, Fred Chiluba, who displaced the corrupt one-party rule of Kenneth Kaunda in presidential elections.

In Indonesia the union called "Solidarity," formed in 1990, is the major center for democratic opposition to the Suharto dictatorship. The industrialization of Taiwan, Hong Kong, and Malaysia has led to increased independent working-class organization in those countries.

Finally, one of the most under-reported aspects of the Tiananmen Square massacre is the role of the Workers Autonomous Federations in provoking Deng Xiao Ping to send in the tanks. It was one thing to have rebellious students on the streets. It was quite another when workers formed independent trade unions and thus took away from the ruling Communist Party its right, however tenuous, to claim to be ruling in the name of the working class. Deng could not allow his own proletariat to teach themselves Polish, as it were. Since Tiananmen Square, reports from China show that independent working-class organization continues to survive, and the Chinese authorities report increased strikes and workplace activity.

To list these new unions and to show how effective they have been in changing the political dispensations in their lands is not to make a Panglossian linkage to some form of socialist transformation. Some theoreticians have sought to describe a social movement unionism qualitatively different from the existing trade unions in the industrial North. This is part of the old hunt for good as opposed to bad unions, for democratic labor structures (i.e. the ones we approve of) as opposed to undemocratic labor practices (the ones we don't like). I read recently a call for postal election of union presidents in the United States, as if this procedure was the ultimate in democratic, worker-participatory trade unionism. Yet in my own country, Britain, such postal ballots were imposed on unions by Thatcher's government, the most reactionary antilabor government Britain has had this century, in the name of taking away power from active trade union members and placing the process in an arena where the media and bosses can maximize their influence. Thus in England a membership referendum was an act of reaction; in the United States it is heralded as a symbol of democratic progress.

Perhaps the way out of this conundrum is to accept that there is no democratic form which guarantees democratic content. That surely is the essence of democratic activity. There is no end result, no final goal, no universal method. We live as pluralists but extend pluralism as widely as possible. All one can do, at least in the labor field, is support organization and internal procedures which are in conformity with generally accepted ideas of democratic trade unionism, and which are ratified by members and opposed by bosses.

But the exciting aspect of current trade union work is not just the example of how workers worldwide are seeking to create independent unions, but that finally the globalization of the economy is penetrating the most conservative of labor institutions as they realize that complementary to national labor organization must be transfrontier linkages. These have to go beyond the rhetoric of labor internationalism, fraternal tourism, or neocolonial sponsorships. An example comes from West Europe where, under the aegis of the European Community, a large number of European Works Councils have been set up. These consist of workers and unions from the same multinational company with plants in different countries. Volkswagen, Europe's biggest auto company, for example, in 1992 signed an agreement with the VW Euro Works Council representing workers from VW plants in Germany, Spain, and Belgium. Soon to join will be workers from the Skoda auto works in Czechoslovakia, now 70% owned by Volkswagen. Workers in different European countries employed by Ford, GM, Gillette, and Digital, to name just U.S. multinationals, are setting up similar bodies.

Although the means of production are similar in all countries, there are now three very different modes of organization: 1) a European one, based on works councils which are legal entities and which function in a dual-power system in parallel to unions; 2) a North American mode, based on adversarial trade unionism as the only institution able to represent workers' interests and suffering from aggressive de-recognition drives by capital; and 3) a Japanese mode, based on total worker incorporation into big companies, with a relatively weak external union representation system.

From the point of view of global solidarity it seems that the European model offers the most hopeful way forward in uniting workers from different countries. The building up of transnational workers' committees will be the only serious challenge to the hegemony of the multinational corporations which are the inheritors of the economic power of the nation-state. Global production requires global worker solidarity at the workplace level. For over a century, worker internationalism actually meant occasional meetings of workers' leaders. From 1920 onwards, these meetings were dominated by the communist-socialist split, which, in turn, provided fertile ground for the KGB, CIA, MI6, and other non-worker bodies to play their games. The end of the Cold War should put an end to that leeching on worker internationalism. A more mature recognition of pluralistic differences should stop childish attempts to exclude, or wasted efforts building, alternative rival international bodies. It is now possible for the power game to be transferred from the hotel rooms where ideologues of the world met to workplace-based linkages confronting international capital. E-Mail, fax, and cheap travel open up immense liberating possibilities.

A word of warning, however. These transfrontier workers' councils cannot be loose networks of activists; they need to be permanent, legal, and company-recognized bodies with—oh dreaded word—a bureaucracy, a secretariat of some sort, and, yes, here it comes, leaders: democratically accountable women and men who can articulate the needs of workers, convince other parts of society of their importance, and mobilize, in conjunction with other groups, to achieve common goals.

The four "E's"—economy, ethnicity, equality (of gender), and ecology—are often rivals in claiming priority as much as they are allies in forging complementary coalitions. Thus the process of working toward one-world community will not be conflict-free amongst supporters of the values contained in the concept. When workers assert their right to work, for instance, a clash looms at once with the new world religiosity which, in particular, has as a goal the return of womankind to *Kinder, Kuche, und Kirche.* The "rights" to smoke, to drink alcohol, to consume drugs, to have certain sexual relations (for example, with school-age boys and girls) all impinge on other sets of rights. The provision of work may run counter to the preservation of certain environments. Diversity and decentralization sound noble. Yet if city A votes for free health insurance, while city B votes to keep it private, or workplace D votes for a 35-hour week and a Friday-thru-Sunday shutdown, while workplace E votes for 20 hours of overtime a week to bump up wages, then the egoisms of localist singularity and competition are what emerge rather than agreeable Arcadian joy in differences.

But in a world of capital without frontiers, where capital penetrates each and every corner of the globe, an essential—probably the only—countervailing force must come from transfrontier organization of workers. A new world order requires new world organization of labor. Existing unions in the industrialized North have less to teach than they have to learn from opening their minds to the organizing ideas and values of the new unions. But the new unions, like the old, have no magic formula. "Don't moan, don't mourn, organize!" remains the call, now as in the past.

Opposing the New World Order in Canada

Elaine Bernard

Canada today is a country in crisis. The neoconservative policies of the federal Progressive Conservative Party are forcing a massive social and economic restructuring. Free Trade, first with the United States and eventually with the whole continent, is a cornerstone in this restructuring, along with privatization and deregulation. Under the guise of a desirable democratic goal—reducing government influence in people's lives—the Canadian federal government is signing away its power to act for the society as a whole. It is subordinating government and democratic decisionmaking to the marketplace and corporate power.

Domestically, in response to the demands of indigenous people, Quebecois, women, trade unionists, and others for social justice and inclusion in decisionmaking, the federal government has initiated a new round of constitutional reforms which threatens to permanently enshrine this business-driven restructuring of the Canadian political system. Conservative Prime Minister Brian Mulroney once boasted, "Give me ten years and you won't recognize this country." Yet, few believed that he could unravel so much of the country's social fabric in his ten years in office.

In spite of the crisis that this business/tory offensive has provoked, the Right in Canada has had a hard time in selling its neoconservative agenda. There are a number of reasons for this. First, Canadians view their society as a more compassionate society, especially when compared to their closest neighbor, the United States. In fact, a popular joke in Canada is that when U.S. President Bush said he wanted "a kinder, gentler nation," Canadians thought he meant Canada. While one should not exaggerate the compassionate image, there is some truth in it. Canada's social safety net, for example, is more generous than its U.S. counterpart. While U.S. social programs lift only one in five families above the poverty line, Canadian programs lift one in two.

Because Canadians have traditionally seen the role of the state as more than simply an instrument of big business, the Right's discrediting of an economic role for government and the attack on public enterprise have met much resistance. There is still a general acceptance in Canada of the need for an interventionist state that provides universal social programs, such as the national healthcare system, equalization programs between provinces and regions, and agricultural supply marketing boards to preserve family-run and other small farms.

A further significant factor in opposition to the neoconservative program has been the strength and mobilized opposition of the Canadian labor movement. Thirty-eight percent of the Canadian workforce is organized, as compared to only 16% in the United States. Contributing to the higher rate of unionization in Canada are more favorable labor laws, won through labor political action. But beyond the legal framework, the Canadian labor movement in recent years has evolved toward social unionism with a broad political program for all of society and away from service unionism with its narrower perspective of simply servicing its own members. Social unionism has brought organized labor into coalition with many community groups and social movements, increasing its influence in society.

As well, Canada's social democratic party, the New Democratic Party (NDP), which was co-founded by the Canadian Labor Congress, has helped to give labor a powerful voice in electoral politics. The NDP has assisted labor in defining political issues and in legitimating a working-class perspective in Canadian politics.

The continued opposition of labor and the social movements to the neoconservative agenda is why the Canada/U.S. Free Trade Agreement (FTA) is so crucial to the neoconservative program. Free Trade is a charter of rights for big business. By removing tariff and non-tariff barriers to trade with the United States, the FTA gave U.S. capital and business the same rights as Canadians to invest, divest, and receive government subsidies. It also placed trade matters under the purview of U.S. law and the supervision of a joint international board, costing Canada control over many economic matters and moving Canadian business toward economic integration with the United States.

The FTA has hamstrung future Canadian governments from taking a variety of possible initiatives to promote social equality, on the grounds that such moves would be challenged by the U.S. government and business as unfair subsidies.

Ontario, in particular, as the industrial heartland of Canada, has been adversely affected by the FTA. Canada's labor central, the Canadian

Labor Congress, has calculated that some 450,000 manufacturing jobs have been lost as a result of Free Trade. For the most part, these job losses are the result of U.S. corporations simply shutting down their Canadian branch plants and shipping products to Canada from their U.S. plants tariff-free.

In opposing Free Trade and the demands of business, a growing number of Canadians have demonstrated a new openness to the idea that the role of the state should be to assure the welfare of the citizens, not simply to create an environment within which business can prosper. This is the essence of the New Democratic Party's social democratic approach, and it appears to have found new fertile ground in recent provincial elections. Since the last federal election, the NDP has won three important provincial elections in Ontario, Saskatchewan, and British Columbia, and in 1993 52% of Canadians are governed by NDP provincial governments.

These election victories are the results of unprecedented public debates throughout the country over the last few years which have forced Canadians into a far-ranging discussion about the nature of their society, social programs, constitution, economic treaties, and, indeed, the social contract that underlies their society. But the debates, political mobilization, and coalition-building started well before the elections and have never been confined to electoral politics.

In 1987, while the Canada-U.S. Free Trade Agreement was still on the negotiating table, unionists, farmers, women, antipoverty, aboriginal, environmental, peace, church, cultural, and senior citizen's groups joined together to form a national organization—originally called the Pro-Canada Network but changing its name to the Action Canada Network (ACN)—to oppose Free Trade and to struggle against the restructuring of Canada along continentalist and market-oriented lines. Many of the groups involved in the coalition had worked together previously on single-issue campaigns in opposition to various conservative government policy initiatives. These earlier experiences allowed the coalition partners to quickly appreciate that Free Trade was part of a larger neoconservative agenda, and it allowed the ACN to quickly move beyond the narrow single-issue focus of most coalitions. The ACN has been successful in showing Canadians that the trade debate is really about undermining many of the fundamental assumptions and fabric of Canadian society. As a register of their success, recent polls show that a majority of Canadians in every region of the country are now opposed to the Free Trade deal.

Most of the groups opposed to the neoconservative program in Canada, including the ACN, recognize that while opposition is important, it is not enough. What is needed is an economic alternative to the corporate program for a low-wage, low-skill international competitive strategy. An alternative economic program, while rejecting the narrow nationalism of protectionism, must seek to assure that the people of Canada, through their democratically elected government, have sufficient powers to pursue the goal of social justice. And in this age of multinational corporations and globalization, social justice can no longer be confined to the borders of the nation-state.

The current crisis in Canada holds out the opportunity to restructure the Canadian state, not according to the dictates of business, but rather to meet the democratic and national aspirations of the population as a whole. With Quebecois demanding their right to self-determination, and a majority of Canadians now supporting indigenous people's right to self-government, Canadians have an opportunity to construct a new federal structure that assures self-government for these national groupings.

As an attempt to provide a progressive direction to this restructuring, the NDP government in Ontario has promoted the idea of a social charter as part of the constitutional reform package for Canada. Similar to an economic bill of rights, a social charter would seek to enshrine in the constitution the right of all Canadians to universal social programs, such as education, healthcare, and social insurance. In the face of a corporate agenda which seeks to "harmonize" social programs downward, the social charter proposal is an attempt to benchmark and preserve the hard-won gains made in social programs.

This crisis also offers the opportunity for the forging of new international ties and solidarity among people. While the building of ties is a dynamic process, some of the elements of this alternative strategy to the tory/business restructuring are starting to appear. Unions, such as the Canadian Auto Workers and the Communications and Electrical Workers of Canada, have forged international links for cross-border organizing campaigns. Unions and the community-based groups are discovering that international solidarity work needs to be done at a grassroots level. While national-union-to-national-union links are important, so are local-to-local, and community-to-community connections. The Action Canada Network and Common Frontiers have worked to bring together Canadian, U.S., and Mexican activists from the labor and popular movements opposed to the North American Free Trade Agreement.

In all three countries, workers are struggling with governments which have adopted neoconservative business strategies of low-wage competition. In order to reject the business program of competitiveness, though, labor and the popular movements need to develop in its place an alternative continental agreement on fair trade and development—a strategy that seeks to replace competitiveness with cooperation. This will also require considerable rethinking of the role of government and sovereignty. Social charters can play an important role. Charters as statements of agreement among movements and people, not negotiated by governments, can help promote working people's rights—and not only their political and civil rights, but also their social and economic rights.

In place of corporate whipsawing with a continued downward harmonization of wages and standards in the name of competitiveness, a social charter and cooperative strategies between workers and popular groups in all three countries can demand an upward harmonization. Canada, with its powerful united social movements and in the throes of constitutional restructuring, has a unique opportunity to lead the process of defining a new world harmony which rejects the corporate agenda of international competitiveness and in its place constructs a program of national and international cooperation which places people ahead of profits.

Ethnicity
and New Constitutive Orders
Elise Boulding

In the closing decades of the 20th century there has been an increasing unease in the relationship between the "10,000 societies"[1]—ethnically-, linguistically-, or religiously-based identity groups spread over the 168 nation-states of the contemporary world—and the states which they inhabit. Modernization theory assumes that ethnic groups will be assimilated into modern nation-states. Yet supposedly extinct ethnicities are reappearing at a rapid rate, and new ones are created as migrant streams from the Third World settle in First World societies and create new hybrid cultural identities, distinct from those of the society in which they have settled.

Strong ethnic identities are today frequently seen as a source of social disintegration, violence, and terror, a regression to a less evolved social condition. Yet over most of human history, as well as in the present, different ethnic, cultural, linguistic, and religious groups have coexisted peacefully on common or adjacent terrains. The current revival of communal identities in all nation-states, from the most to the least "developed," and even the creation of new mythical identities with no actual historical foundation, suggests that these identity groups may have an important function to serve in sustaining the social order. The resurgence may in fact be a response to the failure of the modern nation-state to meet the needs of its diverse populations—not only the need for the equitable distribution of resources and opportunities, but the need for meaning and a sense of self-worth. The widening gap between haves and have-nots within both First and Third World countries, as well as between North and South, has been well enough documented not to need elaboration here, and may in itself be a demonstration of serious inadequacies in the organizational forms of the nation-state.

Identity groups are to varying degrees storehouses of folk wisdom and technical problem-solving skills that increase the chances of survival for their members within polities where they are disadvantaged. These skills include conflict resolution skills for use with group members and with outsiders, and knowledge of how to use environmental resources, rural or urban. That wisdom/skill complex may undergo distortion and even degeneration in interaction with an indifferent or hostile state. If this is true, a viable political future for the 21st century may depend on a new constitutive order substantially modified from the present nation-state system, one that permits much wider participation of identity groups in shaping the polities of which they are a part. The intense and continuing efforts to evolve new constitutional formats in countries with strong identity groups like Canada, Switzerland, Belgium, Spain, the former Soviet Union, and other Eastern European countries, as well as in a number of countries of the South, including Nigeria, Sudan, Malaysia, and India, may be harbingers of a new, more democratic, and more peaceful constitutive order of the 21st century.[2]

Ethnic groups are usually studied as oppressed minorities, or sometimes as oppressing elites. They may also be referred to as nationalities, cultures, or linguistic groupings. Sometimes the ethnicity is in fact a religiously-based cultural form. I will use the term identity group to refer to all groups that have some sense of common history and common fate, recognizing that the common history may be at least in part mythical. Identity groups may or may not be territorially based, and most of them spill over the boundaries of several states. Historically the best known nonterritorial identity groups have been Gypsies and Jews, who can be found on all continents, but now more and more identity groups have subgroup settlements in both hemispheres. The boundaries of identity groups are fluid and change over time, as the consciousness of historical roots and common fate heighten or fade according to social conditions.

Identity Groups: Problem-solving and Conflict Resolution

Identity groups can be thought of as trust groups, mini-societies in which there is mutual respect, some degree of social equality, mutual aid, and regular intergenerational communication. Group practices celebrate a shared history, strengthen communal identity, and provide meaning for life as lived in the present, as well as some degree of predictability for the future. Most identity groups provide the opportunity for regular sharing in neighborhood and locality to their members, although some groups may have members living in widely scattered locations.

Kin relations, actual or fictive, and the family unit, however defined (it may be single-sexed, as in monasteries or lesbian/gay communities; it may be one-, two-, or three-generational), are important to identity groups. The commitment to nurturance and support across generations, the recognition of the individuality of each person and their special place in the family unit, the care taken of children, and the ever-present necessity for conflict resolution whenever human beings live in close proximity to each other, produce in each culture unique patterns of intra-familial and community interaction. Except under conditions of great threat and hardship, and sometimes even then, these patterns have certain characteristics of peaceableness. Challenges from the larger environment, when they are not overwhelming, generate creative problem-solving behavior.

The matter of scale is critical here. The intimate knowledge of local terrains possessed by members of folk societies has been discovered by modern science only recently. Today there are intensive efforts to study the folk agricultural practices, aquaculture, pisciculture, sylviculture, medicinal knowledge, and varieties of traditional crafts, all representing more or less sophisticated knowledge systems developed in some cases over thousands of years. It is not just traditional technologies that are important, however. Wherever identity groups are located, whether in forests, mountains, deserts, islands, or modern cities, they develop adaptive practices that not only enable the group to survive but contribute to the functioning of the larger society. This adaptiveness and creativity is released within a setting small enough to give feedback about how its members are doing, in a setting that supports people economically and psychologically through failures as well as successes. The nation-state does not do this for its citizens. In theory every state provides a safety net, but the holes are so large, both in market and centrally planned economies, that non-mainstream populations fall through the net to sink or swim. Identity groups help their members to swim.

Every identity group has its wise elders, its peacemakers, its negotiators. It also has its troublemakers and violence-prone elements. When an identity group is healthy and in some kind of balance with the larger society, it contains aggression and violence within limits, since violence is clearly self-damaging. But oppression of identity groups is increasing; injustice piles on injustice, to the point where the 20th century has been called "the bloody century." Violence cannot always be contained in the face of escalating wrongs. That is why it is time to explore a new constitutive order, with a place for identity groups as co-shapers of their polity.

One of the most difficult aspects of contemporary life is that individuals and groups are continually having to interact with others who are strangers to them in contexts where little or no possibility of the development of trust arises. Michael Barkun describes how acephalous or leaderless societies are able to live at peace with one another without formal structures to facilitate that peace. He points out that interactions with neighboring groups develop slowly over time, so that familiar routines can be established with the stranger, and the necessary minimum of trust is created. If societies are thrown too rapidly into too close a contact with neighboring societies, new habits of interaction cannot be developed fast enough and violence results. That is the plight of every modern society, industrial or not. When Ferdinand Tönnies wrote about the transition from the *Gemeinschaft*, or community-based society, to the *Gesellschaft*, or contract society, he warned that it would be necessary to continue to develop *Gemeinschaft* relationships within the contract society—that contractual relations could not bear the full weight of human needs for recognition and support.

Identity groups, to the extent that they are able, still practice the traditional trust-establishing ways of dealing with the stranger, and there is no reason why these should not be more widely recognized and accommodated. The Bedouin, meeting a stranger in the desert, feeds her first and asks no questions until an interpersonal relationship has been established through conversation. Some tribes have the practice, when a stranger looms on the horizon, of sending one person out to greet her, and to engage in a dialogue about places and people until some contact point through mutual knowledge of a person, place, or event has been established. If none can be discovered, the two in dialogue create a fictive point of contact. The point of contact established, the greeter brings the stranger back to the group and introduces her; she can then be welcomed as a distant relative, a member of the tribal family. Anyone who has been welcomed as a stranger into an ethnic enclave community in any city anywhere in the world knows the warmth of this type of welcome. Such practices are an important resource in an anomic world.

The point here is not to romanticize ethnic communities. Many have fled them, feeling smothered in their embrace. They practice their own cruelties, and women in particular may be very downtrodden—a situation that does not only happen in modernization-distorted traditional societies. Creative interaction with the larger society limits, modifies, and will eventually erase these cruelties. That is what the worldwide human rights movement is about. But increasingly it is being realized that human rights include group rights, and the right of identity groups to evolve and change *as groups*.

Having considered identity groups within countries, let us look at what has happened to the modern state itself, examining the problems to which identity groups possibly can contribute a solution.

The Modern State: A Vision of Peace and Justice?

The Hague Peace Conference that ushered in the 20th century affirmed a world in which nation-states would no longer use war as an instrument of diplomacy. Not only was war to be abolished, but poverty and disease as well, as Andrew Carnegie optimistically instructed his board of directors when the Carnegie Foundation for Enduring Peace was established in 1911. World War I was a regrettable error, but the vision in the 1920s was once again of a world of peace and justice for all, specifically affirming the self-determination of nationalities. The problem was that for the Eurocentric world holding this vision, the world of the South was a vast blur of land to be colonized, resources to be used for the advancement of (European) prosperity, and peoples to be eventually civilized. There was no recognition of the existence of autonomous nationalities, cultures, and civilizations. The universalism of that era was a false universalism.

The second "mistake" of European culture, World War II, was fought to a not insignificant degree on the peripheries of Europe by the soldiers of the colonized South for the European masters. In its aftermath there was a discovery of the South as peoples with their own agendas. New human rights concepts delegitimized colonialism, so the old colonies were turned into nation-states by definition, regardless of the crazy patchwork of nationalities inhabiting each former colony. Given a voice and the forum of the United Nations, coalitions from the South including the Nonaligned movement and the Group of 77 (now 120 states) kept calling attention to more and more peoples who should be liberated— the island colonies, the trust territories—even while holding on to their own patchwork of nationalities as now legitimate states. The last liberated African trust territory, Namibia, gained independence in 1990; several nations, including the United States and France, however, hold on to island trust territories in the Pacific.

Conventional political theory declares that the long journey from primitive, fractious tribalism to the highly evolved modern nation-state in which tribalism has been absorbed into a new type of citizenship guaranteeing rights, security, and welfare for all, has essentially been completed, in Euro-North America at least. True, the newer states of the South are still troubled by tribalism, but in time they will assimilate their populations as the industrial democracies have done. The emerging modern world system, already at peace in a temperate zone triangle including Australia, Japan, North America, and Western Europe,[3] will be able to relinquish a highly technologized national military alliance system once the former communist states have been absorbed into the world market economy. We are moving toward a world at peace.

The reality that shadows this optimistic picture is that there have been more wars in the 20th century than in the 18th and the 19th centuries combined. As Ruth Sivard has documented, there have been 127 wars since World War II, compared to 88 in the 40 years before that war. Only two of these have been in Europe; most of the other 125 have involved ethnic disputes exacerbated by great power involvement. This means that the world political map has been in more or less constant upheaval during this period. The Eurocentric triangle never was really free of it, but now the struggles are physically entering home territory with the breakdown of the artificial distinction between East and West Europe.

Not only has the modern nation-state system been unable to reduce the havoc caused by war, but it also has been unable to close the poverty gap. The 25% of the global population estimated by Gurr and Scarritt to be minorities at risk[4], peoples experiencing serious deprivation in relation to fellow citizens of a given state, provide a rough indicator of the failure of the nation-state to reduce poverty, victimization, and oppression within its borders. When we learn that 44.9% of the population of Africa south of the Sahara are minorities at risk, no one is surprised—these are not yet "developed" states. But what of the 21 minorities in 13 West European countries, 7.8% of the total population, who are at risk? What of the eight minorities in four North American countries, 15.8% of the population, who are at risk?

As migrant populations move from one region to another trying to escape poverty, and as the 30-million-strong (and growing) refugee stream seeks to escape ethnic and political victimization, the number of identity groups needing accommodation on the planet will increase, Lance Clark argues. Referring to them as minority groups can be misleading, as it suggests they are groups that happen not yet to have been successfully assimilated, but will eventually be absorbed into the national societies where they are settled. It also suggests that there are ethnic groups as opposed to non-ethnic mainstream populations. A more realistic approach would be to think of "minority" groups as differentially treated communal groups in a universe of 10,000 communal groups—

recognizing that everyone belongs to an identity group (sometimes more than one). Majority or mainstream communal groups such as Anglo Saxons are ethnics too, with various subcultures (such as WASP, a categorization used mainly by non-Anglos), but no longer identify their own ethnicity because they think of themselves as "the people" of their country.

The fluidity, shifting character, and sheer numbers of identity groups make it difficult to discuss them in well-defined analytic categories. To a considerable extent they are self-defined, and most of them are primarily oriented toward cultural identity and the protection of their rights as a group to share in the benefits of the state in which they live. However an increasing number are seeking various forms of political recognition and political autonomy as the state fails to respond to their needs. Whether it is the nationalist movements in the Celtic fringe of Great Britain—Scotland, Wales, and Northern Ireland,[5] or the Celtic fringe in France and Spain—Breton and Basque—or the Sardinians of Italy, the Sami (Lapps) in Norway, the native peoples in the Americas, the French in Canada, or the host of dissatisfied ethnic groups in Eastern Europe and the former Soviet Union, the story is always the same: each group is being denied some of the economic, social, and cultural opportunities available to other populations in the state in question. If the trend were toward a diminution of the number and activity levels of alienated identity groups, one could say that the state is evolving in the direction of more effective functioning to provide more equal opportunity for its member populations. The trend, however, is in the opposite direction, toward an increase in the number and intensity of these groups.

The Search for a New Constitutive Order and Local Autonomy

What is not generally recognized is that a number of states, both old and new, are realizing the impossibility of effective administration at the national level of very heterogeneous populations, cultures, and ethnicities. These countries are engaged in various efforts to modify their constitutional structures to maintain the boundaries of the existing state while recognizing the right of certain numerically significant member populations to make decisions concerning resource allocation and social welfare of their own people. This means shifting the locus of authority downward to regional and local units, following the principle of "subsidiarity." Subsidiarity calls for decisionmaking to be exercised as close to the locus of the actual activity being decided as possible. Some examples will be given of these constitutional explorations. An enormous amount of effort is required to achieve modifications of this kind, involving protracted negotiation and continuing conflict resolution. There are no easy alternatives to dispute settlement by military force. Yet to achieve the high goals set for the world by leaders of nation-states at the beginning of this century, this path of protracted negotiation is the most likely path to a peaceful world order.

Constitutional Status of Nationalities in Europe

The examples that follow include political entities that were once old states or empires and became modernizing states that were to merge older ethnic identities in a new state identity in the 19th century. They have been chosen because each has subsequently undertaken some constitutional modification to deal with communal entities within their borders. They are only examples, not a complete listing. The United Kingdom, which is struggling mightily with the issue of the necessary constitutional modifications to deal with Northern Ireland, is, for example, not included. Those European countries that have differentiated communal groups but have not as yet needed to utilize constitutional modification in relating to them are not discussed. Neither are two other categories of differentiated communal groups, migrant workers and refugees; their situation would require another paper.

The most glaring omission is the states of the former Soviet Union. The original version of this chapter, written in 1989, contained a section on the national territorial formations representing a few of the 128 ethnic groups in the USSR as it still existed in 1989, and a discussion of Valerii Tishkov's thinking about creative constitutive formats for ethnic-cultural and political autonomy. Given the extreme complexity of the present situation, with ethnicities asserting themselves at a rate and with a vigor that defies the problem-solving capacities of the new states, no attempt could be made to briefly update that section.

Consociational democracy,[6] as contrasted to majority rule democracy, depends on the segmentation of society into vertical groups which are thus not constantly rubbing shoulders over issues that could generate conflict. Only the leaders of the different groups interact, on the basis of an overarching consensus. Power sharing and divisions of jurisdiction are key characteristics of the consociational model.

Switzerland is often referred to as the prototype of this model. The Swiss Confederation of 23 sovereign cantons of which three are divided into six half-cantons, with four official languages, has its origins in the Middle Ages. It took centuries of warfare and ethnic hostility to achieve the present federation, which has limited powers in relation to the cantons and fairly frequent national referenda, yet has played a very important role as a neutral country in this century. The level of negotiation required to make the federation work, village by village and canton by canton, is very high, but is something in which the Swiss take pride. Equality of economic status has been a continuing issue, and one which has been dealt with more or less successfully through regional specialization. Currently the French-speaking Jura district within the bilingual Bern canton is asking for its own canton, feeling discriminated against by the German majority, so the process of building the Swiss constitutive order still goes on.

Belgium, an independent country since 1830, has struggled for a century with ethnic separatism, stemming from Flemish economic deprivation compared to the French-speaking Walloons. Three cultural community regions have been created over the past 20 years through constitutional engineering, altering profoundly the institutions, jurisdictions, and responsibilities of the state. Each citizen must now be a member of a Dutch, French, or minority German-speaking community; regional governments function in Flanders, Wallonia, and Brussels. Current ethnic power-sharing agreements of a very complex nature require constant negotiation, bilingual Dutch-French conduct of all government affairs, and a careful respect for each identity group's needs. The fact that Belgium has had 32 governments since World War II indicates how difficult the coalition process is. A recent reversal of previous economic advantage as between the Flamands and the Walloons is currently requiring a whole new set of negotiations to redress new imbalances.

In *Spain*, whose predominant identity groups are Spanish, Basque, Catalan, and Galician, the Basques and the Catalans have had autonomous regions since 1979. This was the result of long and, for the Basques, violent autonomy struggles. Economic difficulties have been met by intense educational and cultural development in each province in its national language. Catalonia in particular has a very advanced economic, social, and cultural planning and development process under way, and publishes an English-Catalan magazine, *Catalonia*, to describe the autonomous region's achievements. It will be interesting to see whether these efforts, accompanied by increasing regional pride and economic initiatives, will solve the problems that the central government of Spain failed to solve. Success depends, in fact, on the cooperation of the central government with the region's development plans. How cooperative the central government will be is not yet clear.[7]

Italy, dealing with a well-organized autonomy movement in the South Tyrol, first created an autonomous region in 1947. In the face of vigorous local campaigns including terrorism, the national government repaired the inadequacies of the 1947 arrangement with a revised autonomy statute in 1972. The economic provisions of the revised statute, bolstered by educational and judicial autonomy, have been particularly important in freeing local initiatives for economic development. Full bilingualism has not yet been achieved, however, and the long process of negotiation between the autonomous province and the Italian government continues.

In each of the examples mentioned, the constitutional modifications to meet the needs of communal groups within the country's borders have been undertaken in a context of increasing the viability of the state itself. The state has been able to maintain the allegiance of these communal groups through providing them with the means to take more initiatives to shape their life conditions. Far from heralding a regression into communal warfare, these modifications have made it possible for a diverse society to establish some minimal common identity while giving space for the diversity of its members.

South Asia

The states to be discussed here were all colonies of modernizing European states in the 19th century. The new states' horror of communalism as a basis for political organization is based to a significant degree on the doctrines of the European colonizers. Communalism and tribalism were seen as the great enemies of modernization and political maturity. As the colonies became independent, each state tried to establish a national identity based on colonial borders into which communal identities could be assimilated, regardless of the pre-existing geographical distribution of the communal groups. The complexities of the political situations that followed can barely be touched on here. In the worst cases, all-out communal warfare has replaced earlier patterns of coexistence and is threatening to destroy the post-colonial states. In the best cases, older patterns of coexistence have been translated into negotiated inter-communal political coalitions with some promise of stability. It is useful to remember that, in general, the European states have had much longer to negotiate their coalitions. (It took centuries for Switzerland.)

Sri Lanka,[8] it has often been noted, was thought to have the best prospects of any Asian nation for developing a peaceful, prosperous civil order at the time of its independence from Great Britain in 1948. Hindu and Muslim Tamils predominated in certain areas, Buddhist Sinhalese in other areas. With vastly different languages and cultures, there was nevertheless enough mutual respect to make the prospect of peaceful coexistence in the new state likely. Minority northern Tamils through the advantages of missionary education in the English language represented the majority of the Western-oriented elite of the country, and the Buddhists were a 75% non-Western demographic majority. The Tamils were nervous about the Sinhalese majority, and indeed the first election after independence brought precisely the feared majority into power. The new government promptly made Sinhalese (which most Tamils do not speak) the official language of the state, and the percentage of Tamils allowed in the universities was reduced. In general, the Sinhalese sought to eradicate the colonial heritage, which meant eradicating what advantages the English-speaking Tamils had. The 1972 constitution exacerbated Tamil fears by mandating special protection for the Buddhist religion. The Sinhalese government, recognizing the problem for Tamils, had indeed tried to address their concerns by devolving state power to the provinces (Tamils were the majority in the northern and eastern provinces). But Sinhalese public opinion and powerful Buddhist groups strongly opposed these efforts. Ethnic hostilities increased to the point that by the early 1980s a full-blown war of secession was going on that has so far resisted all attempts at outside mediation and internal negotiation. There has been such a fractioning of Tamil groups, and such a hardening of positions on all sides, that experienced negotiators do not see any resolution of this conflict in the near future.

Malaysia [9] came to independence as Malaya in 1957 (and later as the Federation of Malaysia in 1963) as a deeply divided multi-ethnic society with 50% Malay, 37% Chinese, 11% Indian, and 2% "other." Ethnic cleavages are compounded by language, religious, and cultural differences. The Malays consider themselves the indigenous inhabitants, and the Chinese have traditionally dominated major sectors of the economy. There has been communal violence at regular intervals since 1945. However, an expanding economy brought a degree of prosperity from the 1950s on, and there has been room for Malays to do well without making inroads on Chinese economic turf. Wise management of ethnic confrontations in the 1950s and emphasis by the British on educating an indigenous administration to manage health, education, and community services left the newly independent country with competent administrators in 1963, and a lot of experience in inter-ethnic compromise. While the Malays had the numerical majority, the Chinese were a significant part of the electorate—and a permanent multi-ethnic coalition was developed even before independence. The Malays, the economically disadvantaged group, realized very early that they could not get what they wanted without the help of the Chinese, and vice versa. Unlike the Sinhalese, who wrote Tamil participation out of political life, the Malays drafted a language act providing for continued use of English, Chinese, and Tamil. The Chinese in turn were willing to support an augmentation of Malay economic resources. A combination of luck and some good negotiating skills created a direction that led from ethnic violence to relative ethnic peace. Continued negotiation is very important in maintaining the present political stability. Pressures and hostilities are not absent, but they are contained in a skillful political coalition.

India, Pakistan, Bangladesh

Nowhere in the world has the colonial imprint on traditional multi-ethnic societies created a more continuously contentious situation than in the region of pre-World War II British India—now the three states of India, Pakistan, and Bangladesh. The initial partition of India into India and Pakistan in 1947 was bathed in blood from the start, and at the time of this writing another war looms between these states over the disputed area of Kashmir.

Independent *India* was a determined modernizer. It reorganized the 560 native states that came into the new India, either merging them with adjacent provinces, converting them into centrally administered areas, or grouping them into unions of states. By 1956 another reorganization abolished the unions of states and merged all formerly native states either into one of 15 states, or into one of eight centrally administered areas. In 1962 a sixteenth state was created, and in 1966 the Punjab was partitioned in two states, making a total of 18 states; the annexation of Sikkhim in 1975 made 19 states. These arbitrary reorganizations disadvantaged economically, socially, and politically the majority of communal grouping thus swallowed up. The religious divisions, 83% Hindu, 11% Islam, 3% Christian, and 2% Sikh, don't even scratch the surface of India's ethnic, linguistic, and cultural identity groups. The forced assimilations did not succeed. India's commitment to liberating East Pakistanis from West Pakistan by military might (in what is now Bangladesh) destroyed the possibility of a solid negotiating relationship with Pakistan. Thus the land of Gandhi has, since his death, a poor track record in the negotiation of internal and external differences, and faces more or less continuous communal rioting at the beginning of the 1990s. Grassroots movements to resolve communal differences may in the long run succeed where the government so far has failed.

Pakistan has an even worse track record, but has only three major communal groups challenging the domination of the majority Punjabis. The problem is that these three communal groups (Baluchi, Sindhi,

Pushtun), while only 30% of the population, claim 72% of the land as historically theirs for the past 5,000 to 10,000 years.[10] So far the claims are simply dismissed: for the Punjabis, there can only be one unitary state. Only the Baluchi, however, are considering a war of secession. The other two groups would settle for substantial political and economic autonomy. At issue for these minorities is the need for a larger share of the royalties on natural resources extracted from "their" land, and control over outside entrepreneurial and governmental economic enterprises.

The only hope for either of these two states, and for impoverished Bangladesh as well, is much more constitutional compromise within each state, and a rejection of the current win-lose stance in bilateral relations. This must be replaced by a willingness to negotiate outcomes that will advantage all parties instead of only some.

It is not that bargaining cultures do not exist in these societies, but rather that they never had a chance politically in the particular historical context of the India-Pakistan partition.

Africa

Nigeria is an instructive example of a multi-ethnic society that went through civil war and came out the other side determined to arrange a constitutive order that would keep the state together within its colonial-defined borders.[11] This most populous state of black Africa is a "nation of nations," with from 200 to 400 ethnic groups, depending on how one counts them, with 10 major groups accounting for 90% of the population. Since independence in 1960 it has developed structurally from three regions to the present 21 states, alternating between centralized military rule and decentralized civilian rule. A three-year civil war ended in 1970 with the successful reintegration of the secessionist Ibos into the federal republic. Because of the strength of the traditional emirate subculture, there is a remarkably effective capacity for local government linked to federal structures in a complex linkage system with both vertical and horizontal components. There is much political creativity in Nigerian society, as well as much conflict. The current stage in the new constitutive order, being prepared for with a return to civilian government, has involved the election of 301 local governmental authorities in the transition period.

In Nigeria a Westernized elite and traditional tribal leaders have mingled in ways that they have not in other former colonies. Traditional tribal leaders have been given a share in the national economic pie, and Westernized elites consider traditional tribal titles a valuable asset, so there are many cross-ties between ethnic groups and between federal and local authority-holders based on access to a combination of traditional and modern statuses and roles. The role of tribal elders in conflict resolution, widely recognized locally and nationally, has played a key part in Nigeria's continuity as a nation of nations through a succession of military and civilian governments. Multiple legal systems flexibly administered and flexibly available to requesting citizens supplement the informal tribal elder system of conflict resolution. There is no lack of tension and conflict in the society, but the social resources for dealing with them are sufficiently abundant that Nigeria looks like a model multi-ethnic society worth studying in considerable detail.

Sudan, the largest country on the African continent, rich in resources and traditions, has been in the throes of civil war for most of the years since its independence in 1955.[12] A superficial look suggests an industrialized Arab North exploiting an undeveloped tribal South, but the reality is much more complex. The exploitation is real enough: the mineral resources from the South fuel the factories of the North. However, populations of both North and South are highly diverse. There are 100 languages and about 40 different cultures, with an Arab admixture in both regions. The educational level in the English-speaking South is as high or higher than in the Arab-speaking North. The South, which had been "protected" from Arab incursions during the colonial era, entered independence expecting equal power sharing with the North under a new constitution. However, the earlier period of protectionism left the North looking down on the South and unwilling to share power on an equal basis. Efforts on the part of an authoritarian northern leader, Nimeiry, to enforce Islamic law on the entire nation was not in fact a true northern issue, since many northerners rejected the Islamicization of the Sudan, preferring a secular state.

The war being waged by the South is for a unified Sudan, and for the long-promised constitutional convention, while the governing powers in the North prefer separate states—an unusual twist in ethnic relations. Because the range of ethnic diversity is similar in North and South, and there are educated elites with common interests in both North and South (contrary to appearances), it has been suggested that serious negotiations would reveal those common interests and enable the construction of a constitution which provided for multi-ethnic power sharing. However, the sheer dynamics of protracted conflict may weaken the negotiating capacities of the society so that it gradually fractionates and loses its potential as a viable multi-ethnic society.

In the Asian and African countries we have examined, we have seen that a plurality of cultures need not impede the formation of a stable nation-state if these cultures are recognized, respected, and brought into active power sharing, on the basis of continual negotiation. When historical circumstances erode mutual respect and when negotiating relationships to achieve an appropriate constitutive order cannot be maintained, the state is not viable.

The Americas

Since the importance of negotiating skills, mutual respect, and creativity in modifying the constitutive order has been established in our examples from Europe, Asia, and Africa, I will here only comment briefly on the American scene. A very instructive effort to create a new constitutive order is going on among the ten states in the *Canadian Federation* at the present time.[13] The principle of the multi-ethnic state was affirmed some years ago with the establishment of a ministry for multicultural affairs. However, the formula for the constitutive order, whether in relation to native peoples or French-speaking Quebec, continues to elude lawmakers. Considering how many years of negotiation have been required to work out similar types of arrangements in European plural societies, and how much negotiation is required to sustain new arrangements once agreed upon, it was probably unrealistic of Canadians to think they could romp through the process of a constitutional amendment as quickly as they originally had planned.

The *United States* is still characterized by a melting-pot outlook, and is a long way from being prepared to modify the constitutive order to allow, for example, for bilingual instruction in bilingual states (such as the Southwest with its substantial Hispanic minorities). Only Louisiana, with its French Acadian heritage, has recognized a second language, French, as a mandatory language in the state elementary and secondary schools. The Bureau of Indian Affairs, while it deals with the rights of native peoples, is hardly an example of power sharing. Treaty rights negotiated by native peoples with the U.S. government in the previous century are being continually abrogated or ignored, and are the subject of more or less continuous litigation.[14]

The native peoples of *Central* and *Latin America* are in very early stages of negotiation with governments about their communal rights. Power sharing is a long way off. Unless negotiation with communal groups is undertaken seriously, on the basis of respect for the negotiating partner, relations between ethnicities in the Americas may deteriorate in the coming decades as certain communal groups become increasingly aware of missed opportunities.

Plural Societies in the 21st Century

Pluralism and diversity and accompanying political manifestations will increase, not decrease, in the 21st century. They will increase partly for the following reasons: communal groups provide identity, meaning, and a sense of self-worth to their members; they offer a more manageable scale of management of human affairs; the knowledge of local terrains makes such groups more effective in problem solving; and their cultural knowledge stock and special skills offer problem solving and conflict resolution capabilities that are not available at the national level.

This increasing pluralism will be furthered by the continuing development of human rights concepts and norms, including group rights, and the heightened levels of awareness—associated with the 1990s United Nations Decade for World Cultural Development—of the diverse cultural patterns that give meaning to people's lives. The Decade's research, teaching, and human exploration of the "10,000 societies" will give further positive meaning to communal identities as sources of cultural enrichment for the world society of the future.

One to-be-hoped-for outcome of the research will be greater awareness of the variety of constitutional arrangements for power sharing to be found in pluralistic societies. All of the arrangements we have examined have involved either territorial federations, or a variety of formulae for proportional representation which give opportunities for the political participation of all parties/communal groups of a specified minimum size within the state. A parliamentary system facilitates power sharing in a way that presidential, majority-rule systems do not. However, not all pluralistic societies have formal power-sharing arrangements. Some arrangements are informal, and seem to work. Sometimes the demands for participation by communal groups are met by cultural councils, such as territorial councils for guest workers in certain European countries.

No one set of conditions or arrangements guarantees successful power-sharing. Economic prosperity may help, but is not critical; the absence of a strong dominant group helps, but is also not critical. What does seem to be critical is the willingness to negotiate, to respect the other. Patience and the willingness to take the long view, to spend lots of time on process, is a key factor.[15] Industrial societies do not have much of a culture of patience, and the other set of major actors on the world stage not discussed in this chapter, the multinational corporations, do not contribute much patience either.

There is one encouraging aspect to the contemporary scene, however. The roles of nation-state and corporation alike are being increasingly modified by the growth of international nongovernmental organizations—NGOs—which have multiplied from 200 at the beginning of the century to 18,000 today. They offer both horizontal and vertical linkages within and between countries, independent of the action of the states they span. They act in the human interest, on a human scale, and are already actively engaged in community education, dialogue, and negotiation in many areas where there are serious communal conflicts. In fact, a 1978 count[16] indicated that there were 65 NGOs with branches in 44 countries whose primary purpose was to support separatist or cultural autonomy movements. If there were 65 in 1978, there are many more now. The World Conference of Indigenous Peoples is a good example of an NGO that provides a global network to support native peoples in their local settings around the world. It might be said that the world's polities are coming full circle from tribal-local to global-local formations.

In conclusion, the nation-states of the 21st century will not only be characterized by a greater variety of constitutional arrangements for participation of diverse identity groups within their borders, they also will work more interactively with NGOs and with inter-governmental organizations (IGOs) and the many UN bodies that also crisscross national boundaries. With more vertical and horizontal linkages across borders, and more emphasis on local initiative, one could hope for a gradual transformation of the state from an instrument of military force to a facilitating partner in global networks pursuing an unimaginable variety of peaceable human adventures.

Notes

1. The "10,000 societies" is a term loosely used by some anthropologists. According to Nietschmann, quoted in Gurr, Ted and James Scarritt, "Minorities Rights at Risk: A Global Survey," Human Rights Quarterly, 11, (1989), p. 375: there are "5,000 distinct communities in the contemporary world [that] might claim that they are national peoples on grounds that they share common ancestry, institutions, beliefs, language and territory." In a 1979 study, I identified 6,276 significant ethnic groups in 159 countries (Boulding, Elise, "Ethnic Separation and World Development," in *Research in Social Movements, Conflicts and Change*, Vol. 2, CT: JAL Press, 1979, p. 276). How many groups you find obviously depends on how you count them.

2. See Boulding, E.; Brown, David, "Ethnic Revival: Perspectives on State and Society," *Third World Quarterly,* October 1989, pp. 1-17; Clay, Jason, "Epilogue: The Ethnic Future of Nations," *Third World Quarterly,* October 1989, pp. 223-233; and Ra'anan, Uri, "The Nation State Fallacy," in *Conflict and Peacemaking in Multi-Ethnic Societies,* Montville, Joseph, ed., Lexington, MA: DC Heath & Co., 1989. pp. 5-20.

3. Boulding, Kenneth, *Stable Peace,* Austin, TX: University of Texas Press, 1978.

4. The term "minorities at risk" comes from the Gurr and Scarritt study of 261 non-sovereign peoples who are both numerically significant and accorded separate and unequal treatment.

5. Hechter, Michael, *Internal Colonialism: The Celtic Fringe in British National Development, 1536-1966,* Berkeley: University of California Press, 1975.

6. For recent analysis of the consociational democracies discussion, see *Catalonia Culture,* (Barcelona), 15 (September 1989) on Linguistic Normalization, and 16 (November 1989) on Territorial Planning and Public Works; Eyck, F. Gunther, "South Tyrol and Multi-ethnic Relationships," in *Conflict and Peacemaking,* pp. 219-238; Heisler, Martin, "Hyphenating Belgium: Changing State and Regime to Cope with Cultural Division," in *Conflict and Peacemaking,* pp. 177-196; and Steiner, Jurg, "Power-Sharing: Another Swiss Export?" in *Conflict and Peacemaking,* pp. 107-114.

7. France, which has overlapping ethnic groups with Spain, has so far been able to avoid the issue of autonomous regions and to deal with its ethnics primarily at the cultural level by recognizing four regional languages for instructional purposes in the schools: Breton, Basque, Catalan, and Occitan.

8. For recent analysis of Sri Lanka, see Horowitz, Donald, "Incentive and Behavior in the Ethnic Politics of Sri Lanka and Malaysia," *Third World Quarterly,* October 1989, pp. 18-35, and Horowitz, Donald, "Making Moderation Pay: The Comparative Politics of Ethnic Conflict Management," in *Conflict and Peacemaking,* pp. 451-476; Stubbs, Richard, "Malaysia: Avoiding Ethnic Strife in a Deeply Divided Society," in *Conflict and Peacemaking,* pp. 287-300; and Sundarem, Jomo, "Malaysia's New Economic Policy and National Unity," *Third World Quarterly,* October 1989, pp. 36-53.

9. For a recent analysis of Malaysia, see ibid.

10. Harrison, Selig, "Ethnic Conflict in Pakistan: The Baluchi, Pushtun, and Sindhis," in *Conflict and Peacemaking,* pp. 301-326.

11. Nolutshungu, Sam, "Fragments of a Democracy: Reflections on Class and Politics in Nigeria," *Third World Quarterly,* January 1990, pp. 86-115; and Paden, John, "National System Development and Conflict Resolution in Nigeria," in *Conflict and Peacemaking,* pp. 411-432.

12. Deng, Francis, "The Identity Factor in the Sudanese Conflict," in *Conflict and Peacemaking*, pp. 342-362; and Kasfir, Nelson, "Peacemaking and Social Cleavages in Sudan," in *Conflict and Peacemaking*, pp. 363-388.

13. Maly, Stephen, "In a State of Ambiguity," letter 504-7, Hanover, NH: Institute of Current World Affairs, 26 January 1990; and McRae, Kenneth D., "Canada: Reflections of Two Conflicts," in *Conflict and Peacemaking*, pp. 197-218.

14. Deloria, Vine, *We Talk, You Listen, New Tribes, New Turf,* New York: Macmillan, 1970.

15. Horowitz; Lijphart, Arend, "The Power Sharing Approach," in *Conflict and Peacemaking*, pp. 491-511.

16. Boulding, E., p. 276.

References

Barkun, Michael, *Law without Sanctions: Order in Primitive Societies and the World Community*. New Haven, CT: Yale University Press, 1968.

Clark, Lance, *Early Warning of Refugee Flows*. Washington, D.C.: Refugee Policy Group, 1989.

Heisler, Martin, "Hyphenating Belgium: Changing State and Regime to Cope with Cultural Division," in *Conflict and Peacemaking,* pp. 177-196.

Information Please Almanac, Atlas and Yearbook, 42nd ed. Boston, MA: Houghton Mifflin, 1989.

Montville, Joseph, ed., *Conflict and Peacemaking in Multi-Ethnic Societies*. Lexington, MA: DC Heath & Co., 1989.

Pfaffenberger, Bryan, "Sri Lanka: The Social Origins of Tamil Separation," in *Conflict and Peacemaking*, pp. 214-258.Ra'anan, Uri, "The Nation State Fallacy," in *Conflict and Peacemaking*, pp. 5-20.

Singer, Marshall, "Prospects for Conflict Management in the Sri Lankan Ethnic Crisis," in *Conflict and Peacemaking*, pp. 259-286.

Sivard, Ruth, *World Military and Social Expenditures,* 13th ed., Washington, DC: World Priorities, 1989.

Tishkov, Valerii, "Glasnost and Nationalities within the Soviet Union," *Third World Quarterly,* October 1989, pp. 191-207.

Tönnies, Ferdinand, *Community and Society,* trans. Charles Loomis, New York: Harper & Row, 1976.

Cross-Boundary Sub-States

Jack D. Forbes

A great many national, ethnic, and language groups do not possess their own sovereign states. Many do not even control local units of government or, if they do, these units may be devoid of genuine authority. A large number of such groups are divided by inter-state ("international") boundaries and are prevented from exercising ethnic unity.

Much of the world's warfare and unrest arises from a failure to find means, short of war, for resolving the problems of stateless nationalities, linguistic minorities, and ethnic groups. One has only to list the locations of current or recent wars—Yugoslavia, Turkey, Iran, Iraq, Israel-Palestine, Northern Ireland, Nigeria-Biafra, Uganda, Georgia, Zimbabwe, Somalia, Eritrea-Ethiopia, Sudan, Sahara, Chad, Azerbaijan, South Africa, Timor, West Papua, Mindanao, Guatemala, Spain, Corsica, Angola, Namibia—to realize the human and material cost of thwarted ethnicity.

Unfortunately, the breaking up of the great modern European empires has failed to solve this problem. Most independent states in the Americas possess boundaries which cut across ethnic groups; modern Africa is especially notable for its arbitrary, counter-ethnic borders; few of the states of Eastern Europe or the successor states of the Soviet Union are comprised of a single ethnic group.

An obvious answer for the problems of ethnic minorities and stateless nationalities is, of course, war or armed rebellion. But such violence has not been notably effective in the last few decades. Most modern states possess the military might for inflicting devastation on rebels and ultimately suppressing rebellions. Few states will voluntarily allow an ethnic minority to secede or allow a neighboring nationality to have so much as an inch of state territory. Some means short of war or armed violence must be found to defuse explosive minority situations and to provide some degree of unification and meaningful self-determination for stateless nationalities and other groups divided by international boundaries.

Everyone understands that a given state may contain within its external boundaries units of government which exercise their authority separate from that of the central state. In some "federal" states, the subordinate units possess constitutionally guaranteed powers; in other states, the separate powers are derived from ancient charters; in still others, the central government possesses all authority but delegates power to local units.

In most instances, such local units—be they provinces, republics, cantons, "states," counties, cities, or boroughs—exist only within the territory of a given state. But it is also possible for bi-state (or non-state) institutions to exist and function on both sides of an international boundary. Such crossover institutions or territories have existed in the past, and a few exist today.

Limited Sub-States, Past and Present

Before the rise of the modern nation-state there were many examples of dual sovereignties, trans-state units, and limited sub-states. In pre-Cortes Mexico, for instance, the Triple Alliance (the so-called Aztec Empire) acquired general suzerainty over a vast area, but each local city or region was essentially left to manage its own internal affairs. The Triple Alliance was not a highly centralized "empire," but accommodated a great deal of diversity.

This pattern was also common in the case of many early "empires" in the Middle East and has been a form often used by later colonial systems as well (e.g., "indirect rule" or leaving local governments intact but with limited functions). The Turkish (Ottoman) Empire sometimes allowed religious communities to possess their own courts, legal systems, and local communal governments. Other examples existed during the era of the Holy Roman Empire, as when the King of England controlled lands on the continent as a vassal of the King of France. At times the King of Scotland also ruled as King of England. Such concepts as multiple jurisdictions, dual sovereignties, and limited sub-states may be even more common outside of the European region, and especially among folk peoples, with flexible and democratic political systems.

Current examples of dual sovereignty and overlapping jurisdictions, both formal and unofficial, range from very limited cooperation across international boundaries (as in the rights of Sami people to herd reindeer across Norwegian, Finnish, and Swedish boundaries) to informal quasi-states such as those of the Guajiro people (Colombia-Venezuela) and the Shan states (Burma and Thailand).

In the United States, the Native American nations ("tribes") continue, for the most part, to possess a certain degree of officially recognized sovereignty. (They have been called "domestic dependent nations.") Certain Kickapoo people possess dual-citizenship status (Mexico, United States), as do the Akwesasne Mohawk Nation (with reservations on both sides of the U.S.-Canadian border). Certain Native American people possess the right, guaranteed by the Jay Treaty of 1794, to cross the U.S.-Canadian boundary without observing customs formalities.

Potential Applications

Cross-boundary sub-states provide a possible way of addressing the needs of groups that have been parceled up among other nations. For example, in North America and northwestern Siberia, the Inuit (Eskimo) people share a common heritage and have common problems, but they are divided among the United States, Russia, Canada, and Greenland. At present, Inuit delegates can come together to discuss common problems, but they possess no unified official apparatus.

There are certain functions of government which could be turned over completely to an Inuit governmental authority of multi-state character, such as education, including all elementary and secondary schools as well as an Inuit language center of higher education; communications, including Inuit-language radio and television; environmental regulation, for example, pollution from oil spills; authority over marriage, the structure of the family, the inheritance of personal property, and other matters often left to provincial authority; and all powers of taxation currently possessed in the region by any existing provincial authority.

Such areas are basic to any ethnic group. Who, for example, should control schools for Inuit children? Who will develop curriculum? Who will determine which of the three or more competing orthographies should be used for the writing of the Inuit dialects? Will Inuit students always be forced to attend higher-education facilities operated in Russian, English, French, or Danish and controlled by outsiders? Who will determine whether an Inuit family shall have only a monogamous character? Who will decide how tax laws affect the structure of Inuit society? Alien nationalities should not be conceded authority over a different nationality in such areas as education and family life, even though they possess state power.

The establishment of such an Inuit limited-authority sub-state would require agreement between the United States, Canada, Russia, and Greenland. Such an agreement might involve phases, or it might be limited initially to a single objective, for example, control over pollution.

The O'odham (Papago) people are similarly divided by the U.S.-Mexican border. Such divided peoples should be able to develop agencies which extend across the border in order to protect traditional lands, water holes, and springs, and also to control education, health, and other aspects of social living.

Such an approach may be relevant to some of the most intractible ethnic conflicts. For example, if a Kurdish-language university existed, it might well serve Kurds from any geographical setting. Similarly, an agency designed to further Rom (Gypsy) culture and history might have no fixed geographical territory or service area.

Another application of this approach might be in Northern Ireland. In Northern Ireland there are two major populations, both of which are also found in the Irish Republic in different proportions. At present the British government possesses total control over the region, but Irish sovereignty can be said to also exist, based on the former unity of Ireland both as an independent country and as a unified British colony for over four centuries.

Under the limited-authority sub-state approach, overlapping jurisdiction would be introduced (by agreement) into Northern Ireland. Areas and institutions of an "Irish" character would be combined in a jurisdiction articulated with the Irish Republic, while areas and institutions of a "Unionist" or British character would be articulated with Great Britain. Neutral zones might also exist. In a way, it would represent a "partitioning" of Northern Ireland, but not in a total sense and not in a permanent manner. Both British and Irish sovereignty would be recognized for all of Northern Ireland; all Northern Ireland residents would be granted dual citizenship (in the United Kingdom and the Irish Republic); all citizens of Northern Ireland would be entitled to vote in all appropriate Irish and British elections, and dual representation would exist in both the Irish and British parliaments.

Agreements would also have to include provisions for economic development in all zones, for free trade with both Britain and the Irish Republic, and for the protection of minority rights. The Irish Republic might well have to offer guarantees of complete separation of church and state in order to satisfy the fears of non-Catholic religious groups.

The entire arrangement could be seen as a gradual transition to some form of Irish unity acceptable to all parties. The present contract between the United Kingdom and the People's Republic of China over the future of Hong Kong, which anticipates that for at least half a century more Hong Kong will exist as a limited sub-state under Chinese sovereignty but with a distinctive local system and a British presence, provides a possible model.

Openings

In many parts of the world, the local community, tribe, city, or province often has a juridical existence prior to that of any modern state. A case can be made for a "common law" transmission of unsurrendered sovereignty by such units. Many states will resist this doctrine, since such rights would fall outside of existing constitutional law and limit central state power. But in the case of many indigenous groups in North America, the Pacific, and elsewhere, such prior status has provided the basis for successfully asserting at least limited group rights.

Emerging forms of international integration also open new opportunities for groups divided by national boundaries. For example, the proposed North American Free Trade Agreement (NAFTA) between Canada, the United States, and Mexico provides a possible framework in which tribal groups could insist upon the right to develop unified cross-state institutions across the Mexican, U.S., and Canadian borders.

The evolution of the European Economic Community and other organs of Western European unification also offer an opportunity for innovations with regard to ethnic minorities. In theory, as the region becomes more politically unified, the possibility of self-determination should be enhanced, since regional security will no longer require that the Basques, Alsatians, Bavarians, Bretagnes, Welsh, Scots, Sami, and other groups be denied their own specific membership in the union. At a certain stage, it should make no difference if Corsica, for example, enters the union as a part of France, as a new member, or as a sub-state with an intermediate status. Scotland could both be a member of the union and retain certain ties with the United Kingdom (such as sharing the same monarch with England and Wales).

So far, the unification of Western Europe is almost entirely a coming together of sovereign states and not of nationalities or ethnic groups. It is not yet clear whether its constitutional evolution will ultimately guarantee that sub-units, regions, and nationalities can enter the union on their own, rather than only as parts of existing supranational states.

Conclusion

Absolute sovereignty and the absolute separation of sovereign states are, in many ways, serious obstacles to problem solving in relation to ethnic issues. Divided ethnic groups are not always well served when local units stop at international boundaries. What we are talking about, in essence, is a way that such units can become trans-state entities. By abandoning ideas of exclusivistic and centralized states, we may be able to find ways to solve ethnic clashes without recourse to violence.

Notes

This chapter is revised from an article which appeared in *Plural Societies,* Vol. 15, (1984), pp. 255-264.

An Alternative World Order and the Meaning of Democracy

Evelina Dagnino

Alguma coisa está fora da ordem
fora da nova ordem mundial
(Something is out of order
out of the new world order)

"Fora da Ordem," a song by Caetano Veloso

The reestablishment of democratic regimes has been a widespread phenomenon in the past few years, sweeping the so-called Second and Third Worlds. The events in Eastern Europe reinforced the old idea that the victory of democracy presupposes the victory of capitalism. The Cold War may be over, but its basic equation of a free world with a free market is still very much alive. In Latin America, the people of several countries elected their governments for the first time after decades of struggle against authoritarian regimes. Newly elected governments, facing a serious economic crisis where external debt, inflation, fiscal crisis, and economic recession are inextricable components, have been trying to implement an IMF-monitored neoliberal model, presented both as the last remaining route to salvation and the quintessence of "modernity," the so much yearned-for "entry into the First World." The major result so far has been the deepening of an already dramatic economic inequality, penalizing yet again the majority of the population, which believed that a democratic government would finally represent its interests.

The extension of democracy, which would be welcome as a crucial step towards the establishment of a truly democratic world order, is in fact serving as a fundamental element and a legitimating factor in a very undemocratic New World Order. What makes this possible is the use of democracy as an abstract generalization which conceals the radically different meanings that this notion can assume. Three steps are usually part of this ideological generalization. First, the formal mechanisms of representative democracy are equated to a democratic regime and assumed to ensure the representation of the interests of the majority of the people. Second, institutional political change resulting from the adoption of such mechanisms is seen as indicating the transformation of politics as a whole. Third, such a transformed political regime is taken to express the existence of a democratic society. It is as representatives of these democratic societies that Latin American governments were able to play their role in the configuration of the New World Order as envisioned by former U.S. President Bush.

Resistance to this ideological use of democracy—which pervades the theory and practice of the New World Order—as well as to the new "modern" face of the old dominant elites in Latin America is a crucial dimension in the shaping of an Alternative World Order. The building of a really new order must be based on a new appropriation of the notion of democracy, one which is able to deepen its radical egalitarian meaning and to extend it beyond the institutional limits of politics to include social and cultural practices.

A decisive contribution toward this redefinition of democracy has emerged from the experience of popular social movements as relevant actors in the recent processes of democratization in Latin America. As an exemplary case which can be easily generalized for Latin America as a whole, Brazilian society is one in which economic inequality and extreme levels of poverty have been only the most visible aspects of the unequal and hierarchical organization of social relations as a whole— what can be called a social authoritarianism. Class, race, and gender differences constitute the main bases for a social classification which has historically pervaded Brazilian culture, creating different categories of people hierarchically disposed in their respective "places" in society. Underneath the apparent cordiality of Brazilian society, the notion of social places constitutes a strict code that reproduces inequality in social relations at all levels.

If political authoritarianism reinforced this dimension, its replacement by a formal representative democracy is far from expressing the eradication of this deeply rooted mode of social ordering. The necessary enlargement of the concept of democracy to include social and cultural practices has a significant consequence: the redefinition of what is considered to be the realm of politics and what is or is not relevant when we consider political transformations in society.

The diversity of social movements emerging throughout the world in the '70s and '80s expressed the plurality of political spaces which characterizes contemporary societies and their aspirations.[1] The emphasis on the role of social movements in the process of democratization implies a conception of politics which includes culture as a crucial dimension in political struggle and political change. In this sense, I share the interpretation put forward by Tilman Evers, that the main contribution of the new social movements is of a cultural nature.[2] But I consider the transformation of culture to be a crucial political task in the building of a democratic society.

Such a conception can be seen as a reaction against the view which considers the state as a privileged focus of attention in the analysis of politics and political transformation. Seen as the specific locus of domination in a society, the state is considered to be the only decisive arena of power relations and, therefore, the only relevant site and target of political struggle. Leninist tradition within Marxism, or what the development of Marxism made of it, certainly shares responsibility for the consolidation of that view. But also within the Marxist tradition, the work of Antonio Gramsci contributed to redefine this tendency. First, he emphasized civil society as a crucial focus of political struggle; he presented the notion of a war of position, as opposed to a frontal attack on the state, as a strategy through which a new hegemonic project, one based on the consent of society, would be implemented. Second, Gramsci made culture a constitutive dimension of politics, where a moral, intellectual, and cultural reform able to articulate differences into a common project would constitute precisely the basis for a hegemonic consent.

The theoretical tendency to emphasize the state as analytical category has, from my point of view, its political counterpart in a conception which considers the state as *the main agent of social transformation*. In Brazil, such a conception was formulated in the '30s when the strengthening of the state was linked to the building of the nation, and showed an extraordinary vitality. This principle of our political culture, shared by both the Left and the Right, helped to shape and reinforce the state's strong autonomy with respect to civil society, and its interventionism with respect to the social, economic, and political organization of social forces. The growth of a bureaucracy—which developed its own interests as a social category, and increased its power based not only on its control over the state apparatus but also on the legitimation of technocratic knowledge as the main basis for political decisions—constituted a natural consequence of such a conception. The military authoritarian regime installed in 1964 exacerbated these tendencies and added repression in all its forms to the list of instruments of social control utilized by the state. These characteristics assumed by the state, and the theoretical and political emphasis they received, helped to disguise what in fact they express and reinforce: the deeply rooted authoritarian and elitist nature of Brazilian society.

The New Citizenship

The concrete experience of social movements included a set of processes which introduced an alternative conception of democracy: the building of collective identities; the desire for autonomy; the search for new organizational practices which emphasize more democratic formats; and the constitution of social subjects, based on the development of a notion of rights and, most decisively, of a notion of a new citizenship.

In order to understand these processes, it is important to mention at least some elements of the historical context in which they emerged. Several factors can be seen as underlying the search for new alternative forms of organization of the popular classes. On the one hand, the elimination of traditional channels for political organization by the military regime was partially responsible for the new forms which emerged during the authoritarian period. On the other hand, a critical appraisal of both past experiences of popular organization—subordinated either to the state or to the interests of the dominant classes—and the excluding character of existing political institutions reinforced innovative political practices. Part of this critique was being conducted by members of several groups on the Left, which were trying to cope with both its reorganization after the defeat of armed struggle and the crisis of the classical paradigms of Marxism. The notion of the vanguard and the lack of organic links between the Left and the popular classes, as well as the role to be played by the industrial proletariat, were major points in this critical reappraisal of the authoritarian tradition on the Left.

Another significant influence in the emergence of these new forms of popular organization was the Catholic Church. Threatened by the growth of other religious sects and interested in maintaining its spiritual hegemony among the popular classes, the Catholic Church redefined its strategy toward the popular classes and adopted a "preferential option for the poor," later developed into a Theology of Liberation. Its progressive faction gained a considerable freedom of action and played a crucial role in fostering the organization of social movements.

Finally, a powerful influence over the forms of struggle adopted by the social movements was exerted by the new labor movement, *o novo sindicalismo*, which emerged toward the end of the '70s. The struggle to overcome state control of the unions played a crucial role from the early stages of the transition toward democracy.[3]

The repressive situation in which the social movements emerged contributed to their initial emphasis on communitarian forms of organization which relied on personal, direct, neighborhood relationships. A typical beginning in the experience of the urban social movements would be a small group of people, living in the same neighborhood and sharing a specific problem, such as a need for a school or a sewerage system, deciding to get together to act collectively toward its solution. In a sense, this kind of relationship and context helped make possible some of the processes which constitute the most significant feature of these movements.

Brought together by a specific need, the first crucial task faced by these collectives is the building of a common identity. As has been pointed out, this identity begins to be established through the assertion of a common need, a common lack, through which a basic equality among the members of the group is asserted.[4] This basic equality, built internally as part of the very process of organization and not given in advance by any abstract criteria (such as, for instance, class membership), constitutes the basis for the exercise of new practices in making decisions within the group and in the forms of representation adopted in its relationships with the external environment. Since all members are defined as equal, procedures of direct democracy are emphasized and the adoption of formal leaderships and institutionalized representation is usually avoided or very carefully adopted.

Another important conception held within these social movements is the desire for autonomy. This autonomy has to be understood in the context of the process of building a collective identity and constituting selves as social subjects; it expresses a history in which false promises, manipulation, and paternalism constituted recurrent experiences. Disillusion with the existing mechanisms of institutional politics, disbelief in the possibilities of spontaneous recognition of claims as legitimate rights, and distrust with respect to external help informed this desire for autonomy, defined mainly with respect to the state and to political parties or individual politicians.

Sharing in a collective identity, members of the group are able to recognize the social origin of their needs, identifying the exclusionary nature of social and political relations in society. In the process, collective needs begin to be perceived as rights. The struggle for rights and the understanding of themselves as citizens entitled to rights become the basis for the emergence of a new notion of citizenship and inform a crucial process, the constitution of social subjects.

The building of a new citizenship or an alternative view of democracy was not what people had in mind when they began to organize
themselves into what became known as social movements. Through
their organization and struggle for better conditions of life, they soon
learned that their first task was to affirm their right to struggle, *their right
to have rights*. In a society in which inequality is so internalized as to
constitute the cultural forms through which people relate to each other
in everyday life, the notion of equal rights which characterizes the idea
of citizenship has to transcend its original liberal framework. This new
citizenship is no longer a question of legal provisions, nor is it confined
to the relationship between the state and the individual; it not only
confronts the very nature of social relations as a whole but it points to a
moral, intellectual, and cultural reform within civil society. Moreover, the
idea of a new citizenship goes beyond the mere extension of rights or
the materialization of their abstract and formal nature; it implies the
creation of *new* rights which emerges from concrete practice. In addition,
this conception is able to provide a common basis for the articulation of
the different interests around which different social sectors organize
themselves. The struggles of the urban poor for housing, health, or
education; of rural workers for land; of ecological groups for a better
environmental protection; of women, homosexuals, and blacks for equal
rights point in a single direction: the elimination of inequality in all its
different forms and the building of a truly democratic society.

At the cultural level, this notion of citizenship certainly confronts
the idea of social places by emphasizing the right to be equal. On the
other hand, and at the same time—and this is decisive in the case of
women, homosexuals, and blacks—it also implies the right to be different and the idea that difference shall not constitute a basis for inequality.
But most importantly, this notion of citizenship constitutes an elastic
system of reference able to encompass different expressions and dimensions of inequality: economic, social, political, and cultural. It expresses
the enlargement of the definition of democracy and the multiplication of
political spaces. The constitution of social subjects, based on such a
broad conception of citizenship, points toward the overcoming of previous reductionist theoretical models and their replacement with new
ones which incorporate the plurality of experiences that constitute our
life in society.

The processes set in motion by these social movements have a
double nature. On the one hand, at the internal level, they represent
personal experiences for the people involved in them. On the other
hand, these processes work in terms of the experience of the society as

a whole, which has to face the erosion of previous social classifications and learn how to live with these "new citizens"—*favelados,* domestic servants, women, black people—struggling for the recognition of their rights and for egalitarian social relations. What Brazilian society is beginning to learn, even if in a very limited, fragmentary, and contradictory manner, is the fact that all these people are refusing to remain in the "places" which were culturally and socially defined for them.

Are these processes and conceptions spread throughout the popular sectors? Is this learning process a general movement in Brazilian society? Certainly not. Brazil lives a typical situation where the old is passing away and the new has not yet clearly come into being. The last presidential elections brought the old and the new face to face. It is not irrelevant that the old had to present itself as the new, through a masquerade that fell apart six months after the inauguration. But it was also very significant that Partido dos Trabalhadores (PT) candidate Luis Inacio Lula da Silva—a metalworker who refused to remain in "his place"—came within five percentage points of being elected president of Brazil.[5]

The enlargement of the concept of democracy embodied in the building of a new citizenship is a result of a struggle for the transformation of civil societies and political regimes in particular countries. This should not obscure its significance to the prospects for an Alternative World Order. It raises at least one basic question: will world orders continue to be defined by governments and elites for the defense of their own interests or should they express real options of real citizens, social subjects able to build their own history?

Notes

1. See Laclau, Ernest, "New Social Movements and the Plurality of the Social" and Slater, David, "Social Movements and a Recasting of the Political," in *New Social Movements and the State in Latin America,* Slater, David, ed., Amsterdam: Cedla, 1985.
2. Evers, Tilman, "Identity: The Hidden Side of New Social Movements in Latin America," in *New Social Movements and the State in Latin America.*
3. For the analysis of these three influences, see Sader, Eder, *Quando Novos Personagens entraram em cena,* Sao Paulo: Brasiliense, 1988, chapter 4.
4. Durham, Eunice "A Construção da Cidadania," *Novos Estudos Cebrap,* No. 10, (1984).
5. For more details on the PT, see Lula's chapter, "The Transformations Must Be Deep and Global," in this book.

The Lessons of 1989

John Feffer

From the Hungarian uprising to the Solidarity trade union movement, the struggles of Eastern Europeans provided many inspiring examples of the extraordinary influence that "ordinary" people can have on the flow of history. Although drawing from varied intellectual and political sources, these movements from below all wished to avoid the evils of contemporary ideological systems and to infuse a higher moral responsibility into civic activities (as in Vaclav Havel's exhortation to "live in truth"). These hopes for new political and economic arrangements reflecting greater accountability, sustainability, and popular participation culminated in the revolutions of 1989 that irrevocably changed the social landscape of the region.

Today, sadly, much of the spirit of '89 has dissipated. Most Eastern Europeans are presently living not in truth, but in despair. Yugoslavia has been torn apart by fratricide and ethnic cleansing. Racism and xenophobia have surged throughout the region, most prominently in eastern Germany. From Poland to Albania, economies are being cattle-prodded toward capitalism, with the predictable result of rising unemployment, declining living standards, and all the proliferating ills of divided societies. Even democratic elections, those precious victories of 1989, have yielded insulated parliaments and declining voter turnouts, as indifference has rapidly replaced civic activity.

How has the situation managed to take such a turn for the worse? Was "living in truth" simply an unrealizable ideal, an empty slogan? What happened to the much hoped-for third way in Eastern Europe?

The most readily identifiable culprit comes from outside the region. It has become a truism of the modern era that no society can long resist the pull of globalizing forces. The industrialized world and its international organizations—the IMF, the World Bank, GATT—have in large part shaped post-revolutionary Eastern Europe. These organizations, which control the funds pouring (or not pouring) into the region, hold to a particular political and economic model and have not been eager to see the spread of alternatives.

But it is too easy to pin the blame entirely on outside actors. A less apparent but equally critical reason for the current state of affairs lies with the revolutionary movements themselves and how they conceived of citizenship, of popular participation, of economic reform. These movements made choices—influenced by but not dependent upon models developed externally—that guaranteed the worst of all possible worlds: the emerging problems of Western consumerism, the lingering headaches of Soviet-style communism, and the convulsive bloodletting of omnipresent chauvinism.

This story of failed promise, with both its domestic and international components, holds many lessons for activists from other continents and other contexts. As the world is being ordered anew, from Vladivostok to Mogadishu, these lessons of 1989 will and should continue to resonate.

Civil Society and Nationalism

Central to the theory and practice of Eastern Europeans prior to 1989 was "civil society," a space independent of official life, an arena that pulsed with political action, cultural activity, even economic ventures. Those pre-revolutionary days were filled with unofficial "flying" universities and *samizdat* publications, underground political parties and informal tavern symposia, irreverent cabarets and donated professional services. Ecological groups in Bulgaria, unions in Hungary, guerrilla theater troupes in Poland: these "antipolitical" organizations deliberately avoided formal political participation. They did not, in other words, take communist politics seriously.

On the other hand, they were fully political in the sense of engaging in protest and in re-imagining social life. These groups gave voice to a distinctly domestic expression of discontent, configured to a particular culture and designed for a specific political purpose. As such, civil society functioned as both a revolutionary tactic and a prefiguring of "society-to-be."

Civil society indeed proved to be a successful revolutionary tactic. In creating an independent space free of government control (though not of harassment), activists could gradually mobilize sophisticated mass movements that toppled the regimes throughout Eastern Europe efficiently and, to a remarkable extent, nonviolently as well.

Unfortunately, however, the alternative society that existed during the pre-1989 era did not translate into a society-to-be. The revolutionary ideal—citizen as political activist, cultural producer, community participant, economic decisionmaker—proved to have only a provisional reality. For many of the leaders of the 1989 revolutions and for many of their less inspired successors, the civic activity of the revolutionary days was merely *tactical*, to be called into play for a short time only against a hated regime. What was less understood was the need not simply to reconstruct government—a task of filling bureaucratic slots, reviving some forgotten ministries, reestablishing a functioning legal system—but to reconstruct *society*. This much larger goal required a continuation of civic activity—of civil society in the broad sense—not its attenuation.

Instead, the newly anointed political leaders established a technocracy, in part staffed by former government and Party officials. This group of experts, economic czars such as Leszek Balcerowicz in Poland and Vaclav Klaus in Czechoslovakia, set into motion an economic reform that was largely removed from public debate and withheld from public referenda. This brand of reform—a shock therapy devised and directed from above by putative experts—was presented to the people as irreversible and ineluctable, with other alternatives being merely irresponsible and ill-informed.

As a result, in post-revolutionary Eastern Europe, the ideal of an active and political citizen devolved into the citizen as mere voter (if that). A gulf opened up between the "ordinary" person and the emerging political expert as the technocracy grew with remarkable speed to offset an increasingly apathetic population. The economic sphere, meanwhile, became dominated by the free market, an arena of burgeoning but often illusory choices that contrasted ironically with the shrinking range of options for alternative economic and political models. Culture began either to be overwhelmed by the mass product or to collapse back into the exclusive province of the intelligentsia.

The region has, in other words, been involved in creating not the alternative society-to-be but, rather, a familiar political economy built around a new middle class. Because of the presence of large numbers of "anachronistic" farmers and industrial workers, this middle class is de facto a restrictive body, composed largely of new entrepreneurs and some of the former professional and managerial elite. Eventually, a more homogenous Western-style middle class is expected to emerge; in the meantime (and for many, it will be a very mean time), Eastern Europe's middle-class system translates into sharpening divisions between rich and poor.

Eastern European society now has a complicated three-tiered class overlay. The new middle-class structure is being imposed on a Soviet-style communist class hierarchy that had in turn been laid over the traditional system of intelligentsia, peasantry, and aristocracy. These models—middle-class, Soviet-style, traditional—encourage little more than an impoverished understanding of citizenship. The traditional hierarchy only endowed a small sliver of the populace with any rights at all; the Soviet-style structure provided a full range of rights, but generally only on paper. The middle-class model, now enjoying an unprecedented ascendance in the region, promotes a civic dormancy that approximates public life only with frenzied parliamentary and marketplace activity: an improvement over past systems in many respects, perhaps, but certainly not the endpoint of social evolution.

Some analysts have fancifully suggested that "civil society" was merely a colorful myth designed to propel revolutionary movements, much as communism's "radiant future" sustained earlier insurrections. The argument continues: since the new political leaders no longer need mass participation (and in most cases desperately fear the canaille), the myth has been quietly retired. But civil society was indeed a reality. It represented real groups engaged for years in oppositional activities. Only at the transitional stage, when tactic was to become blueprint, did the reality become myth.

Whatever the political calculations of the new leaderships, the sad fact is that most people in the region have consented to their own withdrawal from public life. After many years of restricted privacy, it is not difficult to understand such an abandonment of the public sphere. But with all the tasks of social reconstruction so in need of energy and attention—from community renewal and social advocacy to political oversight and labor struggles—such apathy comes at a lamentably inopportune time. Ordinary people, in other words, are still needed to do extraordinary things.

Collaborating with both the technocrats and the "average" citizens in this process of privatizing public life has been, as mentioned at the outset, a wealth of external forces. The IMF plan of structural adjustment—so familiar to the peoples of other regions of the world—also requires a limited sense of citizenship. To be successful, structural adjustment requires a "restrained" sense of democracy. In other words, if a populace participates too much, it will inevitably vote against an economic plan so clearly opposed to its own interests. Thus, an apathetic public is the perfect accompaniment to top-down economic reform of the shock therapy variety. Furthermore, for such "therapy" to "work," it must be the sole economic alternative given serious attention. Shock therapy does not permit a plurality of economic choices: cooperatives, community development projects, employee stock ownership plans, industrial planning, and so forth.

Perhaps the only compelling alternative to these atomistic visions of society (the technocratic, the apathetic, the structurally adjusted) has been the nationalistic. This worldview defines citizenship by blood, soil, language, religion, or some combination of these elements and offers a more compelling rationale—or perhaps irrationale—for civic participation. While it is true that nationalist movements can take a measure of credit for contributing to the downfall of the region's communist governments and for preserving culture during the homogenizing years of Soviet influence, the current nationalist definitions of citizenship are indeed troubling. According to the nationalist, a citizen does not have to *do*, simply to *be*. Only when the purity of the society is threatened must the citizen then act: men taking up arms, women bearing children. According to the logic of this nation-building, political tasks such as constructing unions, healthcare facilities, watchdog organizations, or recycling centers take on a secondary importance.

Such nationalism, in a region forced into competition for loans, resources, and international respect, has proven in many cases to be intolerant to the highest degree. The war in former Yugoslavia is a particularly horrific example, but similar tensions exist in currently "acceptable" amounts between other Eastern Europeans: Romanians and Hungarians, Bulgarians and ethnic Turks, and all majority populations and the Romany peoples (Gypsies). Further, tensions between countries may also spark considerable future conflict in such border areas as between Poland and Lithuania, the Czech lands and Slovakia, Greece and Macedonia, Serbia and Albania. It is naive to suggest that nationalism should not exist. But a society in which the nationalist definition of citizen merely coexists alongside, rather than obliterates, other definitions is a much healthier polis.

The nationalist conception of citizenship and that of the international economic community share certain traits, chiefly an incorrigible simple-mindedness. For the nationalist, the citizen can be reduced to genes or some other form of spurious pedigree. For the structural adjustor, a citizen is no more than a faceless rational actor, familiar to all readers of economics textbooks. The communities—of blood, of consumerism—provide a curious balance for each other: the nationalist preventing the predations of the international, the international eroding the nationalist barriers. Sharing simplistic traits at the micro-level, these two worldviews have an eerily familiar push-and-pull relationship at the level of geopolitics.

A world given over to this new bipolarism is a world as unpleasant as the one that just recently shrugged off the dichotomies of the Cold War. For neither of these communities, populated as they are by card-board citizens, ensures a rich civil society, at least not in the radical sense of the term. To avoid the false choices of the previous era, an expanded sense of citizenship must inhabit concrete ("national" if you prefer) settings and accede to principles agreed upon internationally (for instance, the UN Declaration of Human Rights).

The Second World: Between a Rock and a Hard Place

The predominantly tactical use of civil society, the reassuring simplicity of nationalist definitions of citizenship, the inescapable logic of IMF modernization strategies: it is not difficult to understand why Eastern Europe today is so riven with conflict. Moreover, these are not unique problems. Further to the east, in the former Soviet Union, such trends can be observed unfolding on a much larger scale and at a very similar pace (though at a certain time delay).

Nor are such trends significant only within the unraveling Second World. This enormous region spanning two continents retains an importance that cannot be reduced simply to historical role, geographic size, or number of nuclear weapons. A vast experiment is being enacted on this stage, the implications of which will bear heavily on other countries and peoples throughout the world. Will the heart of the New World Order continue to be a laissez-faire economic model that requires political inactivity and cultural conformity? Will the international community find that the chaos exemplified so tragically in the fighting in Sarajevo, the Caucasus, and the former Central Asian republics cannot be prevented from engulfing the entire region or even from spilling beyond its borders? Or will workable alternatives emerge from the Second World, alternatives that can be usefully attempted elsewhere?

Today, as before, the countries of the Second World occupy a special place in the international community. They function as the bastard children of a rich family, discovered after years of neglect, proving somewhat of an embarrassment for all concerned, but worthy nonetheless of special subsidies. Zimbabwe, Haiti, Cambodia: these are the children of another family. If they survive, they survive—it is not of primary filial concern to the industrialized world. Therefore, although the economies of the former Soviet bloc compare favorably to the so-called basket cases of the Third World, the Second World receives preferential treatment in terms of aid programs, educational opportunities, and so on. For it is assumed, though rarely stated this way, that the regions of the East can be and should be rapidly brought up to the level of industrialized nations.

The Second World thus lies in a netherworld. International organizations such as the IMF had naively hoped that the region would experience that contradiction in terms: a cheap miracle, a cut-rate *Wirtschaftswunder*. But the success that would have strengthened the case of structural adjustment could have been bought only with a Marshall-plan outlay of funds, money that the industrialized world was loath to dispense. The European Community and individual governments are thus left to provide bandaid assistance. Further complicating the picture, multinational corporations attracted to the cheap skilled labor and extractable resources of the region hold out the promise of long-term investments but have more frequently been satisfied with short-term gain.

These diverse governmental and corporate strategies ensure that activists in the Second World must struggle with both the attentions and the inattentions of the industrialized world. There are few choices available to those who refuse to accept simply and gratefully whatever scraps and sops are thrown their way. Autarky—the go-it-alone approach—has proven to be an untenable solution. South to South cooperation—assuming for the sake of argument that the Second World is "South" in spirit if not precise location—has proven only intermittently successful over the years, perhaps because it has been primarily intergovernmental.

The outlook improves only when the focus moves away from the governmental level. This is not a plea for the return of the antipolitical. After all, much can be accomplished in the official sphere, particularly in the still shifting world of Eastern European and post-Soviet politics. Here again, the recapturing of the radical content of civil society offers a way out, a way for Second World activists to link up with struggles elsewhere (for in the globalized context, a struggle anywhere is a struggle everywhere). Activists in the East will find it difficult to follow sterile political formulae. As before, they must construct (and indeed are constructing) alternatives appropriate to their particular plight, this time not Soviet-style communism but the carrot-and-stick structural adjustment models of the international economic community.

This new civil society will borrow liberally from the critical spirit of the previous era, shaping it to the requirements of a political environment that permits greater interaction, sharpening it for use against an international system whose centers of power are just as distant from the countries concerned as the Kremlin once was for the Soviet bloc. Such a task will therefore require a citizenry more attuned to global problems and one that recognizes political action as a continuing responsibility rather than either a revolutionary means of last resort or a once-a-year trip to the ballot box.

Lessons for the Future

What, then, can activists elsewhere learn from the recent experience of the Second World? There are perhaps three principal lessons:

•Democracy is both process and goal. The radical vision of civil society—of a citizenry imbued with a full sense of political action—suggests the importance of democratic participation not simply as a *tactic* to build a mass movement but as a blueprint for society-to-be. Moreover, democracy is neither bourgeois nor by definition liberatory. It is rather of varying shades of complexity, ranging from pale parliamentarism to participatory activities of deeper hues. This is not a vision of permanent revolution. Instead, it is a more modest attempt to blur the distinction between activist and citizen.

•Economics is unavoidable. This was a field of expertise in which Second World activists were woefully unversed. Concentrating on short-term political ends, they assumed that economic reform would take care of itself. After the revolutions, however, economic thinking was at such a minimal level that structural adjustment shock therapy, or Reaganomics exported, came to be viewed—by masses and elites alike—as the only viable alternative to what had come before. For the activist today, economics is what nuclear weapons or superpower intervention were in the 1980s. Throwweight, megatonnage, low-intensity conflict, rapid deployment forces: these ideas had to be understood and communicated in order to organize protest. Today, with debt-for-equity swaps, new free trade agreements, and intricate flows of capital, it is incumbent upon activists—citizens—to learn a new language and not to leave these economic matters to the "experts."

•International economic institutions cannot be assumed to be either neutral or benevolent. Indeed, this is not something new for activists around the world. Solidarity, Civic Forum, Democratic Russia, and others should have been paying closer attention to the experiences of Brazil, of Nigeria, of the Philippines. Should the Second World rebel en masse against the strictures of structural adjustment, however, activists around the world will be considerably strengthened in their attempts to mount a counterforce to the current economic consensus.

Whether because of deliberate intent, tragic oversight, or revolutionary expediency, Second World activists neglected these points. They didn't understand post-revolutionary political activity as more than simply voting; they didn't conceive of democratic citizenship except in the vaguest and most abstract terms; they didn't develop a clear understanding of economic alternatives and the pressures of international economic institutions.

Civil society is by no means dead in the region today. Trade unions continue to struggle for workers' rights. A new wave of activists is working on behalf of beleaguered minorities. Environmental groups, women's groups, peace groups: these organizations have reconstituted themselves without anticommunism as their chief objective and are now courageously fighting for better societies.

Perhaps they will be able to recapture the language of civil society. Perhaps they will be able to infuse greater meaning into citizenship. While we follow their activities closely, we should always hold in front of us the examples of the radical spirit of Eastern Europe in 1989 and the spiritless reality of Eastern Europe in the 1990s. And we must strategize about building upon the former and consigning the latter as quickly as possible to history's overflowing dustbin.

Internationalism is dead!
Long live global solidarity?

Peter Waterman

It is paradoxical that contemporary socialists feel much more at home writing about nationalism (for, against, both for the good and against the bad) than they do writing about internationalism—in any tone or manner at all. Yet internationalism is as central to the labor, socialist, and specifically marxist tradition as are the working class, social revolution, the socialization of the economy, and the dissolution of the state. Proletarian and socialist internationalism—seen as the antidote or antithesis to both the economic internationalization and political nationalism of capitalism—have become embarrassments to contemporary socialists. Socialist and proletarian internationalism, it is true, have had both a sad history and a bad press in recent decades. The Berlin Wall, symbol simultaneously of the Cold War and of statist socialism, fell to the bourgeois-democratic anthem, "Alle Menschen werden Bruder" (All Men Will Be Brothers), not to the socialist-proletarian "Internationale."

The few contemporary commentators on the old internationalism consider it as either in crisis, moribund, or *never* to have had any meaning (internationalism as an unimagined and unimaginable community). Internationalism today is more connected in the public mind with the United Nations, famine relief, and development cooperation than with labor and socialism.

Yet if the old internationalism is dead, the internationalisms of the new social movements (women, ecology, peace, human rights) are alive and kicking. The problem is that even those involved in the internationalist activity of the new emancipatory movements tend not to reflect on their own energetic and creative practice. Far less do they refer back to that of the 19th century.

This represents a summary and update of "Understanding Socialist and Proletarian Internationalism: The Impossible Past and Possible Future of Emancipation on a World Scale," *Working Paper, No. 97,* Institute of Social Studies, The Hague, Netherlands. The relevant bibliography can be found in this source.

"Internationalization," understood as the spreading and deepening of capitalist economic, political, and cultural influence to every last corner and cranny of the Earth, continues apace. To such a point, indeed, that the term has been increasingly replaced by one suggesting both the process and its completion: "globalization." Left and democratic forces are today, however, not only confronted by the destructive dynamic of international capitalist liberalization. They are also faced internationally with an authoritarian populist communal response to both capitalist and communist modernization projects. I am thinking of religious and nationalist fundamentalisms, including communist ones like the Shining Path in Peru. Both of these tendencies (Left and Right) are, moreover, militaristic in their international relations.

Confronted by the contemporary combination of increased "interdependency" and continuing threats to democracy, the international solidarity of democratic forces is both more possible and more urgent. Given such a possibility/necessity, we need to come to terms with classical internationalism. A critical appreciation of it may liberate us from chains we did not know we were still carrying, and provide us with both old and new tools for our present work.

Nineteenth-century proletarian internationalism certainly did exist, but its growth was due to unique conditions, and it was a complex and contradictory phenomenon. One needs to distinguish between many types of socialist and proletarian internationalism, between different levels, and their differing relations with non-proletarian internationalisms (religious universalist, liberal cosmopolitan, radical-democratic). One major characteristic of the old type is that it was largely a "nationalist internationalism"—in the sense of attempting to win nation-states for peoples without them, and rights within them for workers without such.

The decline of socialist internationalism (and its transformation into its opposite in a Comintern subordinated to Soviet realpolitik) was due to the disappearance of the specific conditions that gave rise to early internationalism. Early socialist and proletarian internationalism was based on the exclusion of the new class from the polity and the feeling of both labor organizers and socialist intellectuals (often underground or exiled) that their community was thus an international one. It was easy for them to imagine industrialism and capitalism as replacing all other previous processes and structures; as simplifying all relationships into those of international capital faced by an internationalist working class.

Working-class formation, however, coincided with nation-state formation, the states eventually providing a place for worker-based movements, promising minimal welfare standards, and insulating the working class both from international competition and from other working classes. Stalinist internationalism was a last desperate attempt to preserve the doctrine—and the emancipatory aspiration it codified—from an all-encompassing and inevitably isolating state nationalism. Given the impossibility of *surpassing* an international capitalism that was not even mature, communist (and later radical-nationalist) revolutions represented attempts to *escape* from it. This implied the necessity for curtains and walls, a major purpose of which was to insulate the "liberated" local masses from contact with their "reformist" opposite numbers in liberal democracies.

Internationalist theory and strategy, as it descended from Marx and Engels, was a rich, complex, and ambiguous phenomenon. It combined elements of religious universalism and bourgeois cosmopolitanism with radical-democratic and proletarian-socialist ones. It combined utopian and prophetic discourses with those belonging to political economy and sociology. It saw the new industrial proletariat as the concentrated embodiment of all alienation and—simultaneously—as the privileged internationalist revolutionary subject. The communist project for an international revolutionary party combined inappropriate elements. On the one hand was the party—characteristic political organ of the bourgeois nation-state—on the other, global human emancipation—largely reproducing religious universalist ideas (an Elect, with the Word, leading the Chosen People, via an Apocalypse, to the Promised Land). The prioritization of the proletariat in the struggle for global emancipation lent itself to the notion of a vanguard class, vanguard intellectuals, parties, and states. The end product was concrete nation-states and political parties—and an increasingly abstract utopian internationalist doctrine.

It is necessary to draw from this complex and contradictory doctrine the elements of continuing—even growing—human relevance, and to abandon those that are specific to the period of early industrial capitalism, to nation-state building, to Europe, to early male proletarians, and early socialist thought. We are thus today increasingly able to see the world as one complex and contradictory capitalist whole (rather than as divided into a homogeneous West opposed to a homogeneous East, or Three Worlds, or North and South, similarly homogeneous and opposed). This view of a whole capitalist world and civilization is not one that has been common among either alienated social categories or socialist thinkers in past decades. We can now, however, more easily recognize both the interpenetration of the local, the national, and the international, and the increasing global interdependency of not only

conservative and reactionary forces but also of progressive and democratic ones. There are no longer vanguard intellectuals, states, parties, or
movements, the example of which it is necessary to follow. There are
only varying experiences, defeats, and successes—in struggles against
multinationals, militarism, imperialism, pollution, patriarchy, etc.—on
which it is necessary to reflect, or from which it is possible to learn. The
old proletarian and socialist internationalism, demanding or seeking a
simplified unity, has been largely surpassed and replaced by the pluralistic internationalisms of the new social subjects and movements—
movements that recognize a democratic diversity as a source of strength.
But it is not only or even primarily in this that novelty resides. It is in the
shift of attention from "national" problems to "global" ones—economic,
ecological, military, cultural, etc.—for which there are clearly no adequate national (or even *international)* answers. Thus it would seem to
make sense to refer to the new internationalisms in terms of an uneven,
diverse, and rich movement for global solidarity.

  Along with the above transformation we can see an evolution in
the nature of "the internationalists"—the active force for internationalism. If the first generation were primarily Agitators ("changing their
countries as often as their shirts"), the second were often Agents (a word
that nicely covers both paid public representatives and spies). The new
activists of movements for global solidarity are largely Networkers: they
provide the resources (languages, communication means and skills,
access to information) necessary for creating international linkages. They
may be primarily from the middle strata—but so were most of the
previous generations of internationalists. They differ from the middle-
class bearers of the old internationalism insofar as the middle strata today
are waged, include many women, and exist all over the world (not
primarily in Europe). The proponents of the new global solidarities also
tend to be more modest in aspiration and more open to the different
traditions of internationalism. Contributions to a new body of theory and
analysis have been coming from such people in the East and South, as
well as the West.

  As with the old internationalism, however, major problems remain.
One is of communicating the convictions of the active minority to larger
constituencies or communities that are inevitably mired in national or
even local problems. Another is of empowering these for a do-it-yourself
internationalism.

  The death of the old labor and socialist internationalism must
therefore be seen as the death of a particular understanding and practice
of such. The intellectual and political internationalism of socialists has

been reviving in recent decades—usually in articulation with the new social movements. There has also been a revival in union and worker internationalism. This comes from at least two directions. The first is a "shop-floor" or "grassroots" internationalism, often initiated by unionists threatened by the repeatedly changing international division of labor. It is often supported by bulletins or networks, themselves often staffed or supported by socialists. The second is the limited revival of meaningful solidarity work by the old bureaucratic Western trade union internationals, previously incorporated into the discourses of Eurocentrism, the Cold War, or development cooperation.

These efforts have been provoked by the international antilabor offensive, and stimulated by the growth of militant movement-oriented unionism in the East and the South. In both the bottom-up and the top-down case, the new labor internationalism is itself often articulated with that of the human rights, women's, environmental, and other such movements.

The death of the old internationalism and the birth of the new global solidarity require us to reflect on the meaning of solidarity as the value central to both. Solidarity has at least five aspects or components— identity, reciprocity, affinity, complementarity, and substitution. The old socialist and proletarian internationalism was primarily an identity solidarity, asserting or seeking a single international mass interest against a single opponent. It was, by this token, reductionist and one-dimensional. Contemporary development aid is primarily a substitution solidarity, which, isolated from the other aspects, tends to reproduce the relations of superiority and inferiority between the North and South. An understanding of solidarity that also includes reciprocity (equal mutual advantage), complementarity (differential contribution), and affinity (a community of feelings and desires) would not only provide a multidimensional norm but also a useful analytical tool.

It could be argued, finally, that solidarity should not simply be reasserted alongside liberty and equality, but prioritized as the most relevant and urgent of the three. Liberalism and the bourgeoisie prioritized political liberty; the proletariat and socialism, economic equality. Solidarity—a recognition of the common needs of a differentiated humanity, in and against a world of variable freedom and wealth—would seem to be the value typical of the new social movements and the new understanding of global interconnectedness.

Sustainable Dialogue/Sustainable Development

Developing Planetary Consciousness via Electronic Democracy

Nancy Stefanik

You're already a member of the band. The concert is about to begin.
And this time we're all building the rhythm together. And if you
listen you can hear the heart beat of a better world in the wind.

—global youth magazine One Drum

We may never know for sure the precise role of the 1992 United Nations Conference on Environment and Development (UNCED) in the movement to reverse the current trend toward planetary destruction to one reflecting a universal ethic of sustainable development. We do know that it is possible, using existing computer networking technology and spare communications capacity, to provide world leaders the means to report regularly on the progress their governments are making toward the goals to which they agreed at the Earth Summit.

An alternative vision is to use those tools to facilitate ongoing exchange among ordinary people, allowing them to report on and discuss local, national, regional, or international progress toward sustainable development. These technologies can support Jeremy Brecher's notion that "the social world is composed not of sovereign entities of any kind but rather of a multiplicity of interpenetrating entities with relative and overlapping boundaries." Thousands of remarkable examples of the bonding of "virtual communities" that "span the globe and have absolutely no relationship to geographic divisions" add weight to Brecher's argument. The self-defined grassroots organizations Brecher champions are pioneers in using this resource for public interest advocacy purposes.

Significant barriers to access and ease of use of computer networking technology obviously remain, and critical issues related to privacy, censorship, and intellectual property rights require careful and continual consideration and action. But because global telecommunications and global knowledge banks are essential for modern economic systems, this technology has an inherent bias toward expanded access which will increasingly challenge the viability of closed political or corporate systems.

Once universally accessible, computer networks with language translation tool kits will reduce geographic and language barriers and enable all the world's residents to learn from each other. Students of all ages and nationalities will have the opportunity to develop their own value systems based on their interaction with networks that transcend geographical, political, cultural, and religious boundaries. These new technologies provide a means for the "constant vigilance against claims of monocultural uniformity and the superiority of one nation over another" called for by John Brown Childs.

Computer networking greatly facilitates the "self-organization of humanity" called for by Brecher. Descriptions of two very different models of this self-organization follow.

Kidlink

In May 1992, 2,800 children at 46 locations around the world used various combinations of asynchronous and real-time computer networking, fax machines, ham radio, videoconferencing, and videotelephones to learn about each other's cultures and talk about issues of common concern. A cosmonaut aboard the spaceship Mir beamed a message down to participating youth via ham radio.

This event was not centrally coordinated; rather it relied on the initiative and energy of volunteer organizers in about 20 countries who used electronic mail to plan the two-day KIDS-92 Celebration, which culminated a year of global dialogue among 3,500 10-to-15-year-old youth in 37 countries. Although the majority of participants were from countries with well-developed communications infrastructures, children in countries with less developed communications, such as Argentina, Lithuania, China, South Africa, Israel, Czechoslovakia, Honduras, Russia, Romania, Kenya, Peru, Estonia, Mexico, Saudi Arabia, Poland, Costa Rica, Surinam, Ukraine, and Brazil, were able to join as well.

Founded in the spring of 1990, KIDLINK seeks to provide youth aged 10-15 with a forum for communicating with their peers around the world. Each participating youth is first asked to answer four questions: 1) Who am I? 2) What do I want to do when I grow up? 3) How do I want the world to be when I grow up? 4) What can I do now to make these things happen?

They are then free to join the international KIDCAFE, a free-flowing forum where they can seek keypals, survey their peers about local customs, or talk about anything that is on their minds. A separate forum, KIDSACT, is available for those interested in discussing the fourth KIDLINK question further. Teachers interested in collaborating on KIDLINK mini-projects use the KIDPROJ forum, while general discussion among educators takes place in KIDLEADR. KIDLINK also provides two planning conferences for organizers.

KIDLINK is a grassroots phenomenon that continues to evolve. One organizer developed a computer-based promotional show, KID-SHOW, which volunteers in 40 countries use to promote the project. Another started the KIDLINK Gallery of Computer Art, to which a youth in Protvino, Russia, submitted full-color computer graphics illustrations based on Tolkien's *Lord of the Rings*. A third has thoroughly analyzed the thousands of responses to the four KIDLINK questions and all of the dialogue in the KIDCAFE forum.

In 1992, the Canadian government funded the Toronto-based educational network, SciLink, to conduct a pilot project modeled after KIDLINK to involve Canadian youth in a dialogue about the critical issues facing their country. One hundred and twenty schools and more than 2,500 students participated in the first phase of KIDS FROM KANATA which focused on native issues. The pilot reached an unanticipated emotional peak when KANATA teachers and students from all around Canada were able to positively support new friends in a native community of 2,000 people challenged by a series of teenage suicides at 15 times the national rate.

In addition to participating in the open-ended dialogue among their peers around the world, interested youth and teachers can participate in a wide variety of projects, ranging from a week to several months in duration. KIDLINK projects in 1992 included a Peruvian-initiated sharing of folk tales; a globe-time-date calibration effort, teaching students about time zones; an initiative comparing prices of selected grocery items around the world; 50 Brazilian youth reporting daily from the Earth Summit in Rio de Janeiro; and another team of youth reporting from the United Nations Environment Program's global Youth Forum in New York.

Educational initiatives like KIDLINK have already begun to transform the learning and life experience of students worldwide. As of June 1992, 6,200 children ages 10-15 in 45 countries participating in KIDLINK alone had begun to form personal networks spanning the globe, helping them both to make friends and to pursue their personal career aspirations in a global context. According to Norwegian Project Director Odd de Presno, today's youth inevitably will have a greater sense of planetary consciousness than previous generations because their awareness of society extends far beyond what they can experience personally. The top priority of KIDLINK organizers in 1993 and beyond is to involve youth from as many more countries as possible; particularly targeted are those in Africa, the Middle East, and Latin America.

GLOBALink

The World Health Organization estimates that 500 million humans alive today—10% of the world's current population—will die of tobacco-related disease. That the world has to spend an increasing share of its health resources on entirely preventable diseases caused by tobacco use is deplorable; even worse, the U.S. government actively supports the marketing and promotion of tobacco products to women and children in the developing world through aggressive U.S. Trade Representative actions.

In response, at the Eighth World Conference on Tobacco OR Health, held in Perth, Australia in 1990, the American Cancer Society launched GLOBALink, a computer network designed to empower the international tobacco control movement to "match the global reach of the tobacco industry" and generally meet its information and communication needs.

After two years, GLOBALink has nearly 100 members from 30 countries, including representatives of international health and consumer organizations, national health ministries and departments, grassroots groups, and a variety of other organizations. The network features twice-weekly news bulletins, global action alerts, information databases, access to tobacco control experts, and electronic mail capacity so that activists can discuss strategic planning and report on their campaigns.

The network has successfully provided a means for advocates to reach many people at once with relatively low cost and effort. Information provided on GLOBALink is further distributed via traditional means, including newsletters and regular mailings to thousands of health professionals and activists.

GLOBALink has also brought many more people "into the loop," enabling individuals to more easily find their particular niche and contribute to an international movement. John Bloom, former manager of

GLOBALink, says that it offers speed, inclusiveness, and reach to all members of the international tobacco control community, and that it allows individual advocates to speak "with a big voice" larger than that which they can summon in traditional settings. GLOBALink helps to give people an international framework through the introduction and rapid dissemination of information, ideas, and contacts. Individual activists transcend their tendency to focus only on local action, while still continuing to act on that level. Longer-term global industry, governmental, and movement trends become easier to track.

Bloom believes that the world is in the early stages of the computer networking revolution; just as the telephone and fax machines have transformed worklife in the 20th century, so will new communications technologies significantly alter the way global citizens do business. Of course, he notes, the technology must be more broadly accessible and much easier to use. Bloom believes that technological advances will overcome many of the present limitations of computer networking.

One challenge Bloom identifies is effective management of the large volume of information that is generated on computer networks. In the case of GLOBALink, staff have an explicit mandate to actively manage the information flow without censorship; the on-line marketplace dictates the development of additional resources of value to the community.

Despite their potential, computer networks are truly just another tool, meant to complement those already being used. Indeed, GLOBALink is more than a global computer network; it is a communications support system for the tobacco control movement that uses traditional dissemination means such as postal service delivery of Global Action Alerts. In its first two years, GLOBALink aided campaigns in Thailand, Taiwan, Hong Kong, Argentina, Brazil, New Zealand, and Canada.

The computer network itself has been used effectively for private communication among concerned medical and public health professionals in Asia and the United States as the tobacco control community seeks to shame the U.S. government for its trade policies vis-a-vis Asian countries like Thailand and Taiwan. GLOBALink's interactive Strategy Exchanges have been used to keep the movement abreast of late-breaking developments in U.S. Trade Representative or GATT tobacco- or health-related trade cases. European advocates have reported and called for assistance on initiatives related to European Community directives on tobacco issues.

Latin American health officials, with the assistance of the International Union Against Cancer, the American Cancer Society, and the Pan American Health Organization, have set up a system for translating and disseminating highlights of GLOBALink's news service to health professionals in every Latin American country.

In 1993, the management and coordination of GLOBALink is being transferred to the Geneva-based Union Internationale Contre le Cancer, the international counterpart of the American Cancer Society. The network's development over the next two years will be characterized by a regional approach with centers in each region of the world assessing and taking responsibility for meeting the information and communication needs of the region. The network has been portrayed by the tobacco industry as the leading symbol of the globalization of the tobacco control movement.

Revolution of Consciousness:
Toward Sustainable Development

Computer-based communications technologies have already begun to transform the way planetary citizens conduct their public life. The infrastructure that exists is colossal and growing. In 1991 alone, the number of computers connected to what computer expert John S. Quarterman has dubbed "the Matrix" quadrupled. By 1992, an estimated 14 million users of more than three million corporate, university, school, library, or personal computers located in at least 110 countries were able to send messages to each other and participate in global dialogues at relatively low cost.

In developing countries, a large number of initiatives involving a variety of technologies—ham radio, low-orbit satellites, and/or leased-line or high-speed direct dial links to very low-cost ground stations or nodes—are under way to bypass the limitations of underdeveloped communications infrastructures. Some of these projects are commercial enterprises (like Motorola's ambitious Iridium Project, involving the launch of 77 satellites over the next decade, which aims to permit voice communication anywhere on the planet for a few U.S. dollars per minute.) Others are specifically for public interest purposes (for example, Healthnet, a communications system using a satellite launched by the nonprofit SateLife to allow doctors and researchers in developing countries to communicate with each other via electronic mail and receive medical literature previously too expensive for libraries in those countries).

The Association for Progressive Communications (APC) already has linked thousands of activist organizations and individuals in nearly 100 countries around the world, and has connected nodes in Japan,

Australia, Kenya, Zimbabwe, South Africa, Czechoslovakia, Estonia, Sweden, England, Brazil, Nicaragua, Cuba, Canada, Russia, and the United States.

In connection with the 1992 Earth Summit, APC supported a consortium of Brazilian governmental and nongovernmental organizations by providing its users with direct access to official UN and nongovernmental organization (NGO) documents in the year leading up to the meeting. During the two-week conference itself, an estimated 2,000 to 3,000 Earth Summit and Global Forum attendees, largely from the NGO community but also including journalists and government officials, made use of three APC-staffed telecommunications centers in Rio to communicate at no charge with home offices, constituencies, and the global environmental movement at large. This "Freenet" made it possible to involve many more citizens in the formulation of the numerous treaties negotiated in Rio. Patrick McCully, editor of NGOnet and co-editor of *Ecologist* magazine, described its use:

> In Rio, each day two-three features in English and Spanish were sent out on APC via e-mail and fax to 47 NGOs and media outlets in 19 countries....The features were also posted onto APC conferences...and reprinted in NGO newsletters and magazines in the US, UK, Netherlands, Mexico, Uruguay, Australia, and Malaysia....The press releases and other news items posted onto the APC conferences allowed the NGOnet editorial team to keep up to date with the reaction of NGOs and the media around the world to the events taking place at UNCED....Without APC the logistics of this would have been almost impossible and the cost certainly unaffordable.

Every international initiative—be it for educational, governmental, humanitarian, or commercial purposes—serves to develop the global infrastructure. But despite computer networking's explosive growth, its power lies in its ability to support group communications and solve problems, rather than its potential as a broadcast medium. To date, networking has been used most effectively by individuals or groups to address particular issues of common concern.

Two of the most dramatic examples of electronic democracy involved links among activists in China and Western allies during the 1989 massacre of students in Tiananmen Square, and connections made with global networkers during the 1991 attempted coup in the former Soviet Union. In both instances, activists used electronic mail and fax technologies to gather information about what was really happening within the countries and how citizen activists were being supported globally, and then to communicate this information back to the activists themselves. By 1992, the Chinese Students Association was using computer networking extensively to organize around the world, with over 10,000 subscribers to its English-language *China News Digest* and more than 7,000 subscribers to a version published electronically in Chinese. Similarly, the use of bulletin board systems within the former Soviet Union has mushroomed since 1991, when 24 internal systems were used so effectively to get out the news that Boris Yeltsin was opposing the coup.

The implications for social organizations are far-reaching. Global computer networker Dave Hughes has identified some ways that computer-based communications technologies are already being used to support democracy: They provide direct news from people on the spot around the world, thus weakening government and mass media control of information and encouraging those inside a repressive regime to endure. They provide citizens with the means to participate in a dialogue about events, or to organize advocacy groups; they also help to link geographically separated groups and individuals. This linkage allows people to join any number of "virtual communities," thereby enhancing their sense of being citizens of the world.

Sociologist Daniel Bell argues that "the nation-state is becoming too small for the big problems of life, and too big for the small problems in life." Nation-states cannot effectively respond to global problems, such as capital flows, commodity imbalances, job loss, and massive demographic shifts; at the same time the world is witnessing the national, linguistic, religious, and tribal fragmentation of many polities. Bell further states that by 2013,

> the third technological revolution—the joining of computers and telecommunications...into a single yet differentiated system, that of the *wired nation* and even the *world society*—will have matured [resulting in a] change of extraordinary historical and sociological importance—the change in the nature of markets from *places* to *networks*.

The technologies that support the globalizing of the economy are also facilitating political and social action that transcends national borders. Significantly, the development of a truly global communications infrastructure does not depend on the whims or actions of any group of political leaders or elites. The incompatibility of centrally controlled communications systems with modern economic systems represents an important counterforce to statist, corporatist, and fascist regimes.

The development of networks that empower citizen activists around the world and facilitate the formation of virtual communities that transcend traditional barriers to understanding might be described as a revolution of consciousness. Electronic linkages among social movements around the world reveal universal values of simplicity and cooperation, respect for Mother Earth, and concern for generations to come.

It is not enough that we make progress toward cleaning up and tending our planet. More fundamentally, we have to live our commitment to providing future generations with a higher quality of life. And to do that, we must tap more fully into the collective wisdom that exists on the planet. For reasons of survival—not just because it is the ethical thing to do—we must genuinely appreciate the contributions that all ethnicities and sub-groups can make. There are cultures with a lot to teach about conflict resolution, the arts of negotiation and compromise, parenting, preventive health and natural healing, the use of symbols, myths, and archetypes, appreciation for the arts and literature, and living harmoniously with nature.

Computer networking tools facilitate sharing of knowledge and participation in multicultural virtual communities. They can provide all individuals with the opportunity to become activists at any level of public life. They are already helping to cultivate a planetary consciousness in millions of people around the globe.

Resources

If you are interested in joining the on-line world, you first will have to do a bit of research on which network or networks will best meet your information and/or communication needs and then whether your country's telecommunications infrastructure will support your participation on that network. If you are affiliated with a university, there is a good chance you can get an account which will allow you to send and receive global e-mail and join any of thousands of discussion groups moderated by networkers around the world. Contact your university's computer center for more information. If your orientation is more activist, you may want to explore joining one of the Association for Progressive Communications networks:

E-mail: apcadmin@apc.org

APC Secretariat
18 De Boom Street
San Francisco, CA 94107
USA
Tel: 415-442-0220
Fax: 415-546-1794

APC International Secretariat
Rua Vincente de Souza 29 - Botafogo

22251-070 Rio de Janeiro
Brazil
Tel: 55-21-286-4467
Fax: 55-21-286-0541

Many other alternatives exist. A good reference book on the global infrastructure as it existed at the start of the decade, complete with contact information for networks around the world, is *The Matrix: Computer Networks and Conferencing Systems Worldwide* by John S. Quarterman, Digital Press, Bedford, MA, 1990. Digital order number: EY-C176E-DP-SS. Quarterman also publishes, in both electronic and hard-copy format, the monthly *Matrix News,* which tracks the growth of "the Matrix" and features articles on related trends and developments. Contact Matrix Information and Directory Services, Inc., 1106 Clayton Lane, Suite 500W, Austin, TX 78723 USA. Fax: 512-450-1436. E-mail: mids@tic.com.

Moving Peoples and Nations

Cuauhtémoc Cárdenas

Many thoughts come to mind when one compares the world order that emerged after the end of the Cold War with what the people from every continent have been hoping for: an international order that would represent the existence of a true world community.

There is an ideal, shared by women and men of good faith in every nation in every continent: a world of equals, without exploiters and exploited. This is a valid aspiration, within each country and regarding the relationship to be established among nations, if we want it lasting and fruitful. No one above the others. No one stepped upon or humiliated. No individual or nation constituted as an arbiter of the rest.

To turn this ideal into reality demands from our present world a joint effort that could lead to a transformation of the present relations and means of domination—mainly political intervention and economic exploitation—to the means and relations of cooperation, participation, and equality.

Every day in different parts of the world we hear of a general rejection of imposition and discrimination, and of the demands of social sectors and individuals to be taken into account in the decisionmaking process. We are living in times of searching, of creating new institutions, new forms of politics, and new ways of economic management and social organization.

In many lands there has been a decision to overcome and forever leave behind the experiences of totalitarian, patrimonial, dictatorial states, dominated by heavy bureaucracies or economically privileged minorities, one or the other profoundly corrupt, that have been constantly present in this century, in every continent. The state as an institution has not complied with the principles that have justified its existence nor has it performed the functions assigned to it by the different ideologies and most of the political projects and legal norms that are in force at present in the world—procuring democracy, economic progress, and social equality.

If we recognize that the world's people, independent of the political regime under which they live, claim the need to establish and improve their democracies, as well as to benefit from equality and progress, then the state, of whatever system, has to assume new commitments. It must make its primary activity the transfer of real power to society in its different expressions of organization and participation; to overcome backwardness and marginality, social as well as regional; to preserve and improve the production capacity, quality, and use of the natural wealth—environment and natural resources—of each country and of humanity; and to incorporate the advancements of knowledge, science, and technology into the productive system.

In the international order that emerged after the fall of the pseudosocialist regimes of Eastern Europe, and with the evidence of the eminently depredatory character of the pseudocapitalist systems of the West, competition has been moved from the military to the trade arena, and from the development of technologies for new products to that of new processes and the confrontation between two models of capitalism: Thatcher-Reagan capitalism with its priority on a consumers' economy, and communitarian capitalism, such as Japan's and Germany's, with its emphasis on a producers' economy.

In this world order, with its new hegemonic blocs (the United States, the European Community, and Japan with its Pacific rim), a new distribution of the Third World countries is taking place. They have been assigned the role of providing labor and raw materials; serving as captive markets to complement those of the industrialized countries; supplying agricultural products that require mild climates; and providing new zones for the expansion of First World tourism. They are also repacing the North as the site for production that threatens the environment and for disposing of toxic wastes.

The opportunities for real economic development and social improvement for the Third World countries are thus practically canceled. For some countries, like Mexico and the North African nations, there is a possibility of developing in an extremely limited manner, with economies characterized and conditioned by the low salaries of their workers. Such economies will have the effect the United States and some countries of the European Community are looking for: curtailing the migratory flows caused by poverty.

This situation naturally brings about a growing social discontent. Since there is no political will to really solve the problems that generate this social discomfort, the usual response is the hardening of political regimes and the systematic cancellation, through the use of force and repression, of citizen and human rights.

There has to be a transfer of power from the individuals, groups, and institutions that now exert it to society so that people can really decide their own destinies. In practice, we must begin by democratically reviewing and reforming the existing laws, modifying institutions, establishing new systems of relations and new categories for participation, developing new frameworks for analysis, reconciling interests, and working out agreements.

The individual, man or woman, child or adult, young or old, must be recognized as a person with rights, first and foremost to life, but also to the enjoyment of the fruits of nature, which are the result neither of work nor of capital, as well as to share in the benefits of progress. Every person should also be recognized in the full variety of his or her identity: as a minor, a citizen, a worker, a consumer, a user of services, and/or a resident in a neighborhood, a city, a municipality. On the basis of recognizing these multiple and simultaneous categories, mechanisms for participation in decisionmaking should be established. From these recognitions must stem new rights for the individual and the citizen, as well as new political categories, different forms of economic management, labor relations, institutions, and legal norms.

A just and fair international order, different from the existing one, besides sustaining itself on the collective will to transform the prevailing situation should make use of those instruments that contribute to achieve changes and accelerate them.

We must think about the causes of inequality: What is it that places advantages and benefits on one side and disadvantages and impotence on the other? What is the main factor that creates and conditions the present asymmetries and contrasts among the living standards and the economies of peoples? How might these inequalities be reduced and eventually eliminated, in order to attain more effective collaboration and complementarity among the different countries?

In most of the industrialized world it is held that trade liberalization is the most effective instrument to regulate the economy as a whole, correct its distortions, and create social conditions of equality. Practice, however, has not only demonstrated the inconsistency of this argument, but the limited possibilities of using trade liberalization as the main tool to overcome social backwardness and promote fair and balanced economic growth. If one relies only on the effects of market forces, social contrasts become deeper and the gaps in the development of the economies become wider.

It is necessary to use other instruments: to promote new investments in economically and socially sensitive areas, to liberate the Third World from unpayable debts, and to establish a complementary relationship between the different national economies. The rationale for such efforts could be to solve the problems which affect the majority of the population, to develop effective mechanisms of cooperation, and to open possibilities for different countries to effectively share scientific and technological progress.

To achieve these goals, it would be necessary to review the national and international concepts and norms that regulate intellectual property, and to coordinate scientific research, technology transfer, and higher education—having always in mind that the most important goal is to guarantee dignity and offer hope to every human being, as well as to emphasize human values in the area of economic cooperation. An international commitment is necessary to eliminate, through conscious and energetic collective action, hunger, malnutrition, and the diseases caused by poverty, unemployment, and ignorance. Because knowledge is necessary to overcome these problems, top priority should go to strengthening the educational and research systems so every country may have the human, technological, and productive capabilities to generate, use, and share the most advanced knowledge. Under these conditions, a constructive international cooperation fruitful for all parties can be put into practice.

Considering our existing world, to create an order of justice and equality might seem an impossible task. Some, blinded by the interests that move the great powers today, believe that the present order cannot be changed.

They do not want to see that in the heart of every nation there are men and women who fight against any form of oppression, marginality, and exploitation, and that defying injustice has always brought great changes and progress for humanity.

Therein lies our optimism that changes are possible. People are struggling for them, and without doubt they will be attained. In every nation some lights remain. They may seem weak, but history has taught us that these flames are the ones that light up consciences and warm the will to continue. When they become more intense, they move peoples and nations.

We must not forget that the memories and profound roots of the peoples, the constant renovation of ideas that travel beyond frontiers and across oceans and that sometimes are born simultaneously in diverse, distant places, the multiple confrontations between aspirations and realities—all these are giving birth to new desacralizing and anti-dogmatic movements that will collide with old forms, with immobilities, with fears and resistance of vested interests. In today's conditions, as we enter the 21st century, it is these new movements that will open the way to that new order founded in equality, participation, debate, reason, and truth for which the peoples are struggling in every country of our world.

Patriotism and Global Citizenship
Fang Lizhi

Patriotism is a big problem in this country. Criticize someone for being unpatriotic, and it will shut him right up. But in my opinion, and I want to say this very clearly, patriotism should not be our guiding principle. Let me be a little more specific. "Patriotism" can mean many things, ranging from the purest of emotions to the dirtiest of politics, so the word itself is not too clearly defined. In part, certainly, it refers to a deep love for your homeland, your kith and kin. In this sense patriotism is a fine thing, worthy of respect. But the way "patriotism" is being used right now by no means carries such a simple meaning. Especially when you emphasize the "-ism" part, it means that what you love is the nation-state.

In my younger days I would join in the criticism of our poor old teachers, who always defended themselves by saying, "At least I'm patriotic; at least I love my country." Our standard reply to that was, "But what country do you love? A communist country? Or a Guomindang country?" Of course what we were implying was that they really weren't patriotic at all.

In this context patriotism didn't mean loving your native place, its lands and rivers and people; it meant loving the state. Such a sentiment clearly has no business as our guiding principle. Because after all, what is the state? According to standard Marxist-Leninist teachings, the state is the instrument of repression! The most important tools of the state are the police, the courts, the prisons, and the army. Does that mean if we love our country we must love the police, the courts, the prisons, and the army? Obviously, such a patriotism is no lofty principle at all, but only a feeling that some would exploit for political purposes.

The first opposition to this kind of nationalistic patriotism that I know of came about during the first World War. (No doubt there were earlier examples, but this one concerns physics, and I'm a physicist, after all.) Though Germany and England were at war, the German and British physics communities continued to cooperate. Many felt that nationalism

This talk was videotaped in Beijing on February 25, 1989, by Orville Schell.

was wrong. At that time Einstein was setting out his theory of General Relativity, and his theoretical predictions were confirmed by the experimental observations of British scientists. This was an outstanding act of cooperation. Why shouldn't we in China revere the same sentiments? At any rate, there is no way that patriotism, in the sense of "loving the machinery of the state," deserves to be exalted.

A second point I would like to make is that even very pure feelings of love for one's homeland have their limits. They can be quite parochial and do not constitute absolute criteria on which to base our judgments. Of course you should love your mother and the land of your origins. But when you encounter something new, should you automatically assume that it's good because it originates from your homeland or that it's bad because it does not? Such an attitude is the source of serious problems in China, and we need to rethink it very carefully. Einstein was a good model here, as well. Although he was a Jew, he did not feel compelled under every circumstance to speak as a Jew, but only as a human being.

In science, we approach a situation by asking if a statement is correct or incorrect, if a new theory is an improvement over an old one. These are our criteria. We do not ask if a thing originates with our race or nationality. This is extraordinarily clear in natural science: There is no Jewish physics or German physics. There is only physics that gives good answers and physics that doesn't. Where it comes from is irrelevant. There are no national boundaries in scientific thought, and science is not the exclusive property of any one race or nation.

I think that many scientists have a perspective that transcends their own particular culture. Local cultures should, of course, be respected, but not as an immutable principle that must be defended to the bitter end. In China, as well as in the West, there has long been a saying to the effect that "I love my teacher, but I love the truth more." You should love and respect your teachers, but their ideas shouldn't displace your own judgment and convictions. You have to love the truth more—you simply have to. Whether something is or isn't Chinese is not the issue. You can't go tiptoeing around for fear of challenging anything that is labeled "Chinese." That is not the nature of true knowledge. The issue is whether a thing is true or false, not whether or not it's Chinese.

Things are trickier in the social realm than in natural science, but I think humanity has been slowly evolving in this area as well. As time goes on we arrive at principles that are more and more general in their application. Certainly science was the first such domain. The laws of natural science apply under all circumstances. But in the domain of the social sciences, in society itself, I believe we are also arriving at some increasingly universal precepts. As in science, these truths are not a function of skin color, religion, or nationality. They transcend such boundaries.

Human rights are such a precept. Human rights are not the property of a particular race or nationality. Every human being is born with the right to live, to find a mate, to speak and think freely. These are fundamental freedoms, and everyone on the face of the Earth should have them, regardless of what country he or she lives in. I think humanity is slowly coming to recognize this. Such ideas are fairly recent in human history; in Lincoln's time, only a century past, it was just being acknowledged in the United States that blacks and whites should enjoy the same rights. In China we are only now confronting such an issue. The validity of human rights does not depend on the particular culture involved. Cultural biases are fine if you are not asking questions of right and wrong. You can like whatever kind of food you desire; what you eat is a question of preference, not of truth. Taste can be altogether a function of a particular place. But truth cannot. Truth doesn't distinguish between localities.

Of course, when you start asking detailed questions about democracy, such as whether to have a multiparty system, these are things that can differ from place to place. The specific framework of democracy in Britain is a constitutional monarchy, in France a republic, and so forth. These can differ. But they all start with the acknowledgment of human rights, and are built on this foundation. In this sense every place is equal, and China is no exception.

One reason I oppose patriotism is that it seems to become more narrow-minded as time goes on, while even the purest of patriotic sentiments is already too parochial for the world we now live in. Humanity is faced with a very new kind of reality. A century or two ago, a country could be quite isolated from the rest of the world. Relationships based on common interests between nations were rare. But from a scientific perspective today, the interests of all nations have become inseparably linked. We increasingly face common problems, such as energy and the environment. There are many environmental issues which now have to be considered on a global scale, including those of the oceans, the atmosphere, and outer space. Population is another global issue. These are collective problems, and no one nation alone can solve them. It simply can't be done. Desertification in Asia will cause the United States to suffer, and you can't run away from it, not even all the way across the Pacific Ocean. These are global issues, and they demand to be looked at from a global perspective.

In this regard, I would have to say that I personally have been guilty of something common to many scientists, which is believing that science inevitably leads to progress. In fact, one has to acknowledge that science has played a major role in creating many of these massive problems. With the advance of medical science came overpopulation, with the growth of technology came energy problems, and so on. Nonetheless, how do you deal with such problems? I believe that they require a holistic approach, looking at every aspect including the scientific and technological. And above all, they demand the creation of a truly global civilization.

Patriotism has little to contribute to solving problems of this nature. It is a throwback to an earlier stage of history. To restrict your love and concern to your own country at this point in time is completely misguided. We must face up to this. Our activities are now intimately linked with developments in the rest of the world.

You know, the Earth is really very, very small. To those of us who work in astronomy, it is clear how small it is. People think that the atmosphere and the oceans are so vast that polluting them is of no consequence, but in fact, if humanity continues on this course the Earth will not be able to withstand it. Under such circumstances, it is very dangerous not to have balanced, cooperative management of the world's affairs. We need to develop a world culture. National boundaries must be weakened, not strengthened.

So one might speak of what China achieved on its own a millennium or two ago, but in the next century this won't be possible. Progress in China depends on progress in the rest of the world. There are those who speak hopefully of the 21st century as being the "Chinese Century," but I find this prospect unlikely. China can't overcome all its problems by itself precisely because the problems we face today don't involve only China.

Einstein's concept of world citizenship was profound. Of course, many of his ideas were poorly received while he was alive. Many critics called his work on a unified field theory, on which he spent the last 30 years of his life, a dead end. Marxist-Leninists blasted his work as philosophical "idealism." He had surprisingly few students. But time has shown the true profundity of Einstein's scientific thought. His ideas about world citizenship were also severely criticized at the time; they were labeled "cosmopolitanism." But in the years ahead, the human race will have to come to grips with this idea as well. It is in this vein that I say that patriotism is not a primary value. I would even call it narrow-minded.

The Great Tree of Peace

Lynne Williamson

I write as a woman of mixed ancestry, Native American and Euro-American. My father's family comes from the Six Nations Reserve near Brentford, Ontario. We are Mohawk and Mississauga. The family name was Chechock, meaning "crane," an important clan animal among the Mississauga. I cannot speak for all Native people because they have many voices and they can and do speak for themselves. Here I will express my own thoughts on what the future might hold for us, and how it is entwined with our past.

Many Native Americans awaited the end of 1992 with interest and relief. The Quincentenary, with all its mythology and latter-day racism, has passed and we will move on. During this year a number of projects were developed and implemented by Native people to present alternative views on Columbus and the ensuing colonial experiences. By focusing on new scholarship, wider perspectives on history, and traditional Native beliefs, these thinkers and speakers hoped to stimulate public questions about how history has been written, and who writes it. They saw the Quincentenary as an opportunity to teach, to debate, to present other views of "reality" or "what really happened." First peoples took our places at the podium, at the discussion table, in the seminar room, in the media. Our cultures have much to offer the rest of the world, which is so hungry for solutions and connections to real values.

Other Native Americans chose to ignore the entire circus, asking what relevance it has to our lives, our problems, our traditions. As a means of survival, this refusal to engage in debate or to participate in any aspect of mainstream society is one way traditional Native people have maintained our uniqueness and preserved our cultures. More Native diversity, more vibrant languages and traditions exist today than is generally realized. This is true because our grandfathers and grandmothers sought "invisibility" within the safety of their homelands and communities. If forced to leave, as happened so often, they returned whenever possible or kept their memories fiercely alive within their families. The cultivation of separateness, of difference, has aided our survival as Indian peoples.

We belong within our homelands where our ancestors are buried. The Earth is suffused with the bodies and spirits of our grandfathers and grandmothers—this is why we honor her. She provides sustenance, shelter, continuity, and beauty—all the things we need to live. As those who have lived before have become part of the body of the Earth, so we in the present are part of our homelands and our children will follow us. We are all connected in the Earth, where past, present, and future flow together.

The U.S. ideal of "E Pluribus Unum" ("out of many, one") is not generally shared by Native people. Government policies of extermination, economic dependence, assimilation, termination of some tribes, and now homogeneity under the guise of economic independence have been often contradictory but always driven by the goal of mainstreaming us until we no longer exist as separate nations or groups. Historians like Arthur Schlesinger, Jr. in *The Disuniting of America* continue to champion the benign American melting pot while raising the spectre of Balkanization, which he sees as the inevitable effect of the current "ethnic vogue." Schlesinger states, "Within the overarching political commitment, people are free to live as they choose, ethnically and otherwise." I ask those who subscribe to this romantic view: How free have Indian people been throughout our history to live as we choose, except where we live separately and invisibly, governing ourselves?

The current debate about "multiculturalism" does often gloss over some essential points. It seems most often confined to performances and entertainment—an African Day here, a Puerto Rican festival there—which smack of tokenism. It does not engage any understanding of fundamental differences in cultures, in worldviews, in ways of working.

As I see the process of multiculturalism, it is more than a recognition of diversity—it requires power sharing. Representatives from different groups should be integral members of teams, bringing their individual and cultural perspectives to bear on any type of project or endeavor. The world's problems certainly require new paradigms, and we will benefit from incorporating other cultures' expertise into cohesive, innovative solutions. This way, decisionmaking becomes a collective process, not one imposed by one group upon another.

Indian peoples belong to sovereign nations. We govern ourselves. Families and clans are represented in councils by tradition-bearers, elders, clan mothers, faith-keepers. When our leaders negotiate or make

*treaties with other governments, this is a nation-to-nation relationship—
we are equals. In council meetings, there is rational debate and discussion as we work to make decisions by consensus.*

Consensus is a common Native tradition, one that takes a lot of time but produces more cohesive results. The Haudenosaunee (Iroquois), a confederacy of six Indian nations living in upstate New York and southern Ontario and Quebec, have a very strong system of traditional governance. The Onondaga Nation hosts Grand Council meetings, where leaders from each of the nations gather to resolve issues and set policy.

The leaders (sometimes stereotypically called "chiefs" by outsiders) are appointed by respected elder women in each clan of each nation, and can be removed by the clan mothers if they fail to live up to expectations. Clan members have a voice in this process through their leaders. The nine clans form shifting alliances and support systems in council meetings as well as during the important cycle of ceremonies, maintaining a balance of power within the confederacy but also allowing for dissent to be heard. During the meetings everyone is allowed to speak without interruption; there is argument and counter-argument as speakers attempt to resolve disagreements through convincing and rational discourse. Ideally, the goal is to achieve unanimity of opinion rather than allowing the will of the majority to take precedence over minority views. Certainly, constructing compromise is an important part of this process, but its main dynamic is to air differences and work through them rather than merely to paper over the cracks.

Not all Native groups follow this same political model. Even among the Haudenosaunee, some reservations are governed by elected officials. But most share a close connection between leaders and the people. There is constant access, monitoring, and accountability because the system of governance is embedded within a community and exists to serve it. Traditional governments and laws like the Haudenosaunee "Great Law of Peace" are an expression of "natural righteousness," doing what is seen to be right by a community of people who share the same values. This kind of political organization is like a family on a larger scale.

Native oratory has a compelling, straightforward quality of truth-telling, "speaking from the heart." It uses metaphor to suggest subtlety, beauty, and emotion—not as propaganda or exaggeration but to evoke shared understanding. Native speakers, and today's writers, also know the potency of silence, and weigh their words carefully.

Public speech provides a key dynamic within Haudenosaunee governance. Taking place when all are present in council in the longhouse, the recitation of the Great Law is spoken by leaders from memory, in the original languages. Included in the ceremonies are "readings" of wampum belts (visual representations of symbolic metaphors), and the Code of Handsome Lake, Gaiwiio, which gives teachings on how the Haudenosaunee should live based on original instructions from the Creator. Grand Council meetings also include discussion and debate on issues among the leaders and members of the traditional groups who wish to attend. The spoken word is the central guiding force.

The beauty and power of the oratory, its ability to persuade and the evocative quality of the metaphors used, reinforce a sense of Haudenosaunee identity by narrating a common history of the people who are listening and participating. Even while we may be disagreeing or in debate, the essence of the words links us through archetypal principles. The metaphors in the oratory bring us together, just as the recurring image of five arrows, representing the five original Haudenosaunee nations, reminds us that separately we may be broken but, combined as a group, no one can bend or break us.

Another image which recurs throughout Haudenosaunee oral tradition depicts the Great Tree of Peace. This is the white pine standing at Onandaga, the nation centrally placed among the five (now six) nations, where the confederacy council fire is located. The Great Tree of Peace rises very tall, with the Eagle Who Sees Afar sitting at the very top, watching over the Nations for any approaching danger. The Great Tree also runs very deep. Beneath it, four white roots extend in the cardinal directions to bring the words of peace to other nations farther afield. Weapons of war are buried beneath this tree, further signifying peace among the nations of the confederacy and all other nations joining us.

We belong to large family networks. We are related to many people, and also the animals, by ties of blood or mutual respect. Relatives work together, protect one another, and cooperate in raising children. The clan system also links together across nations. When we travel, we find immediate hospitality and support with our clan relatives, no matter how distant.

It is possible to imagine kinship bonds extending in some ways to non-Native people, as long as the responsibilities of such relationships are understood. Just as families live and work together cooperatively, we need to explore ways of collaborating on a global scale. However, indigenous people must not be forced to subsume our concerns or needs to an overarching goal, however noble. That has happened before; that is cultural imperialism.

Native groups expect to participate in developing solutions to global problems, and our leaders will represent us. However, for a great number of us, the first responsibility is toward our own people. The topic I hear most discussed in Indian Country today is the importance of strengthening our communities, because they are threatened. We have to fight to keep them free of the detritus of U.S. society: drugs, alcohol, corruption, toxic waste, and pollution. We have to resist the lure of easy economic development through bingo and gambling and through renting reservation lands for nuclear waste dumps. We must use traditional skills to support ourselves, to remove dependency on any outside government system. Above all, we need to encourage our children to know their languages and their cultures. We have to be aware of the United States, of Canada, of the world—there is no question. But we can do this from a basis of traditional strength. Here is the challenge for all of us: a "new world order" which derives from, depends on, revitalizes, and celebrates our separate and different traditions. There is no map; it has never been done. *This* will be the "new world" to discover during the next 500 years.

Our traditions are still alive, and guide us to live in a good way. Respected elders teach us through their experiences and the wisdom of those who lived before. Stories also remind us of our original instructions from the Creator. We celebrate the many gifts from the Creator, including the spark of human creativity present in every person. When we build homes, teach children, make tools, find balance, solve problems, think with a good mind, create beauty—then we honor the Creator. In our ceremonies we give thanks for all the gifts of the world, so that life may continue forever.

Co-Creating a
One-World Community

Dokun Oyesbola

The collapse of the Warsaw Pact has helped to remove the usual tension between the East and West, but the unfolding sociopolitical situation in the Eastern European republics encourages fear and apprehension: fear of disintegration and civil unrest, and fear of the proliferation of nuclear weapons without anyone in control. In addition, new questions with respect to the world order are emerging. As the world is moving toward a political, economic, and cultural hegemony, will there be room for visionaries and dreamers who may oppose the ethos of the realists and pragmatists? Does the "victory" of the neoliberal free-market system guarantee the rightness and success of its principles? Is the United States prepared to accept that peoples may seek social paths other than those which it favors? Will the development of the Third World be pursued only at the whim of the industrialized nations? Should our world be seen and be related to solely from the perspective of human beings? Should not ecological and environmental issues become integral and prominent on the world's agenda?

Today it is very easy to be discouraged even to the point of despair in the face of injustice and hypocrisy, especially in high places. Yet, more than at any other time, we are in need of dreams and utopias to sustain hope and create a new reality. We must have a one-world community so that instead of wars and violence, there can be peace; instead of death and murder, an improved living standard for all; instead of socioeconomic disparities, the cooperation of North and South to save the environment. It is in the spirit of hope for a better and sustainable world that I write this chapter, having as my primary constituency for mobilization the Roman Catholic Church.

The Setting

The New World Order is influenced by the old, which is primarily a product of the international economic system, a reality that gives the major industrial countries of today a decisive influence over the rest of the world.

The two world wars in particular strengthened the military and economic position of the United States. After the second World War the International Monetary Fund (IMF) and the World Bank were created to form the principal instruments of the world monetary and resource transfer system. Since 1970, the system has changed radically, exhibiting characteristics of greater flexibility and increased instability. Floating exchange rates and the growth of the Eurocurrency market are examples of these trends. There has been an overall increase in resource transfers, but a decrease in finance offered on concessional terms.

In spite of changes in the international monetary institutions, one fact remains constant: the welfare of the central industrial economies is of central concern to the international economic system and its institutions. The World Bank and UN Conference on Trade and Development may be exceptions, but neither of them is really at the center of the system.

The operations of the international monetary system assume an orthodox free-market model. This model affirms the universality of perfect competition, free entry, no externalities, no uncertainty. However, a closer examination of this paradigm reveals that there are indeed imperfections and weaknesses in free-market economy. These imperfections have great consequences for the progress of developing countries. What precisely are these weaknesses?

The free-market analysis assumes that the initial distribution of assets and income is given and unchangeable, and that world markets are basically neutral instruments of a particular pattern of income distribution.

A contrasting view is that markets are creatures of social and political systems. They came into being as a result of deliberate policies. Which markets are allowed to operate and how, which are encouraged and which are repressed, are nationally and often internationally determined. In addition, spontaneous and impersonal forces of markets do not govern the decisions and operations of multinational enterprises in regard to the physical movement of goods and services among their various subsidiaries in different countries. This means that developing countries, including those in Africa, are bound to lose out.

Establishing a Utopia

What is said of the Old and New World Orders in this book—especially in respect to our emerging world and its problematics of growth versus recession, nationalism/racism, dominance of the United States in international politics, and global security and progress—is adequate. However, the debate, at best, seems to marginalize the role of faith as a credible influence on social change. Faith may become a utopia.

In the Christian scriptures, Acts 4:32-35, the early Christian community presented to itself the ideal of the kingdom of God among its people through the sharing of food, prayer, the Eucharist, and so on. No one was in need. This utopia—a community of sharing—was valid then as it is today. No wonder then that Western democracies, rooted in Christian traditions, internalized the principles of the Acts in their sociopolitical machinery and concretized them through social-welfare-schemes. Unfortunately, these principles are fast becoming marginal to the mainstream politics of national security ideology. Individualism and market economy, with its primary profit orientation, have triumphed over "socialist" principles. The crumbling of these principles is a pointer to the moral decadence of our world. Similarly, Israel B. Guerra rightly observed that:

> The victory of the neo-liberal free-market system is not due to the rightness and success of its principles in solving the problems of the world's peoples. To use a sporting image, its victory is due to the withdrawal of its opponent.[1]

In the same vein, Laurence Harris asked whether "leaving the world to the mercy of the market and unaccountable corporation offers much hope?"[2]

In religious terms, individualism has taken on the cloak of sin. Is it possible to have a fundamental religious conversion of the international system and national security mentality? Such a conversion must accept the human needs of everyone, especially the now-marginalized, as the central motivating force in national and international relations. Should not the rich economies of the West accept a limit to growth, so that resources can be made available for production aimed at fulfilling the basic needs of all?

A popular Western argument has it that the developing countries are overpopulated and need to introduce rigorous birth-control schemes. Meanwhile, the world cannot afford to feed all these people, the argument concludes. This is an escapist approach. It ignores the reasons for large families. People living in a poor economy with few social services, no pension, and the prospect of a bleak old age will deliberately have large families in order that the children might help with family responsibility and support the parents when they are no longer able to look after themselves. It costs the family little to feed an extra mouth, which may make the difference for the parents between survival or death in later years.

The Challenge and the Project

One-World Community as opposed to New World Order is a challenge and a project of liberation, especially to people of faith.

In the preceding sections, the world order has been discussed primarily in the context of economic and political relations. Fortunately the world order paradigm does not reflect the totality of our reality: the non-human dimension of the world does not exist! Hence, the One-World Community paradigm is the project and challenge because it encompasses, as constitutive elements, the environmental and ecological dimensions.

The Christian scriptures begin with the account of the creation of the Heavens, the Earth, and all the creatures on Earth, culminating in the human. In other words, in contemporary language, the outpouring spirit of God which hovers the Earth manifests itself in our highly differentiated universe with its galaxies, vast interstellar space, the solar system, and the profusion of life on Earth, all finely tuned into one living community. But each reality in the universe has its own inner radiance and beauty which points to and reflects the ultimate mystery of God.

At the end of creation (Genesis 1), God testified that all He had made was very good. In chapter 3 of Genesis, sin enters to mar the human-Earth and human-divine relationships. And the ripples of that original sin stain and distort everything. They fracture family relations with the murder of Abel and lead to the strange union between the sons of heaven and the daughters of Earth in chapter 6:2. This cumulative evil precipitated the disaster of the flood. After the flood the injunction of Genesis 1:28 (Be fruitful...) is again repeated, but this time in the context of a covenant made not just with human beings but with all creation (Genesis 9:8-17). We are given a second chance!

But instead of seeing ourselves as co-creators with God, often we act solely as namers and rulers of nature. That has caused and is still causing disaster to our world. In the process of naming and ruling nature as a way of "development" and civilization, we have polluted our seas and rivers, destroying habitats and killing marine life. Air in many places is polluted; acid rain is spreading; erosion is common. Global temperatures are rising, making climatic predictions very unreliable.

With these effects in mind, we can no longer see ourselves as namers of and rulers over nature. Our redemption must bring back balance, harmony, and beauty to what has been destroyed in the world: interpersonal, racial, national, and international relationships. The extent of this is seen in Isaiah 11:5-6, where it even includes healing of the predatory relationships in nature: "The wolf lives with the lamb, the panther lies down with the kid; calf and lion cub feed together with a little boy to lead them."

We must think of ourselves as gardeners, caretakers, mothers and fathers, stewards, trustees, priests, co-creators, and friends of a world that, while giving us life and sustenance, also depends increasingly on us in order to continue—both for itself, and for us.

Failure to do this constitutes *sin* for members of the Roman Catholic Church. This is a situation in which a Catholic does not wish to be. For sin in the scriptures not only distorts inter-human and human-divine relations; it also affects the life-sustaining harmony between human beings and the Earth. In the context of One-World Community, sin is the refusal to realize one's radical interdependence with all that lives: it is a desire not only to manipulate others, but also to set oneself apart from others as not needing or being needed by them. Sin is the refusal to be the eyes and the consciousness of our world.

Working for One-World Community from the perspective of the needs of people and planet is the way forward for the realization of a peaceful and sustainable world. This must be preached and labored for with devotion and dedication.

Notes

1. Guerra, Israel B., *Cuba at the Crossroads,* Study Pamphlet 6, World Council of Churches, 1991.
2. Harris, Laurence, *The Guardian Weekly,* 14 January 1990, p. 5.

The Uprooted from the Land

Primitivo Rodriguez

The Chicano-Mexicano movement of the 1970s for justice and self-determination took up its struggle for immigrant and workers' rights with a visionary slogan: "We are a people without borders." In this world where the internationalization of capital and production represents the dominant force of the economy, this slogan focuses on basic strategies for educating and organizing beyond national boundaries. Moreover, "we are a people without borders" promotes a vision with potential to carve out a new order from the aspirations of dispossessed and working people.

We will use this slogan to discuss the phenomenon of women and men, young and old, who were forced to abandon their place of origin, becoming "the uprooted from the land." Further, the Chicano-Mexicano slogan will serve to advance the concept of "people without barriers" as a fundamental perspective in the building of a "common global village."

The Displaced and Coerced

At present in the world, there are more than 60 million refugees, undocumented immigrants, and displaced people. War and political persecution, natural disasters, and lack of opportunity have all compelled these human beings to struggle for their lives on "foreign soil."

Coerced immigrants and refugees represent the social group with few and ill-recognized or protected rights, a fact which makes them easy prey to exploitation and abuse, and frequently victims of abandonment and death.

The tragedy experienced by these men and women shows the crude drama of the current international order—an order without the means or the will to answer the clamor of the uprooted from the land. The international treaties established to protect the legal rights of undocumented immigrants and refugees are inadequate, or not upheld when ratified by nations. At the same time, the moral indignation awakened by the conditions of these millions of people remains weak relative to the political and economic forces that cause their existence.

Quite often, migratory waves are the product of links created by the economic expansion of industrialized nations into Third World nations. Currently, the globalization of capital markets and industrial production is one of the leading factors in explaining massive migration from poor to rich countries. Millions of displaced people and coerced immigrants have become a cheap and flexible labor reserve both within industrialized nations and in the "borderlands" that divide the North and the South. In this respect, the Mexico-U.S. border offers, perhaps as no other region does, a clear example of the dramatic encounter between uprooted workers and industrial production often on the move.

The Broken Line

The Mexico-U.S. border is known as the "broken line." National barriers have been torn down by the collision, on the one hand, between economic expansion pushed by the North and the decapitalization suffered by the South, and on the other, between the rationalistic philosophy of the West and the cosmic vision of indigenous and mestizo people.

At the "broken line" a new proletariat and the most sophisticated multinational corporations coexist. It is a coexistence of two violated boundaries: the entry into assembly-line production by young women of rural origin who make up 70% of a total labor force of half a million workers at the disposal of 1,800 maquiladoras; and the arrival of corporations to their paradise of cheap and inexperienced labor. From their agricultural origin, maquiladora workers took an historic leap into modern industrial production; the corporations leapt in the opposite direction, back to the prehistory of labor rights and benefits.

For reasons different from, but related to, the problems of immigrants, maquiladoras have no roots; they represent "runaway" industry, which follows the path of the highest profitability based on the lowest accountability and responsibility toward workers and their communities. In fact, maquiladoras do not relate well to development or to people's rights.

Growth and economic health are not fertile soil for maquiladoras; nor are fair labor contracts, environmental regulations, and public awareness about the social and economic impact of the industry. Maquiladoras prosper only where people are so desperate for jobs, and where governments have such a great need of hard currency, that low wages, tax exemptions, and violation of labor and environmental regulations become "normal" conditions for foreign investment. Maquiladoras represent the most volatile and unaccountable sector of the global economy.

The maquiladora industry carries forward some fundamental characteristics of the "new order" imposed on the Latin American and Caribbean region by the unregulated internationalization of the economy: integration based on significant economic disparity, industrial growth achieved at the cost of sustainable development, and competitiveness built upon environmental degradation and the exploitation of young working women. Currently, free-market-oriented economies in the Western hemisphere lack social and institutional checks on corporate power; therefore, they represent not the promise of a new frontier, but rather a reenacted economic version of the Monroe Doctrine: the people and resources of the Americas for the U.S.-backed corporations.

As a broken line between the North and South, the Mexico-U.S. border signals the end of "national" identities and announces the birth of a new "country" whose rules and mores are still undefined, but whose workers are bound together by the reality of being citizens of the global economy. This "nation" without borders is one in which the encounter of capital and labor, production and environment, and ideologies and cultures presents unparalleled risks for a healthy future, but also unprecedented opportunities for social change.

Existential Uprootedness

The fall of socialist regimes in the Soviet Union and Eastern Europe has been portrayed by political leaders in the West as the triumph of good over evil, and of freedom over oppression. Yet it is precisely in the world dominated by capitalism that we witness a dramatic gap between the haves and have-nots, and between access to wealth for the few and lack of opportunities for the many. More than half of the population living under capitalist systems have lost access to healthcare and adequate food, education, and housing. The net result of this travesty of values is that the cost of living is much higher than the price of human life.

For this reason, the condition of "landlessness" is not exclusive to refugees, undocumented immigrants, and maquiladora workers. The expulsion from opportunities for a dignified life is the reality imposed on most men and women who inhabit the world. In a violent perversion of priorities, to be a human being does not *per se* entitle anybody to the opportunity to live in dignity.

The uprooting of millions of poor and working people is more than economic; in fact, being "uprooted from the land" is an existential condition that now encompasses humanity. People's persistent yearning for a plentiful life, in harmony with nature, is still unanswered. Thus, in an ontological sense, we all are immigrants forced to live in a world we have yet to understand, in a reality that feels alien to us. Social injustice and ecological decay are crude and cruel manifestations of the fruitless search for happiness through the accumulation of wealth and power by a few individuals, groups, and nations.

Beings without Barriers

The Chicano-Mexicano slogan "we are a people without borders" was born as a response to the surge of the unregulated internationalization of capital and production; the slogan was also a call for identity and solidarity, for the right of being oneself and being with others beyond the limits imposed by the nation-state.

However, the new order cannot be defined only through the falling of political and economic walls. It will have to rise out of the dismantling of the multiple class, racial, gender, and cultural barriers that have so far impeded the building of a "common global village," of a community of individuals and groups bound by the recognition of their dignity, by the free exercise of their potential, and by the sharing of love among themselves and with their habitat.

The globalization of capital, production, and communications has created the conditions in which the peoples of the world can come together across borders and barriers. This opportunity represents more than a common effort in proposing alternatives to the global economy; it is rather an opportunity for the convergence of "world visions," cultural experiences, and long-held aspirations whose dynamics can lead to a profound reevaluation or revolution in our ways of thinking of and relating to ourselves and the universe around us.

The foundations of the "common global village" do not yet exist. In identifying them, we will have to acknowledge the multidimensional character and aspirations of our being. It won't be so much an intellectual task as it will be a challenge to our hope in achieving a liberation beyond politics and economics: freeing ourselves from the belief that the social illnesses or injustices we have encountered in the struggle for a meaningful life are congenital to our existence rather than simply a facet of our evolving nature and understanding.

In its most visionary translation, the Chicano-Mexicano slogan would have to say in face of the future: "we are beings without barriers." Indeed, beings at the doorstep of understanding both the secrets of life and the sacredness of all forms of existence and their unlimited potential.

Notes on Contributors

Nahla Abdo is professor of sociology and women's studies at Carleton University, Ottawa, Canada. Her publications include *Family, Women and Social Change in the Middle East,* and she is active in grassroots politics including the women's, anti-racist, and other community movements.

Ben E. Aigbokhan is senior lecturer in economics at Edo State University in Nigeria. He is the author of *Planning, Employment, and Income Distribution in Nigeria* and of articles on armament and development, structural adjustment and inequality, and privatization and commercialization of public enterprises. He is a member of the African Peace Research Movement, the West African Economic Association, and the Nigerian Economic Society.

Elaine Bernard is executive director of the Trade Union Program at Harvard University and former director of the Labour Program at Simon Fraser University, Burnaby, British Columbia. She is the author of *Technological Change and Skills Development, Working Lives: Vancouver 1886-1986,* and *The Long Distance Feeling: A History of the Telecommunications Workers Union.* She was for many years a member of the Executive body and served as president of the New Democratic Party in British Columbia.

Elise Boulding is professor emerita of sociology of Dartmouth College, former secretary-general of the International Peace Research Association, and former international chair of the Women's International League for Peace and Freedom. She is author and/or editor of many books, including *Handbook of International Data on Women, Women in the Twentieth Century World, From a Monastery Kitchen, Children's Rights in the Wheel of Life, Building a Global Civic Culture: Education for an Interdependent World,* and *The Underside of History: A View of Women through Time.* She also conducts workshops on Imaging a World Without Weapons.

Jeremy Brecher is humanities scholar-in-residence at Connecticut Public Broadcasting. He is the author or co-author of six books on labor and social history, including *Strike!, Building Bridges: The Emerging Grassroots Coalition of Labor and Community,* and *Global Village vs. Global Pillage.*

Cuauhtémoc Cárdenas is president of the Party of the Democratic Revolution (PRD), Mexico's largest opposition party, and its candidate for president of Mexico.

John Brown Childs is professor of sociology and chair of the Race and Ethnicity Research Council at the University of California, Santa Cruz. He is the author of *Leadership, Conflict and Cooperation in Afro-American Social Thought* and *The Political Black Minister.*

Jill Cutler is a dean and teacher of writing at Yale University. She has long experience as a writer and editor.

Evelina Dagnino teaches political science at the University of Campinas, Sao Paulo, Brazil. She has been affiliated with the Worker's Party since its creation in 1980.

Francis Mading Deng was recently named by U.N. Secretary-General Boutros Boutros-Ghali as his representive on the problem of displaced persons throughout the world. He has served as Sudan's Minister of State for Foreign Affairs and is currently senior fellow in charge of the African Studies branch of the Brookings Institution Foreign Studies Program. His books include *The Man Called Deng Majok, Bonds of Silk: The Human Factor in British Administration in the Sudan, Human Rights in Africa: Cross-Cultural Perspectives, Conflict Resolution in Africa,* and *The Challenges of Famine Relief: Emergency Operations in the Sudan.*

Richard Falk is the Albert G. Milbank Professor of International Law and Practice at Princeton University. He is the author of *Explorations at the Edge of Time, The Promise of World Order,* and many other books.

Fang Lizhi was, until 1986, vice-president of the Chinese University of Science and Technology. He was removed from his post and expelled from the Chinese Communist Party for his outspoken advocacy of democratic reform. Following the Tiananmen Square massacre of June 1989, Fang and his wife sought sanctuary in the U.S. embassy in Beijing, where they remained for over a year. He currently teaches physics at the University of Arizona.

John Feffer is the author of *Beyond Detente: Soviet Foreign Policy and U.S. Options* and *Shock Waves: Eastern Europe After the Revolutions.*

Jack D. Forbes is professor of anthropology and director of the Native American Studies Program at the University of California, Davis. He is the author of *Columbus and Other Cannibals, Africans and Native Americans,* and *Tribes and Masses.* His background is Powhaton (Renápe) and Delaware (Lenápe). He is co-founder of the California Indian Education Association and former editor of *Warpath.*

Xabier Gorostiaga is rector of the Central American University in Managua, Nicaragua. He has also served as president of the Regional Coordinator of Economic and Social Research (CRIES) and as a world-wide networker.

Siba N'Zatioula Grovogui has taught at Loyola College in Baltimore, Maryland, the University G.A. Nasser of Conakry, Guinea, the University of Michigan, and Macalester College, St. Paul, Minnesota; he has also worked as a civil servant in his native Guinea. He is fluent in English, French, Fula, Malinke, Susa, Loma, and Kpele.

Petra Kelly was a founder of the German Green Party and until 1990 a Green member of the Bundestag. She was author of *Fighting for Hope* and *The Anguish of Tibet.* Until her death in 1992 she remained an active campaigner for human rights and the environment all over the world.

Martin Khor Kok Peng is a journalist and managing editor of *Third World Resurgence*. He is the author of *The Future of North-South Relations: Conflict or Cooperation* and *The Uruguay Round and Third World Sovereignty*. As director of the Third World Network, he played a major role in organizing an independent Third World response to the 1992 Earth Summit.

Luiz Inacio Lula da Silva, generally known as Lula, has been a metalworker and president of the Brazilian Metal Worker's Union. He helped start the Central Unica dos Trabalhadores (CUT), now the principal union federation in Brazil, and the Worker's Party (PT), of which he is president. In 1989 he received 45% of the vote for president of Brazil.

Denis MacShane works for the International Metalworkers Federation in Geneva. He is the author of several books on labor unions in Western Europe, Poland, and South Africa, including *International Labor and the Origins of the Cold War* and the forthcoming *The New Politics of Global Labor*. He is adviser to the Socialist Group in the European Parliament, associate director of the European Policy Institute, and former president of the British and Irish National Union of Journalists.

Muto Ichiyo is co-president of the Pacific-Asia Resource Center in Tokyo. He is the author of ten books on political philosophy, Japanese state and society, and world affairs and is a regular contributor to *AMPO* magazine. He has been an active participant in social movements since the 1950s. He is also an adjunct professor of sociology at the State University of New York at Binghamton.

Dokun Oyeshola teaches international relations at Obafemi Awolowo University in Nigeria. He is a counselor to an AIDS project, a member of the Nigerian Institute of International Affairs, a member of the Justice, Development and Peace Commission for the Diocese of Oyo (Nigeria), and the author of a series of papers on peace and environmental issues in Africa.

Juan Palacios is professor of social sciences and director of the Center for Pacific Studies at the University of Guadalajara. He is the author of *La Política Regional en Mexico, 1970-1982, Las Contradicciones de un Intento de Redistribucion* and *La Apertura Economica de Mexico y la Cuenca del Pacifico: Perspectivas de Intercambio y Cooperacion*. He is a member of the University of Guadalajara Committee for Social and Political Development and of the Party of the Democratic Revolution Local Chairman Advisory Group.

Primitivo Rodriguez is director of the Mexico-U.S. Border Program of the American Friends Service Committee. He is the author of *Social Change and the Media* and *Public Administration During Civil War and Foreign Intervention, 1850-1867*. He is a member of the Executive Committee of the National Network for Immigrant and Refugee Rights and the Executive Committee of the Citizens Network for Sustainable Development. Before moving to the United States in 1977 he participated in independent political movements in Mexico City.

Saskia Sassen is professor of urban planning at Columbia University and visiting scholar at the Russell Sage Foundation. She is Latin American and works with Latino immigrants in New York City. She is the author of *The Mobility of Labor and Capital* and *The Global City: New York, London, Tokyo*. She is currently working on a book tentatively entitled *Governance and Accountability in a World Economy*. She is a member of the United Nations Centre on Regional Development's project on Economic Restructuring in the U.S. and Japan and the Social Science Research Council's Working Group on New York City and its Committee on Hispanic Public Policy.

Gay W. Seidman is assistant professor of sociology at the University of Wisconsin in Madison and visiting lecturer in sociology at the University of the Witwatersrand in Johannesburg. She is the author of *Manufacturing Militance: Workers' Movements in Brazil and South Africa, 1970-1985*. She has long been involved in anti-apartheid activities and currently serves on the editorial board of the *South African Labour Bulletin*.

Stephen R. Shalom is professor of political science at William Paterson College of New Jersey. He is the author and/or editor of *Imperial Alibis: Rationalizing U.S. Intervention After the Cold War*, *The Phillipines Reader*, *Socialist Visions*, and *The United States and the Philippines*. He has been active with the Philippine Bases Network.

Vandana Shiva is an Indian journalist, the author of *Ecology and the Politics of Survival*, *Biodiversity*, *Staying Alive*, and *The Violence of the Green Revolution* and a contributing editor of *Third World Resurgence*.

Nancy Stefanik works for the Washington, DC-based Advocacy Institute. She led the design and initial technical development phase of GLOBALink and four other health-related model computer networks. She is also a founder of KIDLINK. She has served as deputy director for Rebuild America, a policy center promoting U.S. investment in people and technology.

Hassan A. Sunmonu is secretary-general of the Organizaton of African Trade Union Unity. Trained as a civil engineer, he has been president of the Yaba College of Technology Students Union, president of the Civil Service Technical Workers' Union of Nigeria, and president of the Nigerian Labor Congress.

Haunani-Kay Trask is professor and director of Hawaiian studies at the University of Hawai'i at Manoa. She is the author of *Eros and Power: The Promise of Feminist Theory* and *From a Native Daughter: Essays on Colonialism and Sovereignty*. She is a member of Ka Lahui Hawai'i, a native initiative for self-government in Hawai'i, and of the Nuclear-Free and Independent Pacific Movement.

Peter Waterman teaches on social movements, alternative international relations, and communications at the Institute of Social Studies in The Hague, Netherlands. During the 1950s and 1960s he worked for the international Communist movement in Prague. He is the author of many publications on the new internationalism and alternative international communications and was editor of the *Newsletter of International Labour Studies*. He is currently writing a book tentatively titled *From Labour Internationalism to Global Solidarity*.

Lynne Williamson is director of the Connecticut Cultural Heritage Arts Program based at the Institute for Community Research in Hartford. She has served as curator for numerous American Indian museums and exhibitions and has written many articles and exhibition brochures. She is of Mohawk/Mississauga descent from the Six Nation Reserve in Ontario.

Index

A

AAF-SAP. *See* African Alternative to Structural Adjustment Programmes

Abdo, Nahla, xvii

ACN. *See* Action Canada Network

Action Canada Network (ACN), 209, 210

Adversarial trade, 26-27

Africa: and Cold War, 87-88, 91, 93, 99, 104, 105, 108; communism, 108-9; deforestation, 36; democratization, 87-88, 93-96, 97, 106; economic crisis, 68, 92-93, 97-98; economic liberalism, 93, 95, 97, 105, 192-93, 194; ethnic conflict, 107-8, 109-10, 226; First World blame on, 91-92, 98-99; and globalized economy, 61; humanitarian aid, 105; identity groups in, 225-27; independence, 93-94, 96-97, 99, 107-8; Islamic fundamentalism, 99, 108-9; national conferences, 94-95; nation-state system, 92-94, 107-8, 109; politics in, 90-91, 92-93; and postwar world order, 89-91. *See also* Third World

Africa Peace Research Institute, 37-38

African Alternative to Structural Adjustment Programmes (AAF-SAP), 193

African Leadership Forum, 106

AIDS, 100

Aigbokhan, Ben E., xx

Air pollution, 173

Algeria, 90, 116-17

Alternative Earth Council, xix

Alternative World Order. *See* Globalization-from-below

American Cancer Society, 266, 267

Amnesty International, xv, 47

Angola, 105

APC. *See* Association for Progressive Communications

Arab world, 113-24; activism, 116-18; and global economic institutions, 115, 118; and Gulf War, 5, 32, 114-18; Islamic fundamentalism, 99, 108-9, 116-17, 122-24; and Israeli-Palestinian conflict, 115-16, 120

Argentina, 74

Aristide, Jean-Bertrand, 81, 82

Arms buildup. *See* Military spending

Asia: and globalized economy, 62, 64, 274; identity groups in, 222-25. *See also* Newly industrialized countries; Pacific Basin; *specific countries*

Association for Progressive Communications (APC), 268-69, 271-72

Autarky, 253

B

Backlash, 48

Baker, Pauline, 91

Balcerowicz, Leszek, 249

Baltic republics, 135. *See also* Former Soviet republics

Banda, Kamazu, 95

Banjul Charter, 106

Bank crisis (1982), 64

Barkun, Michael, 216

Barraclough, S., 36

BASF corporation, 10

Behind the Disappearances: Argentina's Dirty War Against Human Rights and the United Nations (Guest), 197

Belgium, 142, 221

Bell, Daniel, 270

Bendix, Reinhard, 185

Benin, 94, 97, 195

Benvenisti, Meron, 125n7

Bernard, Elaine, xx-xxi, xxiii-xxiv

Bhopal disaster, xix, xxii, 141, 142, 147, 168

Biodiversity, 56-57

Bishara, Azmi, 121

Biya, Paul, 95

About South End Press

South End Press is a nonprofit, collectively-run book publisher with over 175 titles in print. Since our founding in 1977, we have tried to meet the needs of readers who are exploring, or are already committed to, the politics of radical social change.

Our goal is to publish books that encourage critical thinking and constructive action on the key political, cultural, social, economic, and ecological issues shaping life in the United States and in the world. In this way, we hope to give expression to a wide diversity of democratic social movements and to provide an alternative to the products of corporate publishing.

Through the Institute for Social and Cultural Change, South End Press works with other political media projects—*Z Magazine;* Speak Out!, a speakers bureau; the Publishers Support Project; and the New Liberation News Service—to expand access to information and critical analysis. If you would like a free catalog of South End Press books, please write to us at South End Press, 116 Saint Botolph Street, Boston, MA 02115. Also consider becoming a South End Press member: your $40 annual donation entitles you to two free books and a 40% discount on our entire list.

Other titles of interest to readers of *Global Visions*

Workers of the World Undermined:
American Labor's Role in U.S. Foreign Policy
Beth Sims

The New Resource Wars:
Native and Environmental Struggles Against Multinational Corporations
Al Gedicks

Colonial Dilemma:
Critical Perspectives on Contemporary Puerto Rico
Edited by Edwin Mélendez and Edgardo Mélendez

Shock Waves: Eastern Europe After the Revolutions
John Feffer

Strike!
Jeremy Brecher

Rockin' the Boat:
Mass Music and Mass Movements
Edited by Reebee Garofalo